PUZZLING SHAKESPEARE

The New Historicism: Studies in Cultural Poetics
Stephen Greenblatt, General Editor

PUZZLING
SHAKESPEARE

LOCAL READING
AND ITS DISCONTENTS

Leah S. Marcus

University of California Press
Berkeley · Los Angeles · London

University of California Press
Berkeley and Los Angeles, California

University of California Press, Ltd.
Oxford, England

© 1988 by
The Regents of the University of California

Printed in the United States of America
1   2   3   4   5   6   7   8   9

Library of Congress Cataloging-in-Publication Data

Marcus, Leah S. (Leah Sinanoglou)
    Puzzling Shakespeare : local reading and its discontents /
Leah S. Marcus.
        p.   cm.—(The New historicism ; 6)
    Bibliography: p.
    Includes index.
    ISBN 0-520-07191-3 (alk. paper)
    1. Shakespeare, William, 1564–1616—Criticism and
    interpretation.
I. Title.   II. Series.
PR2976.M39 1988
822.3'3—dc19   88-15572
                                                                    CIP

All illustrations not otherwise attributed are reproduced with
permission from the Newberry Library, Chicago, Illinois. An
earlier version of portions of chapter 2 appeared in Mary Beth
Rose, ed., *Women in the Middle Ages and the Renaissance: Literary and Historical Perspectives* (Syracuse: Syracuse University
Press, 1986).

For my parents

Contents

Illustrations

Preface

This book was born out of my dissatisfaction with my own previous interpretive methods—at least as an approach to Shakespeare. During the 1970s, when the New Criticism had not yet lost its ascendancy, I took considerable pleasure in demonstrating the deep cultural and political embeddedness of what most scholars still considered ahistorical works of art—the "ethereal" masques and lyrics of Jonson, the "slight," gossamer verses of Herrick. Back then, I was interested in beating formalist interpretation at its own game by showing how historicist readings (in particular, topical readings) of authors like Jonson and Herrick could provide a sudden, gratifying snap of clarity, a revelation of deep structural unities not made visible by other means. But times and critical *mores* have changed since then. In the 1980s, historicism is nearly everywhere; it still encounters resistance, of course, but from a position of much greater visibility and dominance. Moreover, there has been a radical shift in the kinds of historicism we are willing to accept. Sudden moments of interpretive clarity are not as gratifying as they used to be, or as easy to come by. As I gradually discovered in broadening the scope of my own critical endeavor, the kinds of topical approaches which had "worked" for Jonson or Herrick earlier on seemed not to work for Shakespeare, or at least left so many questions unanswered that their effect was more to interrogate the method than to open up the texts. To attempt topical readings of Shakespearean drama is not at all to find reassuring patterns. It is more like entering a murky labyrinth without signposts or exits. In all topical interpretation, there is a point at which the method's power to "explain" a text must yield to intransigent textual elements which disrupt the explanation. But that point comes much more quickly and decisively in the reading of Shakespearean drama than it does for many other Renaissance texts. What we call Shakespeare is somehow mysteriously different, impervious to history at the level of specific factual data, the day-to-day chronicling of events. The present study is designed to probe into this puzzling immunity, its origins, effects, and points of breakdown.

My first title for the project was "Shakespeare and the Unease of Topicality." That label was in some ways more accurate than the present one as a guide to the preoccupations inside. *Unease* is an awkward word, and deliberately so—it captures the unbalancing effect of trying to read Shakespeare through the distracting lens of sixteenth- and early seventeenth-century events, gossip, personalities. *Topicality,* or that which is "temporarily commonplace," as Alan Liu has succinctly defined it in his forthcoming book about Wordsworth, is a word which at least maps out the subject matter I am working with. But not for enough readers, perhaps. It is a technical term which has little resonance for most scholars outside the area of Renaissance studies, and even for Renaissance specialists it carries a faint but distinct odor of disreputability, a stigma which it is part of my purpose to examine. The word *topicality* will come up frequently in my discussion, but often I have preferred the simpler and less value laden idea of the "local" as defined in chapter 1. Even that term is far from innocuous, however, in terms of its impact upon Shakespeare. A "local" Shakespeare is a figure of massive instability, a contradiction in terms, a puzzle which keeps coming undone.

Given the mercurial nature of my subject, it is appropriate that this book, much more than my earlier ones, has evolved through discussion, oral presentation, and debate. My greatest debt in writing it has been to the patience and perceptiveness of audiences: at the Shakespeare Association (1985 and 1987) and Stanford (1987) for materials on Elizabeth, the Armada, and Joan of Arc; at the University of Chicago, MLA (1984), and La Jolla (1985) for the riddles of *Cymbeline*; at Brown (1986), MLA, the University of Texas, UC Santa Barbara, and various points in between (1987) for my analysis of the First Folio title page and other parts of the Introduction. Perhaps the best audience of all has been my friends and colleagues from the Department of English at the University of Wisconsin–Madison who comprise that unique organization affectionately known as the "Draft Group." They argued over two of my chapters with their customary zest and rigor, challenging me as usual to communicate effectively across the boundaries of my own area of expertise. Other readers of all or part of the manuscript have been just as helpful and perceptive. I owe special thanks to John Bender, Thomas Berger, Mark Eccles, Patricia Fumerton, Judith Kegan Gardiner, Stephen Greenblatt, Jean Howard, Arthur Kinney, Mary Ellen Lamb, Philip C. McGuire, Phyllis Rackin, Mark Rose, Mary Beth Rose, Peter Stallybrass, Len Tennenhouse, Jane Tylus, John M. Wallace, Don Wayne, Andrew Weiner, and Barry Weller. Many other debts are recorded in my notes. Institutional support and precious leave time for writing were provided by a fellowship from the John Simon Guggenheim Foundation, by grants from the Graduate School of the University of Wisconsin, and from the Vilas Foundation. My warmest thanks to these institutions, and to the Newberry Library, Chicago, and the Kohler Art Library, Madison, for providing help and congenial environments for research. I also owe thanks to Robert Grotjohn, Susan Rochette-Crawley, and William Soleim, who checked the footnotes. The people to whom I have owed most over the course of the project have been, as usual, my family. Lauren Marcus graciously postponed her birth until the final manuscript had reached the press. David and Emily kept me from succumbing to "Unease" through their healthy lack of interest in matters of Shakespearean topicality, and endured months on end of my glaze-eyed inattention while "that stupid old Shakespeare book" was gradually getting done. Despite their salutary skepticism, however, I have not lost my enthusiasm for the historically particular. It is not at all fashionable to attach a date to one's preface, but in light of the preoccupation in chapter 2 with events of the Armada year, I cannot resist the temptation. I am writing these words in 1988—just four centuries after the great unrecognized watershed of England and Elizabeth's victory in 1588.

I

Localization

Localization.
1. The action of making local, fixing in a certain place, or attaching to a certain locality; the fact of being localized. Also, an instance of such action or condition.
2. Assignment (in thought or statement) to a particular place or locality. Also, the ascertaining or determination of the locality of an object.

Oxford English Dictionary

The word was first used in the nineteenth century. It names a set of processes that have been applied to the figure of Shakespeare, as to his work, by biographers, textual scholars, and historically minded critics. But the idea of a Shakespeare who can be localized—attached to a particular place, institution, or ideology—has also, almost from the beginning, been resisted. He is the Bard, after all, not of an Age but for All Time.

"Of an Age" and "for All Time" are only apparent opposites. It is possible for authors to be localized in the sense that they and their work are given specific coordinates, associated with a specific milieu, without the implication that such activity restricts them within these "local" limits and closes off more general avenues of approach. Indeed, in many cases, localization has aided more general interpretation by giving us access to areas of a text which are culturally alien. When it comes to Shakespeare, however, localization is usually viewed as intolerable, imprisoning. Those critics who have sought to attach the Bard's work to a specific audience or milieu have not, as a rule, fared well with their peers. Even though every interpreter of Shakespeare depends on the work of previous "localizers" for such basic things as determining the order of the plays' composition and establishing the texts in which we read them, we have tended to set such work apart from the mainstream, as though by assigning the localizers to a fenced-in preserve we can minimize their impact on something we are willing to perceive only as universal and without limits. The tendency is not new. Even though the word *localization* dates only from the nineteenth century, resistance to the activity it names goes back, in the case of Shakespeare, at least as far as 1623. More than any other English writer, Shakespeare has been made the bearer of high claims for the universality of art.

THE ART OF THE UNCOMELY
FRONTISPIECE

Let us begin by looking at something we have all seen before, the title page of Shakespeare's First Folio (1623). The image of Shakespeare, the lettering, the verses on the facing page—all are familiar, perhaps numbingly so. But if the First Folio is considered in light of other English folio volumes of the period—volumes with which it had to compete for buyers' attention in the London bookstalls—there is something quite odd about the way it starts out.

The most striking feature of the page is, of course, the engraved portrait by Martin Droeshout, which has been the object of much vilification. It has, we hear, a depressing "pudding face" and a "skull" of "horrible hydrocephalous development." W. W. Greg put the general complaint more mildly: "It is not pleasing and has little technical merit." It is indeed less elegantly executed than many engravings, but why should that make it unpleasing? William Blake, himself an engraver, pronounced it very good.[1] Part of the discomfort may relate, instead, to its unsettling size and directness. By comparison with portraits on other title pages, it is extremely large, measuring more than six by seven inches—nearly as large as the portrait of James I that adorned his 1616 *Workes*. Photographic reductions like that offered here (figure 1) greatly understate its impact. It is also stark and unadorned. Unlike most portraits on title pages, it has no frame, no ornamental borders, even though such embellishments are supplied inside the volume for the rest of the introductory material and for the beginning of each play (figure 2). Nor does the title page include the allegorical figures and devices that might be expected to surround the engraved image of the author in a volume of such size and costliness and which were included in a number of other volumes printed by William Jaggard. The First Folio sold for one pound; William Prynne complained, "Shackspeers Plaies are printed in the best Crowne paper, far better than most Bibles."[2] Yet even the Puritan Prynne could scarcely have complained that the volume was overadorned.

Contemporary engraved frontispieces tended to place the author through visual reference to his métier, his intellectual affiliations, sometimes through highly personalized mottoes and emblems. *The Workes* of James I provides the most elaborate example, with a title page interweaving devices associated with the king: heraldic emblems of the Stuarts, four crowns for the four kingdoms united under his rule, Pax and Religio expressing his major policy goals, and opposite them, a portrait of the author in state with his motto *Beati pacifici* above (figure 3). The two sides mirror each other, the right, defining the king emblematically, the left, displaying the royal person to whom the symbols belong. For less exalted examples, we could turn to the *Civile Wares* of Samuel Daniel (1609) or to the 1625 edition of Samuel Purchas's *Pilgrimes* or to the 1630 folio *Workes* of John Taylor, the Water Poet (figures 4–6). The "comely frontispiece" was becoming so elaborately allegorical that often it had to be explicated, as in Sir Walter Ralegh's *History of the World* (1614), for which Ben Jonson supplied a poem interpreting the "Minde of the Front" and including oblique references to Ralegh's undeserved imprisonment.[3] Jonson's own *Workes* (1616) had a title page equally elaborate and "legible" to the learned as a vindication of the author's work in terms of the classical origins and history of the theater (figure 7). Michael Drayton's *Poly-Olbion* (1612) was even more self-consciously erudite. The author felt obliged to provide readers with a versified decoding and detailed gloss of the engraved title page on the facing page (figure 8). By contrast with these near-contemporary productions, the First Folio of Shakespeare appears stripped down to essentials.

It was, of course, a memorial volume published seven years after the author's death: Shakespeare had not, as the dedicatory epistle puts it, had the "fate, common with some, to be exequutor to his owne writings."[4] Since he had not supervised the edition, it could not be expected to show the personalized signature that the comely frontispiece represented, a display of authorial self-consciousness and pride which was, in any case, quite new in seventeenth-century England. Yet even for a memorial volume the First Folio's frontispiece is chary of elaboration. Lancelot Andrewes's *XCVI Sermons* was, like the First Folio, a collection published after its author's death. It lacks an engraved title page but does have woodcut decorations; it places the celebrated bishop in his contemporary milieu through the engraved portrait on the facing page, the usual place for portraits in memorial volumes. Andrewes wears his clerical garb and holds a book, perhaps the King James Version of the Bible, which he had helped to translate,

To the Reader.

This Figure, that thou here feeſt put,
   It vvas for gentle Shakeſpeare cut;
Wherein the Grauer had a ſtrife
   with Nature, to out-doo the life :
O, could he but haue dravvne his wit
   As well in braſſe, as he hath hit
His face ; the Print would then ſurpaſſe
   All, that vvas euer vvrit in braſſe.
But, ſince he cannot, Reader, looke
   Not on his Picture, but his Booke.

                B. I.

1.   Frontispiece (*above*) and facing title page (*opposite*) to Shakespeare's First Folio (1623).

Mr. WILLIAM
SHAKESPEARES

COMEDIES,
HISTORIES, &
TRAGEDIES.

Publiſhed according to the True Originall Copies.

Martin Droeshout ſculpſit London.

LONDON
Printed by Iſaac Iaggard, and Ed. Blount. 1623.

That *Rosincrance* and *Guildensterne* are dead :
Where should we haue our thankes ?

  Hor. Not from his mouth,
Had it th'abilitie of life to thanke you :
He neuer gaue command'ment for their death.
But since so iumpe vpon this bloodie question,
You from the Polake warres, and you from England
Are heere arriued. Giue order that these bodies
High on a stage be placed to the view,
And let me speake to th'yet vnknowing world,
How these things came about. So shall you heare
Of carnall, bloudie, and vnnaturall acts,
Of accidentall iudgements, casuall slaughters
Of death's put on by cunning, and forc'd cause,
And in this vpshot, purposes mistooke,
Falne on the Inuentors heads. All this can I
Truly deliuer.

  For. Let vs hast to heare it,
And call the Noblest to the Audience.
For me, with sorrow, I embrace my Fortune,
I haue some Rites of memory in this Kingdome,
Which are to claime, my vantage doth
Inuite me,

  Hor. Of that I shall haue alwayes cause to speake,
And from his mouth
Whose voyce will draw on more :
But let this same be presently perform'd,
Euen whiles mens mindes are wilde,
Lest more mischance
On plots, and errors happen.

  For. Let foure Captaines
Beare *Hamlet* like a Soldier to the Stage,
For he was likely, had he beene put on
To haue prou'd most royally :
And for his passage,
The Souldiours Musicke, and the rites of Warre
Speake lowdly for him.
Take vp the body : Such a sight as this
Becomes the Field, but heere shewes much amis.
Go, bid the Souldiers shoote.

    Exeunt Marching : after the which, a Peale of
    Ordenance are shot off.

FINIS.

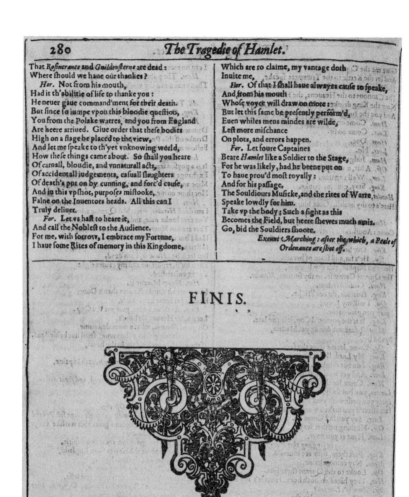

2.   Inside pages from the First Folio showing woodcut decorations.

THE TRAGEDIE OF
KING LEAR.

Actus Primus. Scœna Prima.

Enter Kent, Gloucester, and Edmond.

Kent.

Thought the King had more affected the Duke of *Albany*, then *Cornwall*.

Glou. It did alwayes seeme so to vs : But now in the diuision of the Kingdome, it appeares not which of the Dukes hee valewes most, for qualities are so weigh'd, that curiosity in neither, can make choise of eithers moity.

Kent. Is not this your Son, my Lord ?

Glou. His breeding Sir, hath bin at my charge. I haue so often bluth'd to acknowledge him, that now I am braz'd too't.

Kent. I cannot conceiue you.

Glou. Sir, this yong Fellowes mother could ; wherevpon she grew round womb'd, and had indeede (Sir) a Sonne for her Cradle, ere she had a husband for her bed. Do you smell a fault ?

Kent. I cannot wish the fault vndone, the issue of it, being so proper.

Glou. But I haue a Sonne, Sir, by order of Law, some yeere elder then this ; who, yet is no deerer in my account, though this Knaue came somthing sawcily to the world before he was sent for : yet was his Mother fayre, there was good sport at his making, and the horson must be acknowledged. Doe you know this Noble Gentleman, *Edmond* ?

Edm. No, my Lord.

Glou. My Lord of Kent :
Remember him heereafter, as my Honourable Friend.

Edm. My seruices to your Lordship.

Kent. I must loue you, and sue to know you better.

Edm. Sir, I shall study deseruing.

Glou. He hath bin out nine yeares, and away he shall againe. The King is comming.

Sennet. Enter King Lear, Cornwall, Albany, Gonerill, Regan, Cordelia, and attendants.

Lear. Attend the Lords of France & Burgundy, Gloster.

Glou. I shall, my Lord.   *Exit.*

Lear. Meane time we shal expresse our darker purpose. Giue me the Map there. Know, that we haue diuided In three our Kingdome : and 'tis our fast intent, To shake all Cares and Businesse from our Age, Conferring them on yonger strengths, while we Vnburthen'd crawle toward death. Our son of *Cornwal*, And you our no lesse louing Sonne of *Albany*,

We haue this houre a constant will to publish Our daughters seuerall Dowers, that future strife May be preuented now. The Princes, *France & Burgundy*, Great Riuals in our yongest daughters loue, Long in our Court, haue made their amorous soiourne, And heere are to be answer'd. Tell me my daughters (Since now we will diuest vs both of Rule, Interest of Territory, Cares of State) Which of you shall we say doth loue vs most, That we, our largest bountie may extend Where Nature doth with merit challenge. *Gonerill*, Our eldest borne, speake first.

Gon. Sir, I loue you more then word can weild ye matter, Deerer then eye-sight, space, and libertie, Beyond what can be valewed, rich or rare, No lesse then life, with grace, health, beauty, honor : As much as Childe ere lou'd, or Father found. A loue that makes breath poore, and speech vnable, Beyond all manner of so much I loue you.

Cor. What shall *Cordelia* speake ? Loue, and be silent.

Lear. Of all these bounds euen from this Line, to this, With shadowie Forrests, and with Champains rich'd With plenteous Riuers, and wide-skirted Meades We make thee Lady. To thine and *Albanies* issue Be this perpetuall. What sayes our second Daughter ? Our deerest *Regan*, wife of *Cornwall* ?

Reg. I am made of that selfe-mettle as my Sister, And prize me at her worth. In my true heart, I finde she names my very deede of loue : Onely she comes too short, that I professe My selfe an enemy to all other ioyes, Which the most precious square of sense professes, And finde I am alone felicitate In your deere Highnesse loue.

Cor. Then poore *Cordelia*, And yet not so, since I am sure my loue's More ponderous then my tongue.

Lear. To thee, and thine hereditarie euer, Remaine this ample third of our faire Kingdome, No lesse in space, validitie, and pleasure Then that conferr'd on *Gonerill*. Now our Ioy, Although our last and least : to whose yong loue The Vines of France, and Milke of Burgundie, Striue to be interest. What can you say, to draw A third, more opilent then your Sisters ? speake.

Cor. Nothing my Lord.

Lear. Nothing ?

Crounes haue their compasse, length of dayes their date,
Triumphes their tombes, felicitie her fate :
Of more then earth, can earth make none partakers,
But knowledge makes the KING most like his maker.

Simon Passæus sculp:Lond.   Ioh: Bill excudit.

3. Frontispiece (*above*) and facing title page (*opposite*) to *The Workes* of King James I (1616).

SVPER EST

RELIGIO

PAX

THE
WORKES
OF THE MOST HIGH
AND MIGHTY PRINCE,
IAMES,
By the grace of God, Kinge
of Great Brittaine
France & Ireland
Defendor of the
Faith &c:
Published by IAMES Bishop of
WINTON & Deane of his
Ma.t. Chappell Royall.
1.Reg.3.v.9. Loe I haue giuen thee
a wise and an vnderstanding heart.

LONDON
Printed by ROBERT
BARKER & Iohn Bill,
Printers to y.e Kings mo.t
excellent Ma.tie he.
1616.

Cum priuilegio

Renold Elstrack sculpsit

THE CIVILE WARES
betweene the Howſes of Lancaſter
and Yorke corrected and continued
by Samuel Daniel one of the Groomes
of hir Maieſties moſt honorable
Priuie Chamber.

Ætas prima canat veneres
poſtrema tumultus.

PRINTED
AT LONDON
by Simon Waterſonne
1609

Cockſonus
ſculp.

4. *Above:* portrait title page, Samuel Daniel, *The Civile Wares* (1609), showing symbols associated with the houses of York and Lancaster and Daniel's own motto. This title page, unlike the others reproduced here, is only quarto size.

5. *Opposite:* portrait title page, Samuel Purchas, *Pvrchas his Pilgrimes* (1625), showing King James and Prince Charles (*upper left*), the tomb of Elizabeth (*upper right*), portraits of explorers, maps, and Purchas himself (*bottom*). At the top is the New Jerusalem, to which all explorers must travel in the end.

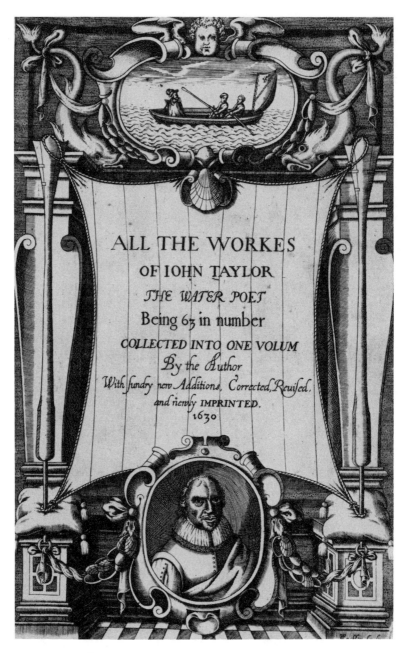

ALL THE WORKES

OF IOHN TAYLOR

THE WATER POET

Being 63 in number

COLLECTED INTO ONE VOLUM

By the Author

With sundry new Additions, Corrected, Reuised,
and newly IMPRINTED.
1630

6. Portrait title page, *The Workes* of John Taylor, the Water
    Poet (1630), showing a Thames riverboat to memorialize
    his trade, along with oars, sail, and seashells, and Taylor's
    portrait at the bottom.

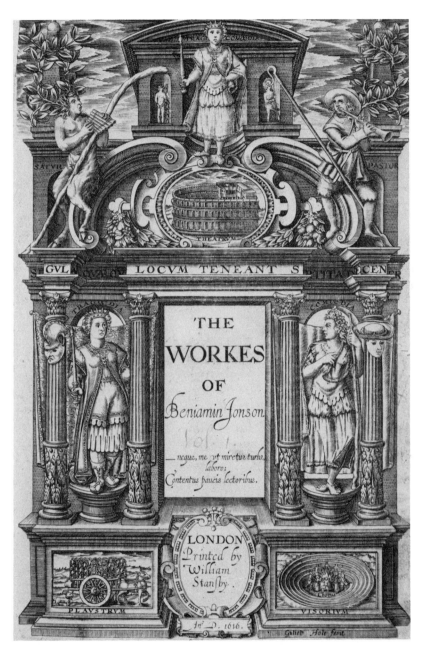

7. Title page to Ben Jonson's *Workes* (1616), showing decorations associated with the classical theater: a satyr, a shepherd, and Tragicomedy at the top; below that a depiction of the Roman theater, Tragedy, and Comedy; and at the bottom, two vignettes depicting the earliest history of the theater. On the left is Tragedy being carried around in a cart; on the right is a chorus dancing around a sacrifice to Bacchus.

Vpon the *Frontispice.*

* *Infula Caruli.*
ᵃ So *Hauillan* &
Vpton anciently
deliuered. I iu-
ſtifie it not; yet,
as well as others
can hit other at-
tributed Arms,
I might.
ᵇ *Obiect* not,
that it ſhould be
the *Eagle*, be-
cauſe it is now
borne by the
Emperors; and
that ſome He-
ralds ignorant-
ly publiſh it, as
I. Cæſars Coat,
Double headed.
They moue me
not; for plainly
the *Eagle* was
ſingle at that
time (vnles you
call it *Olimpi Bæ-*
αſιλ· Αιδϛινου,
as *Pindar* doth
Ioues Eagle) and
but newly vs'd
among the Ro-
mans (firſt by

THrough a *Triumphant Arch,* ſee *Albion* plas't,
In *Happy* ſite, in *Neptunes* armes embras't,
In *Power* and *Plenty,* on hir *Cleeuy* Throne
Circled with *Natures Ghirlands,* being alone
Stil'd *th'Oceans* * *Ifland.* On the Columnes beene
(As Trophies raiz'd) what Princes Time hath ſeene
Ambitious of her. In hir yonger years ,
Vaſt Earth-bred *Giants* woo'd her: but, who bears
Jn ᵃ *Golden field the Lion paſſant red,*
Æneas Nephew (*Brute*) them conquered.
Next, Laureat *Cæſar,* as a Philtre, brings,
On's ſhield, his Grandame ᵇ *Venus:* Him hir Kings
Withſtood. At length, the *Roman,* by long ſute,
Gain'd her (moſt Part) from th'ancient race of *Brute.*
Diuors't from Him, the *Saxon* ᶜ ſable *Horſe,*
Borne by ſterne *Hengiſt,* wins her: but, through force
Garding the ᵈ *Norman Leopards bath'd in Gules,*
She chang'd hir Loue to Him, whoſe Line yet rules.

Merius) as their *Standard,* not otherwiſe, votill afterward *Conſlantine* made it reſpect the two Empires: and ſince, it hath beene borne on a Shield. I tooke *Venus* proper to him, for that the ſtamp of hir face (ſhe being his Anceſtor *Æneas* his mother) in his Coins is frequent; and can ſo maintaine it here fitter, then many of thoſe inuented Coats (without colour of reaſon) attributed to the old Heroes. As for matter of Armory , *Venus* being a Goddeſſe may be as good Bearing, if not better then *Atalanta,* which, by expreſſe Authority of *Euripides,* was borne, in the *Thebanw*arre by *Parthenopæ*. ᶜ *Hengiſt* hath other Armes in ſome traditions, which are to be reſpected as Old wiues fictions. His name expreſſes a *Horſe,* and the Dukes of *Saxony* are ſaid to haue borne it anciently, before their Chriſtianity, *Sable* : therfore, if you giue him any, with moſt reaſon, let him haue this. ᵈ The common Blazon of the *Norman* Armes iuſtifies it. And, if you pleaſe, ſee for it to the XI. Canto.

8. Frontispiece (*above*) and facing title page (*opposite*) to Michael Drayton's *Poly-Olbion* (1612), showing image of Albion with explanatory poem and gloss.

9. Frontispiece (*above*) and facing title page (*opposite*) to the third edition of Lancelot Andrewes, *XCVI Sermons* (1635).

XCVI
SERMONS

BY

THE RIGHT HONOVRABLE,

AND

REVEREND FATHER IN GOD,
LANCELOT ANDREWES,
late Lord Bishop of WINCHESTER.

Published, by His MAJESTIES *speciall Command.*

THE THIRD EDITION,

Whereunto is added an Alphabeticall Table of the Principall Contents.

LONDON,
Printed by RICHARD BADGER,
MDCXXXV.

or perhaps a volume containing the very sermons which were now being published posthumously (figure 9). The words encircling the picture spell out Bishop Andrewes's ecclesiastical office—the "place" from which his effigy and works are offered to the reader.

The First Folio portrait of Shakespeare has none of these identifying marks. It appears on the title page itself instead of the facing page, and that position gives it special prominence. It was probably copied from a miniature painted during the author's lifetime, and preserves the sense of immediacy characteristic of the form, but the fact that it is not trimmed into the customary oval gives it a slightly unfinished look. Except for the stiff wired collar, which was out of date by 1623, it offers no particularizing details—only the raw directness of the image, as though to say that in this case, no artifice is necessary: this is the Man Himself.[5]

That, at least, is what the portrait seems to say; the verses on the facing page say otherwise. Even as the First Folio appears to cast off the conventions of the engraved frontispiece, it includes the expected poem "To the Reader" explicating the "Minde of the Front" and placed opposite the portrait head as though to imply the usual mirroring or continuity between the facing pages. Rather than making plain what appears obscure, however, Ben Jonson's short poem unsettles what seems direct. Shakespeare, the verses tell us, is not to be found after all in the compelling image opposite. The poem undermines the visual power of the portrait by insisting on it as something constructed and "put" there. It is a "Figure" cut "for" Shakespeare in which the engraver had a "strife / with Nature, to out-doo the life." "Out-doing" life suggests exceeding the original in some way rather than merely reproducing it, and the following lines seem to argue that the reader can only "hit" Shakespeare by going beyond his "face" to his "wit":

> O, could he but haue drawne his wit
> As well in brasse, as he hath hit
> His face, the Print would then surpasse
> All, that was euer writ in brasse.

This is a sentiment often found in Renaissance books; there is a version of the same argument affixed to the portrait of Lancelot Andrewes. What makes the idea peculiarly destabilizing in the First Folio is its juxtaposition with the large, compelling image. In *XCVI Sermons*, the portrait of Andrewes reinforces the message of the verses beneath by directing the viewer's attention away from his face and toward the volume in his hands. With eyes averted, Andrewes points at the book, held slightly open as though to invite readers inside.[6] On the First Folio title page, by contrast, the various elements are in competition with one another. The poem and the picture are on opposite pages, vying for the reader's attention. The portrait is not at all self-effacing—Shakespeare appears to gaze candidly outward, establishing a visual connection with the viewer which the verses placed opposite must break.

Ben Jonson's poem is, in a precise sense of the term, iconoclastic, shattering the power of the visual image in order to locate Shakespeare's identity elsewhere, in "wit." The poem invites the reader to look beyond the picture, just as the Andrewes volume does, but without having established the author's identity with anything like the same specificity. In fact, Jonson's poem sets readers off on a treasure hunt for the author: where is the "real" Shakespeare to be found? In "his Booke." It is there, in language rather than physical presence, the little poem assures us, that we will locate the Man Himself. It is there, too, that we will discover the felicitous intricacy missing from the uncomely frontispiece, for indeed the folio's inside is more embellished than its outside. At a time when English writers were asserting unprecedented autonomy and mastery over their own work through allegorical frontispieces, admonitory prefaces, overt and covert declarations of intent, Jonson's poem abolishes Shakespeare as an entity apart from his writings. What the author may have intended becomes void as a category because there is no space at all between the man and his work. Andrewes and other authors may gesture toward their books, but Shakespeare *is* the book.

And what are these writings that constitute Shakespeare? They are specified on the title page as "Mr. William Shakespeares Comedies, Histories, & Tragedies. Published according to the True Originall Copies." This declaration appears to reinforce the message of Ben Jonson's verses "To the Reader" by claiming a kind of truth for the writings inside: they are the "Originall." But the phrase "True Originall Copies" is troublesome. If these are "True" originals, what would a false one be? How can something be both an original and a copy? The *OED* offers numerous definitions of *copy*. A copy could be a transcript, image, imitation, or a "mere" show, hence a pretense; on the other hand, it could be a pattern or text to be copied or a manuscript prepared for printing. It is interesting, however, that the *OED* does not cite the First Folio usage to illustrate any of these meanings even though the First Folio offers such a prominent use of the term. Perhaps the dictionary's editors were unwilling to commit themselves to one or another definition. Even in the Renaissance usages they do cite, *copy* is a slippery word prone to confusion with its opposite; its use in conjunction with *original* makes it even more indeterminate. The phrase "True Originall Copies" operates within itself in the same way that the transition from portrait to verses does, seeming at first to set forth something direct and immediately apprehensible, then undermining the authenticity of what it presents.

Moreover, the title-page announcement of "True Originall Copies" undoes the certainty offered by Jonson's poem just opposite. Is Shakespeare to be found "in his Booke," as the poem suggests, or is the book itself a copy, a mere reproduction, as the portrait has turned out to be? Even contemporary readers, for whom the issue of textual authority was probably far less pressing than it is for us, might have been uncertain about what was being offered them. The First Folio opens with an implicit promise to communicate an authorial identity, which it instead repeatedly displaces: Shakespeare is somehow there, but nowhere definitively there.

From time to time Bardolaters have advocated the exhuming of Shakespeare's body so that, assuming that his remains have survived as well as others in the Stratford area, his actual physiognomy could be known, and the "mystery" of the frontispiece portrait be solved. At similar times, anti-Stratfordians have argued that there was, indeed, no playwright named Shakespeare: Jonson's iconoclastic advice "To the Reader" was a cryptic message that the man in the portrait was not the author—unless, as some anti-Stratfordians have suggested, what the portrait actually depicts is the real author wearing Shakespeare's face as a mask.[7] These reactions are generated at least in part by the folio title page itself, with its teasing postponement of a promised "True Originall." Readers have delighted in pulling apart Droeshout's engraving. Shakespeare, it is complained, has lopsided hair and a doublet with two left armholes, a displaced nose, eyes that don't match, a head much too big for the body. Such complaints blame the picture for a broader discomfort arising out of the endlessly circulating interplay among all elements of the title page—the portrait, the words above, the poem.

Shakespeare, as presented through the rhetorical anomalies of the First Folio, is an author who is simultaneously not an author in the proprietary sense that contemporaries were beginning to claim for themselves. As the volume sloughs off devices that would "localize" the author's identity, so it resists the creation of a localized audience. The comely frontispiece of the late Renaissance was like a veil covering a book's contents and preserving it from vulgar eyes: only those learned enough to "read" the book's visual schematization on the title page had earned the right to enter the text itself. Elaborate engraved frontispieces thus served contemporary authors as a way of preselecting their audience, or at least of favoring some segment of it. Ben Jonson's title page prominently cites Horace in Latin, borrowing the citation to suggest that he, like his classical progenitor, is *Contentus paucis lectoribus* (figure 7). He writes not for the crowd but for the discriminating few, and the vignettes at the bottom of the page would indeed have been unintelligible to all but the very learned.

Yet authors like Jonson, who were beginning to take the trouble to prepare their work for the press and see it through publication, clearly had hopes of attracting a wider public. The veil could not be so impenetrable after all. And so we find that some authors, like Drayton in his *Poly-Olbion*, felt obliged to provide explanatory materials that would help prospective readers overcome the frontispiece's resistance to interpretation. There was a tension, often quite explicit in these volumes, between the intellectual elitism claimed for authorship and the broader appeal required if authorship were to prosper in the marketplace.

Shakespeare's First Folio addresses the claim of elitism by appearing not to do so. The title page, unlike the usual engraved frontispiece, offers no obvious barriers against perusal by the unlearned. Its apparent simplicity suggests the type of directness associated with popular materials—news books or ballads or devotional manuals, particularly those with a strongly Protestant cast. For contemporaries the iconoclasm of the title page may have given the volume a distinctly Protestant aura: the contemporary portrait engravings that come closest to Droeshout's Shakespeare are those of the early Protestant martyrs in Henry Holland's strongly anti-Catholic *Herωologia Anglica* (1620); moreover, the earl of Pembroke, the First Folio's major dedicatee, was known for his support of strongly reformist causes.[8] If the title page conveyed such a message, however, the fact that it "veiled" a collection of plays—works of the devil in the eyes of many of the "hotter Protestants"—would have dispersed its aura of sanctity, or perhaps served as a silent vindication of the volume's contents against such opinion. In any case, the unadorned title page creates an appearance of openness to all manner of readers.

Heminge and Condell's prefatory address "To the great Variety of Readers" lumps all potential readers of the First Folio together, urging them to buy, buy, as a street pedlar might hawk ballads: "Well! It is now publique, & you will stand for your priuiledges wee know: to read, and censure. Do so, but buy it first. That doth best commend a Booke, the Stationer saies. Then, how odde soeuer your braines be, or your wisedomes, make your licence the same, and spare not. Iudge your sixe-pen'orth, your shillings worth, your fiue shillings worth at a time, or higher, so you rise to the iust rates, and welcome. But, what euer you do, Buy." The language so strongly echoes the Induction to Jonson's *Bartholomew Fair* that many are convinced Jonson wrote the preface himself.[9] However, the strategy of his Induction is inverted. There, Jonson enumerated the various segments of his audience so that he could order them into a hierarchy of "understanders"; here, the preface melds the various segments of the readership into a single group, irrespective of their special "priuiledges" and "wisedome." The learned who come to the First Folio schooled in the art of the comely frontispiece will not go away empty-handed: its title page and accompanying verses offer complexities aplenty for those who choose to read within the conventions of the form. But "understanding" readers will not be rewarded with any special information that will set them apart from others. If anything, they will be subjected to special frustration, since the title page refuses to yield a clear message about the author. In the First Folio, Shakespeare is made immediately available, yet withheld, and the effect is to blunt distinctions among different groups and forge a more generalized readership.

An escape from the game of withholding a "localized" Shakespeare is finally effected by Ben Jonson's commendatory poem, which comes after Heminge and Condell's address "To the great Variety of Readers." Jonson's poem displaces the author yet again, but assigns him to a place which is not a place and lacks "local" character. The title of Jonson's commendatory poem "To the memory of my beloued, The AVTHOR Mr. William Shakespeare: And what he hath left vs" suggests that the First Folio has an author after all. "His Booke" is indeed only a copy; the suspicions induced by the title page turn out to have been justified. In Jonson's commendatory poem, Shakespeare is no longer to be perceived as coterminous with his writings, but exists somewhere else, apart and above, in a place which we can, I suppose, call Art. He is part of a starry array of comedians and tragedians, European, British, Latin, and Greek, who shine down from the heavens. Of this glory, "his Booke" provides a mere reflected light:

> But stay, I see thee in the *Hemisphere*
> Aduanc'd, and made a Constellation there!
> Shine forth, thou Starre of *Poets*, and with rage,
> Or influence, chide, or cheere the drooping Stage;
> Which, since thy flight from hence, hath mourn'd like night,
> And despaires day, but for thy Volumes light.

This realm of transcendent perfection is a place where we have long been accustomed to finding Shakespeare and the place where many have felt most comfortable imagining him. It is outside contingency, purged of the nagging, petty details "of an Age" that might threaten the Bard's status as a universal "for All Time." But this final place to which Jonson assigns him is no more "natural" or inherent to Shakespeare than the more localized set of milieus which the producers of the First Folio (and more recent generations of readers) have set aside as marginal.

Ben Jonson's idealizing poem dominates the First Folio's dedicatory epistles and poems. In this portion of the front matter, unlike the title page itself, there are vestiges of a Shakespeare who can be localized in terms of specific personal traits and institutional affiliations. His name heads a list of "Principall Actors in all these Playes"; he and his work are said to have been shown "much fauour" by the earls of Pembroke and Montgomery; his "flights" "did take *Eliza*, and our *Iames*"; he is asserted to have had "small *Latine*, and lesse *Greeke*"; the editors claim that what "he thought, he vttered with that easinesse, that wee haue scarse receiued from him a blot in his papers" (the idea of the "True Originall" again); his "dainty Playes" made the "Globe of heau'n and earth to ring"; one contributor even refers to his "Stratford *Moniment*." But these scattered pieces of information are only admissible because the Bard himself has been placed in a realm apart. Unlike other memorial volumes, the First Folio defers identifying details about the author until he has been established as transcendent.

Moreover, the pages of front matter that give the most historical specificity to the idea of Shakespeare—the pages containing the list of actors and the poems by Leonard Digges and James Mabbe (I.M.)— are floaters, with no fixed place in the volume. The list and the two poems are part of the same unsigned sheet apparently included as an afterthought and appearing in different places in different copies of the First Folio. Sometimes they come after the editors' preface "To the great Variety of Readers" and before Ben Jonson's commendatory poem (between [A4] and [A5]). Sometimes they appear after the "Catalogue" of plays ([A6]).[10] But whichever position the extra pages occupy, they fail to fit in: the list of "Principall Actors" interrupts the sequence of introductory materials and jumbles the organization. Once again, the First Folio resists localization. The elements that seem most immediate in terms of their evocation of the author as a man who existed at a definite time and as part of a specific cultural milieu are out of place, as though alien to the transcendent image of Shakespeare that Jonson's poem constructs.

The Bard generated by the First Folio is a figure for Art itself as Renaissance humanists like Ben Jonson wished to imagine it, existing in lofty separateness from the vicissitudes of life, yet capable, from its eminence, of shedding influence, "cheere," and admonition. However hackneyed this idea may appear to us, it was quite new in 1623, particularly as applied to someone who wrote for the stage. The folio offsets the lowly social status usually assigned to the "common player" by presenting Shakespeare as a gentleman. In the portrait he wears a garb specified by contemporaries as typical for the "English Gentleman" and the accompanying material nearly always uses his name with the honorific prefix "Mr."[11] Like similar volumes, the First Folio claims for its author an exalted status based on his actual accomplishments: even *The Workes* of James I had praised the king for the "knowledge" displayed therein (figure 3). But unlike other such volumes, the First Folio exacts as the price of this elevation the individualizing details which make the author identifiably himself. The usual folio volume encouraged readers to perceive continuities between "local" particularities about the author and the higher and more generalized realm of fame and permanence to which the author laid claim through the work: the author was both "local" and transcendent. The First Folio disrupts the perception of such continuities. It makes high claims for "The AVTHOR" while simultaneously dispersing authorial identity, so that "Mr. William Shakespeare" becomes almost an abstraction, a generic category, while remaining an unstable composite. Given the rhetorical turbulence of the volume's introductory materials, constructing Shakespeare requires almost a leap of faith, like Jonson's, and depends upon the suppression of a host of particularities that recede into indeterminacy when an attempt is made to pin them down. If we insist upon clinging to such ephemera, the volume seems to tell us, we will lose the "essence" of Shakespeare and fragment the unstable, generalized figure that the First Folio constructs. Then there will be no Shakespeare after all. That is a very powerful inducement against localization—at least if authorial identity is something we wish to value.

THE DEMISE OF THE
TRANSCENDENT BARD

If Shakespeare is for All Time, as Jonson's dedicatory poem asserts, then the well-turned and "true-filed lines" in which his "minde, and manners" shine forth should be similarly timeless. Just as it omits differentiating details about the author, the First Folio suppresses particular data about the plays that might undermine the appeal to universality. The quarto editions had regularly included information about staging on the title page, as though to assure buyers that the playtext they were about to read would bring them as close as possible to the experience of attending a performance. They were offered *Romeo and Juliet* "As it hath been often (with great applause) plaid publiquely, by the right Honourable the L. of *Hunsden* his Seruants," *Richard III* "As it hath been lately Acted by the Right honourable the Lord Chamberlaine his seruants," *Hamlet* "As it hath beene diuerse times acted by his Highnesse seruants in the Cittie of London : as also in the two Vniuersities of Cambridge and Oxford, and else-where," *King Lear* "*As it was played before the Kings Maiestie at Whitehall vpon S.* Stephans *night in Christmas Hollidayes.* By his Maiesties seruants playing vsually at the Globe on the Bancke-side."[12] All this information is omitted from the folio texts: the acting companies are not even mentioned by name.

This reticence can be understood in terms of the First Folio's elevation of Shakespeare and his work. Contemporaries disparaged quarto playtexts as mere "riff-raffs" and "baggage books"; the folio was much more respectable.[13] But other folio volumes were less thorough about winnowing out details relating to the conditions of artistic production. The only previous collection in English with a high preponderance of plays had been Jonson's 1616 *Workes*. Jonson did not suppress all basic information about the performance of his plays—quite the contrary. For each, he carefully supplied a date and a list of the players who had performed in it. There is none of that in the First Folio; even listings of the "Names of the Actors" occur only rarely, seemingly more to fill up white spaces than for any other reason. It is as though, in the case of Shakespeare, the very fact that the plays had been acted (and were still being acted) was in some way peculiarly damaging—as though they had to be cut off from the milieu of their production in order to be lifted into the timeless, transcendent place inhabited by the Author himself.

Again, this is a not-unfamiliar gesture, this transformation of the playtexts from records of performance to a form of literature in its own right, part of the realm called Art. I would like, as before, to call attention to the startling newness of the strategy. The First Folio has taught us (and readers and editors before us) to bracket off particularizing details that might link the plays to a specific sixteenth- or early seventeenth-century milieu. Such details, to the extent that they survive at all, are to be treated as ephemera, indispensable for dating the plays, perhaps, but thereafter sloughed off as distractions from the essence of the work, in the same way that the First Folio "disowned" title-page matter from the quartos. The First Folio's valorization of the general neatly reverses the set of priorities which Renaissance audiences habitually brought to the theater.

Then, it was the particular that made plays most meaningful, most memorable, most dangerously attractive. Hamlet calls players the "Abstracts and breefe Chronicles of the time" (TLN 1565). He is, of course, a mere character in a play himself and has his own ax to grind—he is about to use a play (*The Murder of Gonzago*, extant in "choyce Italian") to test the culpability of his uncle. Yet his characterization of players captures something about Renaissance drama almost too obvious to require spelling out. When contemporaries attended and talked about plays it was the currency of the stage, its ability to "Abstract" personalities and "Chronicle" events in the very unfolding, that was the primary object of fascination. Local meaning was at the center—an "essence" inherently unstable in that it altered along with shifting circumstances. More generalized meaning was peripheral. By detaching Shakespeare's plays from specific milieus of performance, the First Folio turned contemporary reactions to the drama inside out.

Instability is not necessarily comfortable. Even vicarious immersion in the frantic environment of contemporary interpretation may convince us that there was something to be said for severing connections with it. Given the feckless, highly ingenious, almost ungovernable gusto with which contemporaries found parallels between stage action and contemporary events, there are few things that plays could be relied upon *not* to mean. In early Tudor times, plays were openly used both for official propaganda and for political agitation. Heavy-handed moralities glorified the Reformation; one play displayed Henry VIII cutting off the heads of the Catholic clergy with a two-handed sword. On the other hand, according to Holinshed it was at a play that leaders of Kett's Rebellion (1549) incited followers to "enter further into thir wicked enterprise."[14] During the early years of Elizabeth, the drama was no less embroiled in events and personalities. Plays like *Gorboduc* and *The Comedy of Patient and Meek Grissell* took up the vexed matter of the royal succession. During the 1560s Elizabeth herself regularly interpreted comedies presented at court as offering advice about the succession: she was to follow the "woman's part," a part she professed to dislike, and marry as the heroine inevitably did at the end. Given her ability to find "Abstracts of the time" even in seemingly neutral materials, no comedy performed before her was safe from topical interpretation.

Her subjects were no less agile. The fact that some plays like *Gorboduc* and the Tudor moralities commented so directly on contemporary affairs encouraged audiences to find similar resonances nearly everywhere else. During the 1580s court plays like George Peele's *Arraignment of Paris* built the presence of the queen into their very structure: the *Arraignment* could not be performed at all unless the queen played her part. But even when such connections were not made structurally necessary, they were regularly found out. Negative examples are the most prominent in the surviving records if only because censorship caused them to receive special scrutiny. So, in 1601, a sudden rash of performances of Shakespeare's *Richard II* was taken by Elizabeth and her chief ministers (and not without reason) as propaganda for the Essex rebellion.[15] The next monarch faced similar affronts. During the early years of James I's reign, the king, his ministers, and his favorites were regularly lampooned; so were figures like the duke of Buckingham and the Spanish ambassador in the 1620s. Even contemporary folk drama "Abstracted" and "Chronicled" the times. May games regularly included highly charged topical materials. In a 1537 May Day play in Suffolk, actors told "of a king, how he should rule his realm"; one actor playing the part of "husbandry" said "many things against gentlemen, more than was in the book of the play." During early Stuart times, "scurrilous and slanderous matter" against the government or local magnates was still such a regular feature of the May games that they were included, along with the drama of the professional companies, in official orders of censorship.[16] Plays were caught up in a whirl of intense if nebulous topical speculation in which meaning was multiple, radically unfixed, but also capable of settling into temporary fixity as a result of interpretation.

If this indeterminacy was exhilarating, it also struck some contemporaries as wearisome or worse. State censorship can itself be understood as an agenda for stabilizing meaning, at least in the sense that a play licensed for production is officially declared free of a whole range of potentially subversive significations. But censorship was as erratic as the interpretation it sought to control, and did not necessarily dampen the fervor for interpretation. Sometimes it merely increased the fascinating subtlety of the game. In psychoanalytic treatment, dreams are often accessible early on; however, with the repeated intrusion of interpretation, they become wily and multiple, fragmenting among a number of figures and situations motifs that would earlier have been rendered more simply. Similar evasive strategies were available to Renaissance dramatists, and we shall discuss some of them, like Shakespeare's "double writing" of texts, at a later point.[17] For the moment, however, we need to notice how efficiently the First Folio's bald presentation of the playtexts distances them from the maelstrom of contemporary interpretation. Some of those most obviously embedded in contemporary affairs, like *Coriolanus* and *Macbeth*, or the three plays that will be given extended analysis in the following chapters, appeared in print for the first time only in the First Folio—in a generalized context that made their topical resonances fainter and easier to overlook. In attempting to date these plays, we must rely almost entirely on internal evidence and chance records of performance from other sources. Memorializing the topical was no part of the First Folio's construction of a transcendent Shakespeare.

It has been suggested that the new Renaissance creation called The Author was itself the product of censorship: who had written a book or play and what was intended by it only became issues when officialdom took up the task of determining its range of potential meanings. Many Privy Council and Star Chamber investigations, like that surrounding the Essex faction's sponsorship of *Richard II*, focused almost entirely on the issue of intent.[18] For writers who wished to be Authors, to own and "own up to" the meanings of their texts, there were compelling reasons for attempting to limit the field of meaning within which their work could be interpreted. In seventeenth-century England, we begin to hear anguished cries from authors about "inuading interpreters" who make connections that the authors have not intended and are unwilling to accept.[19] Even when authors constructed elaborate allegorical commentaries upon specific contemporary events, as Jonson and others did, for example, in entertainments and masques at court, they regularly devised strategies for deflecting interpretation away from the "local" and toward the "more removed" and general—as though the very attempt to build identifiable and relatively stable topical meanings into a text was a tawdry secret that could not be openly acknowledged.[20] Authors wanted to be recognized as individuals with their own identifying attributes—hence the flowering of the "comely frontispiece" with its personalized mottoes and symbolism. But at the same time, they wanted to claim for their work some of the protective distance associated with the Greek and Roman classics, texts in which topical references could certainly be identified, but for the era in which they had been written, at a safe remove from the seventeenth century.

That does not mean, of course, that seventeenth-century authors did not want their work to influence contemporary and future generations, only that they were beginning to want such influence to be transmitted in ways that were (or at least could be made to appear) general, unexceptionable, and hence unthreatening to themselves and their reputations. In reading the classics, Renaissance schoolchildren were taught the art of "application"—reading was to be a continual weighing and connecting whereby unhealthy materials were rejected and moral lessons culled and applied to personal and public situations.[21] This learned readerly activity was strongly pluralist in that there was no set limit to the range of "applications" that could be drawn. But it was far more orderly than the interpretive maelstrom surrounding the drama in performance. And perhaps more to the point, it encouraged readers to redirect their energies away from the evanescent thrill of time-bound topical readings in favor of more generalized interpretation with the goal of self-knowledge and moral instruction.

Just such an interpretive situation is established for Shakespeare by Jonson's commendatory poem to the First Folio. The author is in the heavens, from which nothing but benign influence can be imagined to flow. His plays offer "light" to those capable of recognizing the good, "cheere" to those needing inspiration, and chiding to those needing correction. For lack of a better word, I will call this suggested mode of reading *humanist*, even though the term is much too broad. *Humanism* as used here will refer not to the whole spectrum of Renaissance attitudes that have been associated with the name, but to one late and codifying set of attitudes associated with the creation of a special realm for art. [22] In the First Folio, the plays are covered by a humanist overlay that protects them against the marauding inroads of irresponsible interpretation. As in other "authored" works of the late Renaissance, there is an implicit contract between writer and readers, or in this case between the volume's compilers and readers, governing the terms in which the contents may be read. Shakespeare is, Jonson's poem asserts, "proofe" against "seeliest Ignorance," "crafty Malice," and "blinde Affection, which doth ne're aduance / The truth, but gropes, and vrgeth all by chance" ([A4r])—safe, in other words, against the perils of ungoverned topical interpretation, in which meaning is shifting and transient, at the mercy of the whim or vices of a mercurial audience.

It is hard, perhaps, for us to think ourselves back into a cultural situation in which such insulation could have been exhilarating. The construction of a transcendent, independent place for art was a project that empowered seventeenth-century authors and opened up a whole range of new possibilities for their lives and work. There are twentieth-century cultural contexts in which the creation of a separate, autonomous space for art is similarly associated with release from preexisting perils and limits—we may think immediately of Eastern Europe, for example, where the idea of artistic transcendence can have much the same enabling function it had for authors of the late Renaissance. [23] In Anglo-American culture of the late 1980s, however, the humanist project carries far different associations. It is implicated in a system of values and institutionalized hierarchies that many of us— British cultural materialists, American new historicists, poststructuralist critics of many different varieties—find more deadening than invigorating.

Shakespeare enskied may be a symbol for the transcendence and permanence of art, but any closed-off space inhabited for too long is likely to become confining. As we have become increasingly distant in time and culture from the First Folio, the humanist *credo* that art can promote self-knowledge has been generalized to the point that it amounts to a kind of formalism. Shakespeare's "universal" temper and "oceanic mind" have been enshrined for so long that these concepts, once so thrilling for readers and critics, now function less to preserve the vitality of the figure we call Shakespeare than to condemn it to slow asphyxiation.[24] It can be argued that by the 1960s and early 1970s, interpretation governed by humanist assumptions about the transcendence of Shakespeare was already playing itself out. During that period, the sheer mass of Shakespeare criticism was a wearisome burden for many scholars. There were attempts to curb the production of articles and books, as though everything worth saying about Shakespeare had already been codified as dogma. The decline of the humanist Shakespeare was accelerated by the political activism that burst upon universities and other public institutions during the 1960s and early 1970s. For many scholars and students of that era, the formalist enclosure of art was not just barren but reckless and irresponsible. As the "ivory towers" of learning painfully reengaged with a milieu of action from which they had held serenely aloof, the transcendent Shakespeare began coming apart.

In his dedicatory poem, Ben Jonson proposed Shakespeare as the strongest English contender for a timeless canon of great authors. But in the late twentieth century, the idea of canonicity has become problematic in itself: it sets unnecessary limits and links up with too many other institutionalized hierarchies that have become confining. Jonson's poem established Shakespeare as a figure for the universality of art. But if his readers are unable to accede to the Neoplatonic assumptions behind his elevation of the Bard, that universality may appear less a single, unitary thing than an amalgam of particular instances. What we call human nature itself now appears less general than it once did and less separable from particular cultural situations. With the demise of what has been called the "transcendent subject," the construct called authorship has itself lost much of its élan because it appears implicated in an idealist aesthetics that many of us now find neither attractive nor philosophically tenable.[25] As part of our assimilation of poststructuralism and postmodernism in their various guises, we have developed an appetite for dissonance, for an art which is multicentric, shifting, provisional, implicated in other things.

The First Folio gives readers two choices: either we must accept the transcendent Shakespeare, or there will be no Shakespeare at all, only an untidy pile of fragments that cannot be assembled. If those were indeed our choices, many of us would opt for the pieces. The idea of fragmenting Shakespeare has lost some of its terror because the transcendent Shakespeare has already begun to come apart; such an assault upon one of our chief symbols for the autonomy of art will not be particularly devastating if the autonomy was an illusion in the first place. But there are possibilities beyond the false dilemma posed by the 1623 folio. One of these would be to collect and assemble the very particularities the First Folio was at pains to suppress, but without tying them to its transcendent version of the Bard. That is the project here called the localization of Shakespeare. It is already under way, particularly in the work of scholars who came of age during the 1960s and 1970s. The First Folio's humanist covering has broken apart and, in gingerly fashion, we have begun to sift through what lies beneath. But there are inhibitions that hover about the enterprise.

TOWARD A NEW TOPICALITY

The unease associated with topicality is at the very least threefold: what bothered Renaissance writers about topical reading was not the same as what may bother us, and there have been various other attitudes in between. For the compilers of the First Folio, particularizing details were to be dispensed with if only because they interfered with the project of constructing a generalized Shakespeare. The Renaissance unease with topicality tended to focus on changing definitions of the place of art: authors were caught between the need for currency, the need to attract an immediate public, and a newly emerging desire for permanence and monumentality. A more massive unease is associated with nineteenth- and twentieth-century formalist methodologies—with New Criticism, for example, which tended to view all attempts at "local" reading as incompatible with the essential nature of literature as a thing apart.[26] The dismantling of the humanist enterprise in its Renaissance and its twentieth-century forms has cleared the way

for a renewal of interest in local reading. In theory, we are able to tolerate—even to welcome—the indeterminacy that topical interpretation seems inevitably to carry with it. Yet despite the surge of interest
in exploring the tangled connections between art and other things,
there is still an unease about topicality—particularly when the approach is applied to Shakespeare. Local reading tends to be associated
with antiquarianism and the valorization of origins, with an older
mode of historicism that deciphered texts in order to discover and fix
the meaning of Shakespeare, thereby buttressing his place in the canon
in much the same way that Bardolaters have advocated the exhuming
of Shakespeare's body in order to prove that the Bard was really
himself.

The scandal of topical reading is, of course, that it has accomplished
no such thing. When sudden waves of enthusiasm for topical reading
have swept over Shakespeareans in the past, the effect has almost invariably been not to confirm the power of historical research to establish the definitive meaning of a text, but rather to expose significant
weaknesses in traditional historicist methodology. Each critic has felt
obliged to discredit previous topical readings to make space for his or
her more probable reading, only to be discredited in turn by the next.
One such exercise was the controversy over *Love's Labor's Lost*, whose
male leads all bear the names of actual French heroes of the Henrician
wars. The search for solutions to the play's topical puzzles became so
intense that, in the complaint of Alfred Harbage, it acted upon otherwise reputable scholars "as catnip acts upon perfectly sane cats."[27] Another type of topical reading popular during the heyday of traditional
historicism in the 1920s revived the seemingly paranoid tendency of
Elizabethan and Jacobean audiences to read the same set of events into
every play. According to this approach, specific details recalling one or
more traumatic public episodes like the succession crisis or the Gunpowder Plot, the Gowrie conspiracy or the Essex affair, can be found
interlayered in *Macbeth* and *Hamlet* and *Lear*, so that the works of the
Bard become impressionistic composite renderings of burning issues
of the day. This is the methodology Richard Levin has ridiculed as
"Fluellenism"; but he might just as well have called it Elizabethism,
since the queen and her subjects practiced it with as much zeal as the
character in *Henry V*.[28] Like the search for keys to *Love's Labor's Lost*,
the effort collapses from within, since it defeats its own goal of finding
stable meaning. And more serious than that, it makes scholarship look

undignified, exposes the search for truth about literature as a pursuit no more weighty than the Renaissance passion for decoding which it uncannily reproduces.

But I would suggest that there is a yet deeper threat to authenticity associated with traditional topical reading—a threat that those who have used historical approaches have not taken sufficiently into account. Topical interpretation is a favorite method among the anti-Stratfordians, who respond to Shakespeare's failure to possess a stable authorial identity by reassigning his works to someone else, usually the earl of Oxford. In the present century, whenever topical approaches to Shakespeare have flourished, the anti-Stratfordian movement has been particularly active, as though following as the inevitable corollary of historicism. Topical interpretation and anti-Stratfordianism have both proliferated during and after the major wars, when the highly charged atmosphere of national crisis has broken down customary barriers between art and other things. In 1924 E. K. Chambers took on the "heresies" of contemporary historicism in the Annual Shakespeare Lecture of the British Academy. His address, entitled "The Disintegration of Shakespeare," began, "The rock of Shakespeare's reputation stands four-square to the winds of Time. But the waves of criticism beat perpetually about its base, and at intervals we must stand back and re-affirm our vision of the structural outlines." The "Disintegrators" Chambers was most interested in challenging were textual scholars who broke down the idea of the Shakespearean "Originall" by investigating the collaborative methods of Renaissance dramatists and playhouses. The worst of these assaults upon Shakespeare, he claimed, "amounts to an alien invasion." The wartime language is unmistakable: Shakespeare is a national rock, a Gibraltar, which must be heroically defended against all attempts to undermine it. Chambers numbered among the "invaders" the anti-Stratfordians, ultimate Disintegrators, "small minds" following in the wake of more respectable scholars who chipped away at the Rock.[29] But the anti-Stratfordians themselves explained their mission differently.

Thomas Looney, the most influential advocate of the earl of Oxford, saw his *"Shakespeare" Identified* (1920) as part of the British war effort. He, like Chambers, was defending British culture against the inroads of the barbarians, but his method was to hammer away at the shaky substructure of the Shakespeare monument in order to topple it and replace it with something worthier and more secure. In the name of "spiritual interests" and the "claims of Humanity," the "butcher-boy of Stratford" had to give way to the earl of Oxford.[30] The American branch of the anti-Stratfordian Shakespeare Fellowship was founded in 1939 when the pressures of World War II caused the British branch to be suspended. Its founder wrote, "As war raises its ghastly figure among the most enlightened and cultured peoples of the earth, art and literature flee into hiding places. The pages of European magazines are full of pictures of men burying priceless stained glass in the earth, hiding rare statues and paintings." In the same way, the Shakespeare Fellowship would save Anglo-American culture by moving "Shakespeare" to a safer identity.[31] The plays had to be assigned to someone less shadowy than the picture on the front of the folio, someone with a full and detailed life story and impeccable upper-class credentials, someone easier to assimilate to the honorable role of author.

The research by which these advocates of the high place of art have defended their candidate for Bard is a devastating unconscious parody of traditional historical methodology. They claim to have the same interest in establishing truth and make the same use of topical allusions for such matters as dating the plays, but their conclusions wildly disrupt the efforts of Shakespearean historicism. Using topical methods, anti-Stratfordian researchers can confidently demonstrate that *Measure for Measure* relates to the earl of Oxford's love affair with Queen Elizabeth, that *As You Like It* must be assigned to 1582 because of its reference to half-pence, or, for that matter, that all of Shakespeare's plays can be traced to a time before 1604, the year of the earl of Oxford's death. This fringe movement, which has dogged topical approaches to Shakespeare like a dark shadow, has been more corrosive than we have been willing to admit (it convinced Sigmund Freud, for example) and has had the effect, along with the First Folio itself, of casting a faint yet lingering odor of inauthenticity over all Shakespearean historicism. Even as the present study is being written, anti-Stratfordians have become active again, with brand new topical readings designed once and for all to expose the "great hoax" of the First Folio title page and shatter the false god called Shakespeare.

Anti-Stratfordians have suggested that one of our major research centers be renamed thus:

FOLGER SHAKESPEARE LIBRARY
(A PSEUDONYM)[32]

Such gestures, so richly evocative of the mystifications of the First Folio title page itself, undermine the credibility of all critical work on

Shakespeare by challenging the *idea* of Shakespeare. Even those of us who speak out with most vehemence against the humanist creation called the Bard, and against the foibles of traditional historicism, still seem to want to keep a thing we can call Shakespeare if only to magically guarantee the authenticity of our own revisionist enterprise. Shades of the humanist endeavor are still with us: even as we lash out against the excesses of transcendent formalism, we want to be able to validate our own new methodologies, teach our own revised notions of truth and virtue, through our interpretation of something we still call Shakespeare. "Local" reading threatens that enterprise by turning us away—temporarily at least—from a Shakespeare who can be perceived as self-cohesive and universal.

"Localization" is an idea we need to apply to ourselves as readers as well as to what we read. In the same way that we have begun to explore the "local" circumstances that have shaped past critical efforts (like John Dover Wilson's encounter with a fragmented *Hamlet* during the First World War, for example, or E. M. Tillyard's construction of an ordered "world picture" during the Second), we need to locate our own attempts at reading, or at least never lose our awareness that our activity has local coordinates of its own.[33] British cultural materialists are not at all reticent about placing their work in terms of broader cultural and political goals: one of their aims is to appropriate Shakespeare for the British left. On this side of the Atlantic, we are more quizzical and guarded about what it is that we mean to do, and may associate localization with a kind of retrograde regionalism. But it can be more positive than that: "local" reading can be—and should be—a suspension of our ruling methodologies, insofar as that is possible, in favor of a more open and provisional stance toward what we read and the modes by which we interpret; it should be a process of continual negotiation between our own *place*, to the extent that we are able to identify it, and the local *places* of the texts we read. Local reading may thus have affinities with more radical varieties of regionalism like those which Fredric Jameson has identified with European critiques of "totalization" in all of its cultural forms.[34]

Topical reading conducted along these provisional lines will not be a mere search for historical figures and situations which seem to correspond to dramatic situations in the plays. We can be sensitive to Renaissance climates of interpretation without reenacting them. Instead of participating in the passion for decoding names and political references, we can look more carefully at what such a passion might mean. We can ask whether some texts are more susceptible to topical interpretation than others and if so, whether we can identify structural mechanisms by which a fierce desire for decoding is stimulated. We can explore connections between particular "local" details which would have been immediately available to contemporary audiences and broader ways in which the text can be seen to function if those details are taken as central to meaning instead of marginal. These broader functions are unlikely to have been perceived or understood by contemporaries in the same ways that they will be articulated by us. "Local" reading operates in the space between different systems for generating meaning—between the evanescent interpretation which fascinated Renaissance audiences as they looked for juicy, provocative links between plays and contemporary events, and the broader kinds of interpretation facilitated by our own more general explanatory models.

Very useful paradigms for "local" reading have been developed by anthropologists and historians. Clifford Geertz has shown how what he calls "local knowledge" of a non-Western society can be constructed through techniques of "thick description" that assemble many detailed observations from diverse elements of the culture, including its art and drama, in order to find important recurring patterns.[35] Geertz's "cultural poetics" is capable of accommodating change and pluralism, but as adapted by scholars of Renaissance literature, the method sometimes rigidifies. Topical reading helps us to interrogate and expand cultural *explication de texte* by coming to terms with the materials that appear to resist systematic modeling. In its very indefiniteness and provisionality, topicality cuts across closed, static explanatory systems and closed cultural forms, opening them to the vagaries of historical process. Historians of the Renaissance have used such eclectic, hybrid techniques for the analysis of European social rituals and political events, with spectacularly interesting results.[36] The localization of Shakespeare is based on the assumption that a similar cross-fertilization between the mapping "cross-sectional" analysis favored by anthropologists and the longitudinal, sequential analysis characteristically practiced by historians will create a range of new vantage points from which to consider how the plays create meanings.

The project does not need to be as atomizing or (worse yet) mechanistic as it may sound. The meanings generated by a given text may well be multiple or self-canceling, or both. Instead of striving for a single holistic interpretation of a text, we may find ourselves marking out a range of possibilities or identifying nexuses of contradiction. Local reading, like every other kind of reading, is bound to be provisional in that it will inevitably be limited by the tools we are able to bring to it. The project demands a capacity for methodological diversity if only because the specific "places" we may wish to explore are so diverse. But the effort needs to be capable of generating new perceptions of unified structural patterns just as readily as it allows for the articulation of dissonances. The project seeks to avoid the deconstructionist (and Renaissance) abyss in which all meaning dissolves into dispersal. Like the nineteenth-century novel as analyzed by recent post-structuralist critics, Renaissance drama carries with it its own generic mechanisms for undoing meaning in the very act of accumulating it.[37] Rather than merely pointing out those mechanisms, however, we can look for specific ways in which a given text sets them in motion or arrests them; we can contextualize Shakespeare's deconstruction by analyzing its effects in terms of specific local conditions.[38]

The analysis of the First Folio title page with which this chapter began was intended as a brief and partial glimpse of how a local reading might be conducted. Uncharacteristically, the reading began not with topicality but with its absence in a place where it would have been expected. The reading was not particularly rich in terms of its assembly of detail, but it was local in the sense that it sought to reembed the folio in the cultural milieu of its production and interpret it by working between seventeenth-century expectations created by other folio volumes and late twentieth-century ideas about the genesis of authorship. The reading identified an area of the text in which meaning was dispersed—the self-canceling circulation of identity on the title page. But it also pointed toward devices by which meaning was stabilized and collected, most notably, the dedicatory poem by Ben Jonson. It sought to interpret both motions in terms of specific functions they may have served for authors and readers at the time of the volume's publication. The precise methods by which localization will be conducted cannot be specified in advance, since they will vary along with the phenomena under study. But the wider and deeper our efforts to assemble detailed information, the more telling our interpretation. We need to adopt and redirect various research methods associated with traditional historicism while at the same time shaking off the critical assumptions with which they were previously bound up.

The reading of the First Folio was also unlike the readings which will be offered in later chapters in that it was a reading of a text *as* text, even though the text was composite. The interpretation of Shakespeare's plays is necessarily more complicated and provisional, since the texts are not the only things we need to take into account. There was also the elusive matter of their production on stage, which could alter a play's written form in any number of ways which we are only beginning to explore. Like the decline of humanism in the universities, the "End of Humanism" in the twentieth-century theater has opened up new modes for the interpretation of Renaissance drama.[39]

The period of institutional ferment associated with the demise of the transcendent Shakespeare was also a time of proliferating innovation in the theater. During the late 1950s and 1960s, the American "avant-garde" theater went through a phase of intense experimentalism, trying out new places and modes of performance. Some of this theater was politically engaged, overtly polemical, thriving in an environment of crisis. Often its plays, or "theatrical events," were a product of collective authorship that resisted precise documentation. Sometimes they were not scripted at all. This theater adapted techniques from non-Western drama, from primitive rituals, from various forms of popular entertainment—the circus, traveling jugglers and mountebanks, street magicians. Its intense experimentalism, which borrowed heavily from earlier twentieth-century revolts against the decorous boundaries imposed by the proscenium stage and author-centered dramaturgy, has helped stimulate our thinking about what the theater may have been like in the Renaissance, before the drama had been institutionalized as a branch of "authored" literature. Then, as in the avant-garde or postmodern theater, plays were bound up in an atmosphere of intense political and social ferment. Playing space was relatively unstructured. The drama was intermingled with other popular and courtly cultural forms—disguisings, bearbaitings, May games, and other holiday ceremonies. At the London theaters in late Elizabethan and early Jacobean times, for example, the performance of a tragedy would regularly be followed by jigs and other entertainments on stage.[40] How might our acknowledgment of such alien practices jostle our customary ways of imagining the Shakespearean theater?

In twentieth-century performance, a version of the Renaissance Shakespeare has become overly familiar. The historical reconstruction of Elizabethan costume, stage combat, and pageantry has rigidified into a set of expected patterns. Directors often feel the need to "localize" Shakespeare by placing him somewhere else, and we are offered a Kabuki *Macbeth*, a multimedia *Hamlet*, an *As You Like It* set in the antebellum South or in Edwardian Bloomsbury. Part of this need for relocation may be a simple desire for novelty, but there is more to it than that. Directors want to create an edge of defamiliarization about what has become too well known, engineer a set of encounters between disparate cultural situations in order to open up ways for audiences to rediscover the plays at the point "where remoteness and accessibility meet."[41] When such performances fail, they usually fail miserably, but when they succeed they can be electrifying. That dynamism is much like the revitalizing otherness local reading seeks to create through its own more prosaic acts of interpretation. The difference is that local reading is also historical reconstruction of the first milieu of performance. It circumvents the overfamiliarity of the traditional Renaissance Shakespeare by showing us the cultural otherness of what we thought we understood.

It is time and past time, however, for an obvious caveat. Shakespeare was not postmodern. Our own situation as we throw off the set of attitudes that I have been calling humanism does indeed give us access to areas of Renaissance culture in which humanism had not yet taken hold. But as we shake our heads over the sins of earlier modes of interpretation, we need to acknowledge our own tendency to practice a similar appropriation in the name of the revolt against formalism. Thus far, this discussion has been conducted with a deliberate and obvious polemical bias. I have presented Shakespeare as though he was a preauthorial innocent turned into something else by codifying editors who wanted to establish the autonomy of art. In terms of Shakespeare's dramatic production, there is some justification for this viewpoint. So far as we know, he took no particular interest in "authoring" his plays; he did not collect and publish them himself. But there are other places where we encounter a Shakespeare every bit as captivated by the humanist enterprise as contemporaries like Ben Jonson. I am thinking in particular of the Shakespeare of the sonnets, who asserted in poem after poem the transcendence of his "powrefull rime": it would outlive stones and monuments, last to the "edge of doome."[42] These flamboyant assertions are themselves in need of contextualization; what gets said in the middle of a love poem is not necessarily the poet's settled belief, and there are numerous ways in which the sonnets undercut the defiant assertion of transcendence. Nevertheless, we cannot construct a Shakespeare for whom such authorial attitudes were unknown unless we split the poet of the sonnets off from the dramatist. The monumentality of art in the sonnets is very much like the construction of architectural edifices and obelisks on the late Renaissance "comely frontispiece" by which authors claimed the right to immortality. When Ben Jonson placed Shakespeare in the heavens in the First Folio dedicatory poem, he was making direct allusion to the sonnets, paying Shakespeare the supreme compliment of locating him as a dramatist in the magical, exalted place which Shakespeare had already claimed for his poems. Moreover, the plays themselves, particularly the late plays, show suspicious inklings of some of the same yen for an art that can be transcendent.

To recognize Shakespeare's complicity in the humanist enterprise is by no means to undo our project for localization as it has been outlined above. We simply need to acknowledge the Renaissance drive to regularize and generalize meaning as one of the local conditions that we have to take into account. To inveigh against humanist assumptions is, in a curious way, to show their continuing power over us. If we are able to achieve sufficient distance from the humanist project, we will find it no less amenable to defamiliarizing analysis than other aspects of Renaissance culture. The reading of the First Folio title page with which we began could not have been performed if we had not been willing to set that text within the milieu of the developing seventeenth-century enterprise called Authorship. At times, we may find it revealing to attempt something similar with the plays, even though the conditions of theatrical production made authorship in that setting almost impossible to bring off—hence the bristling resentments of "authoring" dramatists like Jonson at the fates suffered by his works. To be an author, as the case of Jonson illustrates, was not necessarily to give up the seductive lure of theatrical topicality. Rather, "authoring" poets and dramatists looked for ways to regularize and elevate topical issues so that they could be linked with more abstract moral concerns. The extent to which the claims and strategies of authorship impinge on Shakespearean drama is quite variable and nearly impossible to generalize about. Nevertheless, to suppress that factor entirely would be to lose the chance to observe interesting ploys by which Shakespeare invoked and evaded humanist modes of interpretation through the manipulation of "local" particularities.

We need to bring back, among many other methodological tools of

the old historicism, an idea called the Author's Intent or putative intentionality. It is a construct, of course, and always has been—even when
authors baldly state their purpose, we do not necessarily take them at
their word. But it is a very useful construct, particularly when it is
demoted from its traditionally privileged position as the overriding
determinant of meaning. We need to ask ourselves why we have suppressed that particular cultural construct called intentionality while at
the same time insisting upon others. Often, when we appear to banish
the Author's Intent from the field of critical discussion we are not so
much disallowing it as displacing it—relocating its sovereign authority in ourselves as reader-critics.[43] If Shakespeare avoided the appearance of intentionality, it was at least some of the time by design.
We must try to distinguish between a lack of intentionality and the
avoidance of intentionality, which may be a radically different thing.

There are other critical commonplaces inherited from traditional
historicism that cry out similarly for fresh investigation. These will
surface from time to time during our readings later on, but a few of
them are perhaps worth mentioning in advance. One is the matter of
Renaissance audiences and their embarrassing heterogeneity. We have
tended to interpret the generalizations made by Renaissance authors as
class analysis of their public: those praised as select and discriminating
viewers and readers were gentry and aristocrats; those damned as
monsters of the pit were the illiterate masses. But such generalizations
need to be reinterpreted in light of the new Renaissance enterprise
called authorship and the new demands that were being made on the
reading and viewing public. When authors ordered their audiences
into hierarchies of "understanding," they were often referring less directly to class or education than to degrees of acquiescence in the authorial enterprise. Those viewers or readers who were willing to limit
the scope of their interpretive activities within boundaries set by the
author were a favored elite; those who were not, whatever their social
place and origins, were lumped together as an inchoate and ungovernable mass.[44] As we attempt to interpret playtexts caught up in this
shifting arena of expectations, we will find that if we are willing to
undertake seemingly traditional activities like the explication of political allegory, we will be able to identify points at which "authorized"
reading breaks down—nexuses of contradiction or unexpected gaps
that hint at a text's broader cultural functions while disrupting orderly
interpretation. This matter will be addressed below in chapter 3. For

the moment, it is enough to suggest that such disruption of "authorized" interpretive modes is a key device by which Shakespeare triggered an unease with topical references even in the process of evoking them.

Finally, to conclude this hasty and partial survey of methodological problems, we need to come to terms with the vexed matter of the status of the texts we depend on for interpretation. Again, we need to confront and redirect received historicist techniques. During the last decade, criticism has invaded the closed terrain of those traditionally licensed "localizers," the editors of Shakespeare. The results have been both shattering and liberating. Before launching into specific topical readings, we need to consider the impact of the new textual work on the project; for texts, as it turns out, can have—perhaps always have—embedded local identities of their own.

TEXTS AND EVASIONS

This is how Heminge and Condell describe the playtexts collected in the First Folio to potential readers of Shakespeare: "where (before) you were abus'd with diuerse stolne, and surreptitious copies, maimed, and deformed by the frauds and stealthes of iniurious impostors, that expos'd them : euen those, are now offer'd to your view cur'd, and perfect of their limbes; and all the rest, absolute in their numbers, as he conceiued the*m*. Who, as he was a happie imitator of Nature, was a most gentle expresser of it. His mind and hand went together : And what he thought, he vttered with that easinesse, that wee haue scarce receiued from him a blot in his papers" (A3r). Like the title page and accompanying verses, this statement arouses—and claims to satisfy—a deep thirst for authenticity. The defects of all earlier quarto editions have been repaired and Shakespeare's texts restored to their "True Originall," as "he conceiued them." The original is, of course, perfect, "absolute," a kind of automatic writing that has proceeded effortlessly from the mind of the Bard to the pristine, unblotted page.

One of the effects of Heminge and Condell's preface is to tie the idea of recovering the "Originall" Shakespeare to the reading audience's *amour-propre*. To offer them less than the "Originall" would be to "abuse" the respect to which they, as readers, were entitled. Those disreputable enough to consult foul quartos when they could be reading the folio texts are cast beyond the pale, excluded from a privileged, nascent world of timeless communication between the Author and his Readers. The writing and reading situation established by the preface is centered on the recognition and felicitous imitation of something generalized and elevated called Nature. Once again, there is a subtle, devastating devaluation of that which is contingent and time-bound, as though Shakespeare's essence ("what he thought" and "vttered") is immediately apprehensible, intrinsically separate from local conditions.

However, as readers and editors recognized very early on, there are problems with accepting the folio as pure and authentic Shakespeare. Even by contemporary printing standards, it is less than completely reliable: it introduces errors that do not exist in some of the quartos and leaves out choice bits like the mad scene in *King Lear* which are hard to discard as non-Shakespearean. Rather than settling the issue of textual authority, Heminge and Condell's statement had, by the eighteenth century, sent readers and editors into a "jungle of disbelief": the folio texts were scrutinized, found wanting, and demoted from their claimed status as the "True Originall." And yet, most textual editing still operates under the assumption that a Shakespearean Ur-text can, ideally at least, be reconstructed through diligent effort over time. Even the Disintegrators who splinter the folio texts up among various dramatists generally do so with the goal of recovering those precious segments which can be called unadulterated Shakespeare.[45]

All of these efforts give Shakespeare the dramatist the respect and editorial diligence worthy of an Author and his Works. But what if there was no "Originall"? What if, rather than flowing effortlessly and magically from Shakespeare's mind onto the unalterable fixity of paper, the plays were from the beginning provisional, amenable to alterations by the playwright or others, coming to exist over time in a number of versions, all related, but none of them an original in the pristine sense promised by Heminge and Condell? Nothing we know about conditions of production in the Renaissance playhouse allows us to hope for single authoritative versions of the plays. Shakespeare wrote his own name in many different ways; his spelling of other words appears also to have been unregularized in the extreme. His dramatic language was "prelexical," to use Margreta de Grazia's apt phrase, in that it failed to conform to codified notions of language which had not yet been invented. He appears to have punctuated quite sparsely, opening the playtexts up to a variety of "senses" rather than establishing a single governing interpretation. We have no reason to suppose that the larger structures of the plays were less malleable and open to the proliferation of meaning. To put the matter in intentionalist terms, Shakespeare may not have thought of his plays as existing in some single fixed form. He may, in fact, have been more interested as a dramatist in fending off the rising tide of authorship than in conforming to its emerging demands. There is no Shakespearean "Originall"; what we have instead is a series of "local" texts varying in ways that correlate with shifts in external circumstances and in the conditions of performance.[46]

To do local interpretation, we need to use texts that are close to the period of production we are studying—not because those texts are more "valid" than others, but because their language and shaping of events may reverberate with immediately contemporary ideas in subtle ways that later texts do not. One thing that happens in modern editions as part of the construction of a universal Shakespeare is that ideology—words, ideas, and dramatic structures that would have carried distinct resonances for a sixteenth- or seventeenth-century audience—gets edited out. Stanley Wells has provided a good example in his discussion of the mysterious stockings of Sir Andrew Ague-cheek. The folio version of *Twelfth Night* has Sir Andrew respond to Sir Toby's mock encomium of his talents as a dancer (his very "legge" formed "vnder the starre of a Gaillard") with the modest observation, "I, 'tis strong, and it does indifferent well in a dam'd colour'd stocke" (TLN 240–43). Nearly every modern editor has disallowed the phrase "dam'd colour'd stocke," replacing it with "flame-colour'd," or "dun-coloured," or "divers-coloured" (the last being Wells's own suggestion).[47] Why is it that Sir Andrew's stockings can be any color but "damned," which would appear the most obvious reading? The idea of "damned coloured stocks" would reverberate with the play's other subtle evocations of contemporary controversy surrounding the moral valuation of flamboyant dress and Christmas revelry. Sir Andrew wears stockings of a cursedly bright color and skips about to the condescending amusement of Sir Toby and the other holiday celebrants, but to the outraged indignation of Malvolio, who is several times likened to a "Puritane" by the less sober characters and for whom all such excessive behavior is evidence of spiritual perdition. As a result of the ruse of the letter, Malvolio violates his usual "sad, and ciuill" demeanor and puts on "dam'd colour'd" stockings of his own—yellow, cross-gartered, and probably more garish than Sir Andrew's. That act licenses the other characters to turn Malvolio's original scruples (which replicate a set of attitudes associated with late sixteenth-century Sabbatarianism) back upon him. They find him to be possessed by various devils and place him in the private "hell" of the enclosed room. By allowing Sir Andrew's stockings to be any color but "damned," editors rule out a reading that gestures toward the play's embeddedness in contemporary polemics. Shakespearean comedy is purged of the unwholesome "dross" of ideology.

Even the quarto and folio texts which will be relied upon for the present investigation are, of course, at some distance from any given performance. In fact, the three plays which will receive extended analyses exist only in folio versions, which gives us the advantage of a single text to work with but the disadvantage of a considerable gap in time between the text we have and the period of performance. However, the folio version may in some cases be closer to a play as staged than the earliest quartos are—the classic example is *Richard II*, which omitted the key scene of King Richard's "wofull" abdication from every quarto before 1608.[48] In the light of topical investigation, textual configurations which traditional editors might regard as barbarous "irregularities" can become interesting indeed. Despite our continuing dependence on the work of Shakespearean editors (and that dependence must not be forgotten), we need to go back to the early texts in order to keep ourselves from premature closure, from passively accepting readings which may have been generated by the ordering activities of editors. To be stripped of the comfortable securities offered by modern editions is unnerving, but not a sufficient reason for giving up interpretation. All we have to give up is the fond belief that our interpretation has to be infallible and "for All Time," like the universal Bard himself, in order to have any value.[49] Shakespeare criticism has always been precarious in terms of its textual underpinnings whether we have acknowledged that fact or not. Local reading is, if anything, less vulnerable than many other interpretive modes to the problem of textual indeterminacy in that it does not rely on texts alone as the source of meaning. Instead, it finds meaning through the identification of patterns that have the "validating" mark of repetition, that are echoed and refigured in disparate areas of Renaissance culture.

Within Shakespeare's plays, mere playtexts are accorded scant authority. One of the reasons topical reading has traditionally been disparaged is that it acts in complicity with the plays themselves to undermine the sacredness of texts. Shakespeare's metadramatic episodes involve texts that are always wooden and pallid in themselves. All of the interest arises out of the complex energies that swirl around them and envelop them. *Hamlet* is (among other things) about author-ity and its evasion. To "catch the Conscience of the King," Hamlet chooses a play-text based on a printed book, then alters it in order to bring it closer to the circumstances of his father's murder. By adding a few lines he creates what is in effect a new play, a "Mouse-trap." In his advance precepts to the players, Hamlet airs the set of ideas which we have been calling "authorial": he thinks playing should hold the mirror up to nature; he divides the audience on the basis of "understanding," arguing that the "Iudicious" should be preferred above the "Groundlings"; he urges respect for the written text. "Clownes" are to "speake no more then is set downe for them" so that they do not detract from "necessary" questions of the play. During the actual performance before Claudius and Gertrude, however, his decorous advance scenario runs amok, largely because Hamlet will not trust the text to do its work. Like a clown who speaks more than is "set downe" for him, he disrupts the play's orderly transmission of meaning in a series of carnivalesque asides. He calls himself "your onely Iigge-maker," and recasts his father's death as the demise of the ludicrous hobbyhorse of the May games (figure 10) "whose Epitaph is, For o, For o, the Hobyhorse is forgot." This antic posturing could, of course, be a cover for politically dangerous intent, as May games frequently were in the Renaissance, but Hamlet continues in the same carnivalesque mode in his private comments to Horatio when the pose is no longer necessary. By his own advance criteria, the performance has succeeded rather well in unmasking the guilt of the king. Despite its success, however, or perhaps *because* of it, Hamlet disperses its potential political impact by calling for musical entertainment like that which would have followed a contemporary play staged in the theater:[50]

> For if the King like not the Comedie,
> Why then belike he likes it not perdie.
> Come some Musicke.
>
> (TLN 2164–66)

Various motives for this behavior could be adduced; what is important for us is the author's ambivalence about a text's demonstrated power to generate topical meaning. Hamlet claims to have earned, for his efforts, "a Fellowship in a crie of Players." Has he earned his share (or as

10. The hobbyhorse from the May
games. Nineteenth-century engraving of detail from Tollett's
Window, Betley Old Hall, Staf-
fordshire (1621).

Horatio corrects him, "Halfe a share") through his authorial success in
shaping the play's meaning toward a single tremendous revelation, or
through his mercurial strategies of evasion and dispersal?

In *A Midsummer Night's Dream*, the playtext used by the Mechanicals is preauthorial—apparently garbled to begin with and mangled
further through their misreadings and literal-minded alterations for
performance. What we have is not an elite author who seems to abrogate intent and author-ity, but base amateur players who claim no intent at all beyond a desire for honor and financial gain. Much of the
energy of the play scene hinges on the obvious (but apparently un-
planned) topical relevance of *Pyramus and Thisbe*. The playlet, centering on tragic star-crossed lovers in a moonlit forest, can easily be read
as a demeaning burlesque of recent excesses committed by members
of its audience under similar circumstances. Moreover, the play's prologue, being improperly "pointed," speaks hostility toward the auditory: "If we offend, it is with our good will." However, these possible meanings have been evacuated in advance by Duke Theseus's
overriding interpretation of what the Mechanicals will intend. They
mean nothing but "loue"; "Neuer any thing / Can be amisse, when
simplenesse and duty tender it" (TLN 1879–80). The duke's insulating
paternalism protects both audience and performers. The lovers are
spared the prickly ordeal of being made to recognize the play's "application" to themselves; the Mechanicals are saved from the unconscious
sedition that comes of an inability to "stand upon points." The effect

of the duke's "legislation" is to redirect the scene's latent hostility back against the performers, whom the male members of the audience flite unmercifully. The women, however, remain silent. Theirs is an "open silence" which can, depending on whether they participate in the mockery or show repugnance for it, either reinforce or undercut the duke's suppression of "local" meanings generated by the playtext in performance.[51]

In *The Tempest* there are masques and visions apparently designed (in the humanist mode) by Prospero to "chide" or "cheere" their several audiences through generalized images of vice and virtue. These performances are for the most part effective. By the end of the play only Antonio is silent, possibly untouched by the process of enlightenment through art that has regenerated the others. *The Tempest* enacts a fantasy of near-total authorial power and control in which What the Author Intends comes close to infallible execution. It is the play that offers the closest analogue to the scene of reading portrayed in Heminge and Condell's preface to the First Folio, in which Shakespeare's thought and utterance are fully available on the unblotted page for the audience of readers to assimilate. Perhaps that likeness accounts for *The Tempest*'s odd placement as the first play in the folio. Except, of course, that Prospero's triumphs of "authorship" are managed quite without playtexts. His masques and visions are apparently not scripted at all; they are supernaturally produced either at Prospero's instigation or through his direct orchestration from "on the top (inuisible:)" (TLN 1535–36). The author never has to abandon his work to mangling violation by those who are not "Understanders" (although he does cut off the wedding masque in order to deal with three rebels who clearly belong in that category). On the other hand, the author's "works" are only performance, ephemeral and completely subsumed within the exigencies of the moment. Without texts, there is no violation of "authority" but also no monumentality: that potential is either lost or deflected onto the larger work in which Prospero's evanescent productions are embedded.

To make these observations is to do little more than suggest the extreme variability from one Shakespearean play to the next in terms of the interrelationships among texts, their creators, actors, performance, audience, and the local circumstances within which they function. If we were to arrange the three examples chronologically from *A Midsummer Night's Dream* to *Hamlet* to *The Tempest*, we could produce a pattern of expanding authorial control over the conditions and meaning of production. Nevertheless, in each case, the playtext (if it exists at all) is devalued and overridden as the nexus of meaning. What we wish to make of that fact will depend on our critical presuppositions. From the standpoint of traditional historicism, the three episodes can demonstrate the value of topical investigation: like the plays within them, Shakespeare's plays need to be placed within their larger cultural milieu if their "real" significance is to be understood. For readers hostile to the approach, however, the scenes can function in just the opposite way: although they may demonstrate how texts with little or no intrinsic literary value can be infused with a vitality born of circumstance, the parallel with Shakespeare himself does not hold because his plays are by no means so impoverished as the playtexts within them, and have no need of such demeaning supplement. From this formalizing perspective, Shakespeare's metadramatic episodes function talismanically to ward off the depredations of topical reading upon his own far superior texts. The two critical camps intersect in one significant way: both associate "local" reading with the heterodox idea that Shakespeare's texts are not sufficient in themselves.

Let's put the matter differently. The issue is not whether texts *can* stand alone, but whether we want them to. Localization is part of a major epistemological shift whereby we free ourselves from a demanding allegiance to the "truth" of the "Originall." We rework received opinion about the Shakespearean text in order to find—even to celebrate—new, less rigidly positivist vantage points from which to confer and interrogate meaning and identity.

2

Elizabeth

Shakespeare is very English—too English.
Victor Hugo

In "To the great Variety of Readers" Heminge and Condell guaranteed customer satisfaction: "Reade him, therefore; and againe, and againe: And if then you doe not like him, surely you are in some manifest danger, not to vnderstand him. And so we leaue you to other of his Friends, whom if you need, can bee your guides: if you neede them not, you can leade your selues, and others. And such Readers we wish him" (A3r). It is a stimulus to recuperative interpretation, individual and collective: readers are bound to "like him," either on their own or with the guidance of those who are already his "Friends." Even as applied to the Bard, however, the promise is too optimistic. Readers and editors have indeed needed to "like" Shakespeare, but in order to do so they have sometimes felt obliged to sacrifice another idea equally associated with the First Folio's editors—the idea that the plays are pure Shakespeare. What could not be "liked" was cast off so that the universal called Shakespeare could remain intact.

The *Henry VI* plays were among the first to fall to the salvage operations of the Disintegrators. Beginning with Edmund Malone in the 1780s, numerous editors argued that only the trilogy's best scenes are "Shakespeare"; the rest were fragments of older plays or contributions by other dramatists—Marlowe, Nashe, Peele, or Greene. Part 1 of the trilogy has been particularly vulnerable to the strategy: unlike Parts 2 and 3, *1 Henry VI* does not exist in any early printed version, and its apparent date is hard to reconcile with its apparent place in the cycle.[1] Even more than Parts 2 and 3, *1 Henry VI* is steeped in topical materials, using events from the French wars of 1422–50 to evoke numerous details of England's ongoing campaigns in France during 1591 and 1592. The play was enormously popular. It is one of the few attributed to Shakespeare for which we have a record of audience response. Thomas Nashe commented sometime before August 1592, "How would it haue ioyed braue *Talbot* (the terror of the French) to thinke that after he had lyne two hundred yeares in his Tombe, hee should triumphe againe on the Stage, and haue his bones newe embalmed with the teares of ten thousand spectators at least (at seuerall times), who, in the Tragedian that represents his person, imagine they behold him fresh bleeding."[2]

That Talbot had been a "terror" to the French was part of the play's appeal at a time of extreme Francophobia and "war fever." But the blatant patriotism that helped endear *1 Henry VI* to its 1592 audiences has repelled more recent readers. Those who have insisted most strongly on its "newsreel" topicality have also been its most avid Disintegrators, finding it little but "crowding, clamour and confusion," a "thing of threads and patches"—a piece of crude wartime propaganda which could not be "true" Shakespeare because it was too insistently local to be "liked."[3]

We will never know precisely how much of *1 Henry VI* is "true" Shakespeare. It is interesting, however, that when the play was reinstated in the canon during the 1930s and 1940s, there was one element that continued to carry the taint of inauthenticity. Readers and critics began to develop sophisticated arguments for the integrity and artistry of the trilogy as a whole, but held out for composite authorship in the portrayal of Joan La Pucelle, who appeared an impossible pastiche of laudable and despicable traits; the scurrilous, "shameful" spectacle of her trial was particularly singled out as spurious.[4] The exposure of the sublime Maid of Orleans as a witch and strumpet was a low gesture that had to be separated from Shakespeare, lest both idealized figures fall together.

Local reading of *1 Henry VI* needs to focus on the disquieting figure of Joan. She is a key to the other topical issues engaged by the play, the unstable center of a whole set of strong contemporary resonances which we have been oddly reluctant to pick up. A third highly idealized (and deidealized) figure has to be brought into the discussion—Queen Elizabeth herself. She bore ultimate responsibility for the French campaigns of 1591–92, but her lukewarmness in pursuing them caused massive frustration among her subjects. In some ways during those war years, at least to those among her subjects who fretted under her extreme caution, Queen Elizabeth was altogether too comparable in terms of her effect on English militarism to a stage figure like Shakespeare's Joan La Pucelle.

We are accustomed to thinking of the Virgin Queen in terms of a set of clearly female identities. As celebrated in the 1580s and 1590s, she was the divine Astraea returned or, in place of the Holy Virgin banished from Protestant spirituality, a secularized Virgin Mother to the nation. She was a Queen of Shepherds, a new Deborah, a Cynthia or Diana, the unreachable object of male desire and worship. But alongside such womanly identifications, which she certainly did nothing to discourage, the queen possessed a set of symbolic male identities which are much less familiar to us, in part because they surface most frequently in her speeches and public pronouncements, in part, I suspect, because her rhetoric confounds our own preconceived notions about gender. Her subjects had similar difficulties. They were far better acquainted than we are with her complex balancing of male and female attributes, but not necessarily comfortable with her strategies. In *1 Henry VI,* Joan La Pucelle functions in many ways as a distorted image of Queen Elizabeth I. She, like Elizabeth, is a woman who "acts like a man." She collects about her a markedly similar set of idealized symbolic identities. Yet she belongs to the enemy camp. The figure of Joan brings into the open a set of suppressed cultural anxieties about the Virgin Queen, her identity, and her capacity to provide continuing stability for the nation. Elizabeth was loved by her subjects, but also feared and sometimes hated. She was, in the wry formulation of one of her own officials, "More than a man, and (in troth) sometyme less than a woman."[5]

THE QUEEN'S TWO BODIES

To recognize the power and pervasiveness of the queen's disruption of ordinary gender categories, we need to plunge—for a few brief pages—into the morass of historical data, the records of sexual anomaly. As a virgin queen who steadfastly clung to her singleness, Elizabeth was unprecedented in England. Her virginity exempted her from most of the recognized categories of female experience, allowing her to preserve her independence while simultaneously tapping into the emotional power behind the images of wife and mother through fictionalized versions of herself. But the identity which lay behind all the others and lent them much of their authority was her identity as ruler. Elizabeth envisioned this primary public identity in clearly male terms. Like the earlier Tudors, she relied heavily on the juridical concept of the king's two bodies and referred to it explicitly in speeches: the monarch is at once a frail earthly being, subject to death and disease, and an immortal being, the incarnation of a sacred principle of kingship which exists along with the merely mortal body from the monarch's first anointing as king. The Boy King Edward VI's advisers had insisted that the transcendental powers of his office resided in him despite the childish weakness of his person; so Queen Elizabeth frequently appealed to her composite nature as queen: her "body natural" was the body of a frail woman; her "body politic" was the body of a king, carrying the strength and masculine spirit of the best of her male forebears.[6]

Even when she did not invoke the doctrine directly, as she did as early as 1558, she used it to structure an interplay between male and female royal identities. In her famous Armada speech before the troops massed at Tilbury in 1588, for example, she offered herself as a model of kingly courage: "I have the body of a weak and feeble woman, but I have the heart and stomach of a king, and of a king of England too; and I think foul scorn that Parma or Spain, or any Prince of Europe, should dare to invade the borders of my realm; to which, rather than any dishonour should grow by me, I myself will take up arms, I myself will be your general, judge, and rewarder of every one of your virtues in the field." Spanish invasion would be a "dishonor" linked to her womanly weakness, a violation of intact territorial borders that would "grow" through the Virgin Queen in particular because it would bring with it a shame like that of sexual violation. To avert the peril, Elizabeth temporarily sloughed off the marks of her vulnerable female identity and portrayed herself as a king prepared to "take up arms" and lead the troops into battle. Her costume at Tilbury gave visual embodiment to her verbal appeal. She carried a truncheon as she rode between the ranks and wore, according to some accounts, a "silver cuirass"—appropriate covering for the "heart and stomach of a king."[7]

Her strategies were successful—perhaps too successful. After the initial dispersal of the Armada, the Spanish forces never returned to renew the invasion as everyone expected them to. The queen's martial self-presentation at Tilbury was a glorious moment of patriotic triumph, but also (as we will note later on) a spectacle that aroused distinct uneasiness among Englishmen. Poets and balladeers rose gamely to the occasion, however, celebrating her Amazonian bearing and attire, praising her "tough manliness," her "*mascula vis*," and her resemblance to her father, Henry VIII, "Whose valour wanne this *Island* great renowne." As a young woman, Elizabeth had liked to place herself directly in front of the giant Holbein portrait of Henry VIII at Whitehall, challenging those present to measure her own bearing and authority against the majestic "splendour" of her father. At Tilbury, she claimed for herself her father's military éclat.[8]

The appearance at Tilbury was the only recorded occasion on which Elizabeth went to the extreme of adopting male attire. She and the earl of Leicester, who helped orchestrate her visit to the troops, appear to have felt that the extraordinary threat posed by the presence of the Spanish Armada off the coast demanded an extraordinary display in response.[9] But the basic rhetorical strategy Elizabeth employed on that occasion was by no means atypical. Her manly garb was not a mere warlike accoutrement, but a revelation of essence for a queen who claimed to be "man and woman both." In dealing with internal affairs, Elizabeth placed special emphasis on her composite nature when she needed to enforce her will upon groups of recalcitrant men. As early as 1563, for example, when she began to encounter parliamentary opposition, she argued, "The weight and greatness of this matter might cause in me, being a woman wanting both wit and memory, some fear to speak and bashfulness besides, a thing appropriate to my sex. But yet, the princely seat and kingly throne wherein God (though unworthy) hath constituted me, maketh these two causes to seem little in mine eyes, though grievous perhaps to your ears."[10] Or to take a more elaborate example from 1566, in response to a petition that she do the proper womanly thing—marry and declare a successor:

> As for my own part, I care not for death; for all men are mortal. And though I be a woman, yet I have as good a courage, answerable to my place, as ever my father had. I am your anointed Queen. I will never be by violence constrained to do anything. I thank God I am endued with such qualities that if I were turned out of the realm in my petticoat, I were able to live in any place in Christendom.
>
> Your petition is to deal in the limitation of the succession. At this present it is not convenient. . . . But as soon as there may be a convenient time, and that it may be done with least peril unto you—although never without great danger unto me—I will deal therein for your safety, and offer it unto you as your Prince and head, without request; for it is monstrous that the feet should direct the head.[11]

These passages adapt the theory of the king's two bodies to a rhetorical formula which Elizabeth I was to use successfully throughout her reign. She concedes to male discomfort at being commanded by a woman through her open acknowledgment of her weakness. But that disarming confession of the visible truth disables her audience's resistance to the invisible truth that follows. As monarch she exceeds them all; her participation in the undying principle of kingship outranks their masculinity. Small chance that she would be turned out of the nation in her petticoat! That belated reference to her femininity in the 1566 speech, appearing after the appeal to her father's authority and her continuation of his "place," takes on almost the quality of self-inflicted sacrilege. Her self-demeaning corners the market on that potential strategy and renders it unavailable to her subjects. In the meantime, she has forced her audience to accept a slight reworking of the language of sexual hierarchy. John Knox's *The First Blast of the Trumpet against the monstrous regiment of Women* (1558) had argued vehemently that allowing a woman to govern was as ungainly and incongruous as requiring the "head" to "folowe the feet." [12] Elizabeth's speech corrects the analogy: she is a woman, but also the "Prince and head." The truly "monstrous regiment" would be for her male subjects, her "feet," to direct her.

We could argue that such appeals to kingship do not amount to the construction of a second, male identity. But Elizabeth I used a number of other strategies which reinforced the sense of her "body politic" as male. For one thing, she took great care with the vocabulary used to describe her position on the throne. She had no objection to the term *queen* and used it herself throughout her reign. But more habitually, she referred to herself as *prince*. The word's most basic sixteenth-century meaning was ruler, especially male ruler; it was also applied to the eldest son of a reigning monarch. The equivalent female term was *princess*. But although Queen Elizabeth was frequently called "princess" in the early years of her reign and used the word of herself, with the passing of time that feminine epithet tended to disappear in favor of the more masculine *prince*. *Princess* was quite often, in the queen's own later usage, a term of disparagement applied to discredited female monarchs like Mary Queen of Scots. In her policy statements weighing the fate of the deposed Scottish "princess" Mary, Elizabeth calls herself "prince."

We can trace the gradual masculinization of Queen Elizabeth's epithets quite clearly in the formulaic openings to her proclamations. Mary Tudor's proclamations had, as often as not, begun "The Queen our sovereign Lady," with explicit reference to her sex. That formula is also quite common at the very beginning of Elizabeth's reign, but tends gradually to be replaced by more sexually ambiguous formulas: first "The Queen's majesty," then more elaborate formulas like "the Queen's most excellent majesty in her princely nature considering" or "Monarch and prince sovereign" substituting for the earlier "sovereign lady." In the early years proclamations frequently referred to her as "princess," in the later years, almost never. The formula "The Queen our sovereign Lady" lingered on in contexts for which an evocation of her feminine nature was particularly appropriate: during a plague, when the measures she took assumed the aura of maternal concern for her stricken people, or in famine, in connection with feeding the hungry.[13] But otherwise she was almost always a "prince." In parliamentary speeches or court audiences, it was quite common for the queen to be addressed as "princess"; in her response, she would deftly underline her own authority (and chide the presumption of her interlocutor) by referring to herself as "prince." Subtly, perhaps not always consciously, she constructed a vocabulary of rule which was predominantly male-identified. Gradually, perhaps not consciously, her subjects yielded to the symbolic truths she sought to convey through her precision with vocabulary and modeled their language upon her own.

At the very end of her life, as her "mortal body" became older and frailer, she insisted more strongly upon the male component of her regal identity and began to refer to herself with increasing frequency as "king"; for "King," Tudor jurists argued, "is a Name of Continuance."[14] In her famous Golden speech of 1601, for example, which was printed and disseminated throughout England, Elizabeth protested, in a variation of the rhetorical formula which had served her well for forty years,

> I know the title of a King is a glorious title; but assure yourself that the shining glory of princely authority hath not so dazzled the eyes of our understanding, but that we well know and remember that we also are to yield an account of our actions before the great Judge. To be a King and wear a crown is a thing more glorious to them that see it, than it is pleasant to them that bear it. For myself, I was never so much enticed with the glorious name of a King or royal authority of a Queen, as delighted that God hath made me His instrument to maintain His truth and glory. . . . Shall I ascribe anything to myself and my sexly weakness? I were not worthy to live then; and, of all, most unworthy of the mercies I have had from God, who hath given me a heart that yet never feared any foreign or home enemy.

In a message to Parliament that same year, the speaker noted, "She said her kingly prerogative (for so she termed it) was tender."[15] "For so she termed it": the queen's contemporaries were aware of something distinctly anomalous in her adoption of male epithets for her "body politic." But they also grasped what she was trying to convey, commenting that in her "Stately and Majestick comportment" she carried "more of her Father than Mother," and that she had "too stately a stomach to suffer a commander"; she was "king and queen both."[16]

It was not only officialdom who encountered the idea of the queen's composite identity. Her proclamations were usually both printed and read with fanfare in towns and villages throughout the kingdom; her most important speeches were printed and others circulated widely in manuscript versions through alehouses and other gathering places. She herself appeared frequently in public in London and the counties. Nearly everyone living in southeast and central England would have seen her in person at one time or another and she may have used elements of her usual formulas in extemporaneous speeches on many such occasions.[17] In sermons and public entertainments, she was associated with male heroes along with the more familiar female ones. As she was a Belphoebe or Astraea, so she was often portrayed as a St. George or a David, Moses or Solomon, an Alexander, an Aeneas who (symbolically) had sacrificed the Dido of her own femininity out of duty to the future of the nation. Then too, for the most educated segment of the public, the notion of the monarch as androgynous may have had a certain familiarity; this quality was not uncommonly claimed as an attribute even by male rulers like François Premier, who had himself painted with the head of a virago emerging from his breast.[18]

On at least one occasion, a subject's sudden apprehension of the queen's composite nature appears to have saved her life. The Catholic conspirator Dr. William Parry revealed in 1583 that he had approached the queen intending to assassinate her as she walked alone in the Privy Garden. Just as he raised his dagger to stab her, he stopped himself, wonderfully "appalled and perplexed," for he saw· "in her the very likeness and image of King Henry the Seventh." What he saw was the sacred image of kingship, of "Continuance." The royal composite did not always arouse such awe, however. Among ordinary people, there was rife covert speculation as to what the queen's precise gender was.

A carter at Windsor complained once in her hearing that at last "he knew the Queen was a woman," since she had repeatedly countermanded his orders. The remark is brief but revealing: like others among her subjects, he had been doubtful whether she was female or not.[19]

As king and queen both, how could Elizabeth accommodate a husband? The politically expedient courtships which she entertained, sometimes in apparent indifference to the anxiety of her subjects, allowed her to create a particularly complex interplay of sexual identities. When actual marriage was not at issue, she won male allegiance by giving rein to her flirtatious, feminine side, as she did in the symbolic, half-playful courtships of admirers like Sir Christopher Hatton and Sir Walter Ralegh. But genuine courtship was a more complicated matter. During the years of her reign when she at least appeared to entertain the possibility of marriage, she frequently used her chosen epithet "prince" to cool potential suitors: the subtle masculine identification of her language repulsed the potential lover even as she seemed in other ways to encourage him. The duke of Anjou (earlier Alençon) was a prime victim of the tactic: through her teasing, bewildering shifts in sexual attitude and identity, she kept her "frog" dangling for years.[20]

One of Elizabeth's usual ploys when Parliament or her advisers pleaded with her to marry was to insist that she was already married to her kingdom. On one such occasion early in her reign she held up the hand bearing her coronation ring, seeming to portray herself symbolically as the nation's wife. She continued to use the same analogy in later years, as in an exchange recorded by Sir John Harington:

> The Queene did once aske my wife in merrie sorte, "how she kepte my goode wyll and love, which I did alwayes mayntaine to be trulie goode towardes her and my childrene?" My Mall, in wise and discreete manner, tolde her Highnesse, "she had confidence in her husbandes understandinge and courage, well founded on her own stedfastness not to offend or thwart, but to cherishe and obey; hereby did she persuade her husbande of her own affectione, and in so doinge did commande his"— "Go to, go to, mistresse, saithe the Queene, you are wisely bente I finde: after such sorte do I keepe the good wyll of all my husbandes, my good people."[21]

Toward the end of her reign, however, Elizabeth more and more frequently placed herself in the role of husband. In 1596, for example, she claimed, "Betweene Princes and their Subiects there is a most straight tye of affections. As chaste women ought not to cast their eye upon any other than their husbands, so neither ought subiects to cast their eyes upon any other Prince, than him whom *God* hath given them. I would not have my sheepe branded with another mans marke; I would not they should follow the whistle of a strange Shepheard." This language was not some sudden, isolated reversal of expected gender roles; by the 1590s it was familiar.[22]

One of Queen Elizabeth's most clearly womanly self-portrayals was as virgin mother to her people. She used this role throughout her reign, but particularly when the matter of the succession reared its ugly head: how, she would protest, could her people demand that she marry and produce an heir when she was already mother to them all? In an interesting recent paper, Carole Levin has shown how versions of the unsolved problem of the succession would surface to plague her at moments of political vulnerability. There were persistent rumors that the Boy King Edward VI was still alive and ready to claim his throne and a series of impostors claimed to be the long-lost king. There were also persistent rumors that Elizabeth had given birth to illegitimate children: in 1587, for example, a young man claimed to be Arthur Dudley, her unacknowledged son by the earl of Leicester. The longing for a male succession got expressed in other ways as well: one particularly impudent rebel protested "that the land had been happy if Her Majesty had been cut off twenty years since, so that some noble prince might have reigned in her stead"—that prince, of course, being male.[23]

The longing for a male successor to Elizabeth was intense, even among the queen's most adoring subjects. One of the ways she tried to assuage that longing was by depicting herself, on a subliminal, symbolic level, as a son, her own son. Her favored term *prince* conveys this to some degree: even though it was a generic term for monarch, its more specific use was for a male heir apparent. Her perpetual status as young virgin or "virgin Prince" even as she passed far beyond the childbearing years may have fostered the idea of her sonship, since in the sixteenth century women were commonly regarded, like boys, as immature men.[24] Costume emphasized the connection: young Tudor boys wore skirts just like their mother and sisters, with only a sword at their sides to suggest their sexual differentiation. So long as Elizabeth I's identity continued to allow the symbolic potential of growth into manhood, however irrational that hope given the fact of her womanhood, she was able to alleviate at least some of the longing for an heir.

Occasionally, she seemed to deploy her public language in ways that fostered the fantasy. When Mary Queen of Scots gave birth to a prince, Prince James, the English still hoped for the like from Elizabeth. The issue became particularly delicate when James was hailed by the Scots as "Prince of Scotland, England, France and Ireland." Queen Elizabeth issued a proclamation denying reports on the Scottish succession, rumors that Prince James was to "be delivered into her majesty's hands, to be nourished in England as she should think good" and that Elizabeth meant to control the Scottish succession "after the decease of the young prince or King without bairns." In this context, the word *prince* is used to mean male heir to the throne. But the language that follows seems subtly to suggest that the English have no need of such a prince and such rumors. Elizabeth herself is their prince: she "is (and by God's grace intendeth during her life to be) a prince of honor and a maintainer of truth."[25] Like the emblematic phoenix, a device closely associated with the queen, she embodied— or tried to embody—her own succession.

Non-Western cultures offer frequent analogues to the dazzling multiform figure of Elizabeth: a woman, either a young virgin or an aging woman past menopause, who is set apart from the usual female functions and allowed access to otherwise exclusively male activities, who is perceived as androgynous and given hieratic status. In Protestant sixteenth-century England, however, there was no established institutional niche for such a figure to occupy. If it partook of the sacred, it nevertheless lacked the defined cultural status that would have allowed it to be separated from the merely deviant.[26] By emphasizing the maleness of her "body politic," Elizabeth was able to alleviate some of the anxiety her subjects felt about the "monstrous regiment of Women." In effect, she was denying that there was a woman on the throne, or at least that she as ruler was no more than a "mere" woman. But the very strategies by which she preserved received cultural assumptions in one way violated them in another.

In Renaissance England, the image of a ruler who dressed like a woman but acted with the force and leadership of a man was an image associated with riot and festival disorder. As part of the holiday overthrow of normal hierarchy, a "disorderly woman," often a man in female disguise, could be placed on top: a Maid Marion or a Robin

Hood disguised as an old hag, or "Lady Skimmington," the central figure in one of the English versions of the *charivari*, who was impersonated by men dressed as women and led a raucous procession which commonly boiled over into riot.[27] The opposite form of cross-dressing aroused the same fears. During the 1580s, women who followed the mode for wearing doublets, jerkins, and hats "as men haue" were furiously castigated by moralists for violating the Book of Deuteronomy's injunctions against cross-dressing and creating a dangerous confusion of "kinds": "If they could as wel chaunge their sex, & put on the kinde of man, as they can weare apparel assigned onely to man, I think they would as verely become men indeed as now they degenerat from godly sober women, in wearing this wanton lewd kinde of attire, proper onely to men."[28] Queen Elizabeth's self-portrayal as both man and woman, a "woman who acted like a man," perpetuated a complex of attributes associated with danger and "misrule."

The queen had ways of stifling this set of potential associations. One of the most important was that she almost never allowed her composite identity to be depicted visually. Except at Tilbury in 1588, she did not violate sexual boundaries through her actual attire. Nor, it would seem, did she allow the composite to be suggested in portraiture, except through subtle and esoteric iconography. Pictures of Elizabeth as an Amazon are all of foreign origin, or date from after her death. There is, for example, a Dutch engraving from the 1590s that depicts Elizabeth in the threatening posture of Amazonian combat which she had assumed at Tilbury. With sword raised in bellicose threat against an invading Catholic fleet, she both incarnates and protects Protestant Europe (figure 11). But such images did not proliferate within England. In the "official" Armada portraits, Elizabeth appears as a female monarch, an intact virgin whose boundaries and powers remain inviolate as a result of the dispersal of the fleet (figure 12).[29] Visualizations of her *mascula vis* like that offered in the Dutch engraving were perhaps too disquieting for domestic consumption, too disruptive of the delicate balancing of male and female identities which she had imposed through language.

James Aske's *Elizabetha Triumphans* (1588), one of the most elaborate of the Armada poems, shows inklings of such disquietude. The poem sets out to record the "wonders passing strange" accomplished by Elizabeth, wonders which surpass those of her "Sire" Henry VIII, exceed everything, in fact, but the miracles of God. All of her "strange" feats are triumphs over international Catholicism. By the rising of her "Sunne," the wolfish pope has been made to slink away and all "Popish reliques" are "burnt." She has routed the French out of Scotland, defeated Mary Queen of Scots and the many conspirators who supported Mary's claim to the English throne. She has also dispelled the "devillish arte" of popish magicians, seminary priests, and Irish rebels, and—finally and climactically—triumphed over the pope and his minions through the defeat of the Spanish Armada. Aske's poem includes bits of paraphrase of Elizabeth's speech at Tilbury. He also attempts an epic description of the strangest of her "wonders," her appearances before the troops. She came before them a "Queen most like herselfe" when she was most like a male warrior:

> Not like to those who coutch on stately doune,
> But like to Mars, the God of fearefull Warre,
> And heaving oft to skies her warlike hands,
> Did make herselfe Bellona-like renowned.

Despite the murkiness of his attempts at epic elevation, Aske's poem is fairly specific about Elizabeth's attire and demeanor. On the first day of her visit, she "marched King-like" to survey the ranks as they knelt in submission before her sacred majesty. On the second day, inspired by the "warlike show" of her troops marching in display and mock combat before her, she adopted their prowess for herself:

> Most bravely mounted on a stately steede
> With trunchion in her hand (not used thereto)
> And with her none, except her Liutenant,
> Accompanied with the Lord Chamberlaine,
> Come marching towards this her marching fight.
> In nought unlike the Amazonian Queene,
> Who beating downe amaine the bloodie Greekes,
> Thereby to grapple with Achillis Stout,
> Even at the time when Troy was sore besieged.[30]

According to Aske, Elizabeth's donning of male battle gear was an act of courage inspired by the valor of her men. And yet, once equipped, she marches out against them as though they are the enemy—she is likened to the Amazon queen (Penthesilea) who battles her way through the Greek ranks in order to fight Achilles. Once activated, her androgynous power is a threatening, implacable force that annihilates anything in its way.

Aske's account was almost certainly based on eyewitness informa-

11. Dutch engraving of unknown attribution (1598), showing Queen
Elizabeth as an Amazon with sword raised to protect Protestant Europe. Photo courtesy of the Ashmolean Museum, Oxford.

tion. Probably he was there himself. Along with the thousands of soldiers, there were numerous civilian onlookers at Tilbury. But it is
unlikely that he or anyone else there saw the queen mowing down Englishmen. The menacing overtones of his description register suppressed anxiety over the uncanny image of the queen in warlike male
attire. After her appearance, according to Aske, the soldiers talked of
nothing but how she had showed herself before them. The dominant
reaction was fervent acclaim suggestive of a "marvellous concord, in a
mutual love, betwixt a queen and her subjects." One Spanish agent
who visited Tilbury reported, "All that day, wandering from place to
place, I never heard any word spoken of her, but in praising her for her
stately person, and princely behaviour."[31] On the great day itself, discomfort at the "strange wonder" of the queen's violation of sex roles

12.   The Armada portrait of Elizabeth I (1588), attributed to George Gower. Photo reproduced by kind permission of the marquess of Tavistock, and the Trustees of the Bedford Estates, Woburn Abbey.

was apparently not articulated, at least not in public. But there were signs of anxiety later on of the kind that had been expressed earlier by John Knox. He had speculated that if ancient Greeks who had argued against the rule of women were brought back to life in the Renaissance to see

> A woman sitting in iudgement, or riding frome parliament in the middest of men, hauing the royall crowne vpon her head, the sworde and sceptre borne before her, in signe that the administration of iustice was in her power: I am assuredlie persuaded, I say, that suche a sight shulde so astonishe them, that they shuld iudge the hole worlde to be transformed into Amazones, and that such a metamorphosis and change was made of all the men of that countrie, as poetes do feyn was made of the companyons of Vlisses, or at least, that albeit the outwarde form of men

remained, yet shuld they iudge that their hartes were changed frome the
wisdome, vnderstanding, and courage of men, to the foolishe fondnes
and cowardise of women.[32]

At Tilbury, the soldiers were indeed, for a time, living under the regi-
men of an Amazon. Where could the blurring of sexual identities be
expected to stop: if the queen, a woman, was also a man, did that
mean, according to the fears of contemporary moralists about the
effects of cross-dressing, that men were turned into women? In a dedicatory preface to Julius Caesar (one of Elizabeth's Masters of Requests),
as Aske is discussing proper requital for benefits received, he suddenly and illogically expresses a concern "least, I should make myselfe
suspected to be of both sex." This seemingly gratuitous remark relates
to nothing in the immediate context but reverberates insistently with
the subject matter of his poem, which he describes in quasi-maternal
terms as the "first fruit that my barren wit yeelded." Other popular
materials from the immediate post-Armada years display an upsurge
of similar fascination with, and horror of, the Amazonian confusion of
gender. Long Meg of Westminster provided a living London example:
she dressed in male clothing, fought men and bested them (particularly if they were French or Spanish), and was overtly likened to the
queen.[33] Aske's anxiety was a common cultural phenomenon after
Tilbury. He is able to praise the sexual multivalence of his "King-like"
queen, but shows signs of fearing a like sexual indeterminacy for
himself.

In Shakespeare's *1 Henry VI*, the warrior Joan of Arc has a similar
uncanny, befuddling effect on English warriors and their accustomed
roles. The play was staged less than four years after England's victory
over the Armada, and after Elizabeth's glorious, troubling appearance
at Tilbury. On that memorable occasion, she had vowed to lead a life
corresponding to her mode of dress: "I myself will take up arms; I
myself will be your general, judge, and rewarder of every one of your
virtues in the field." Joan of Arc in *1 Henry VI* performs the military
roles Elizabeth had promised to play in the event of Spanish invasion.
Joan, however, acts the victorious soldier through nefarious super-
natural means. The figure of Joan airs a wide range of anxious fantasies
which had eddied about the English queen in the years leading up to
the Armada victory and in the Armada year itself, fantasies which
could be allowed to surface only after the worst of the Catholic threat
had receded.

ASTRAEA'S DAUGHTER

In Shakespeare's play, the dominant man-woman is demonized. Almost from her first appearance at the court of the Dauphin, Joan of Arc is associated with a mystique of virginity and power like that which surrounded Elizabeth. She is a "holy Maid" who can work "wondrous feats," who has sacrificed the usual womanly roles in order to serve the nation and "free my Countrey from Calamitie" (TLN 283). Her public rhetoric often sounds like a tinny echo of Elizabeth's habitual tactics with Parliament. Joan promises the French courtiers, "I exceed my Sex. / Resolue on this, thou shalt be fortunate, / If thou receiue me for thy Warlike Mate" (TLN 291–93). She claims to enjoy an infallible election and divine support which has some of the quality of Elizabeth's sacred "Continuance." And the heroic language with which her adoring "subjects" honor her is also markedly like that which surrounded the English queen. What Elizabeth did to her recalcitrant subjects through rhetoric, Joan manages through combat. When she fights with the Dauphin Charles and "ouercomes" him, he hails her, "Stay, stay thy hands, thou art an Amazon, / And fighteth with the Sword of *Debora*" (TLN 307–8). Her prowess overturns normal hierarchy—"head" and "feet" change places. Charles vows to be her servant, kneeling to the "Amazon" warrior as the Tilbury troops had knelt before Elizabeth, or as her parliamentary opponents had more than once yielded to the "male" authority of her "body politic."

After the victory at Orleans, Charles hails La Pucelle as "Diuinest Creature, *Astrea's* Daughter" (TLN 644) and vows to honor her through processions, images, and "high Festiuals": "No longer on Saint *Dennis* will we cry, / But *Ioane de Puzel* shall be France's Saint" (TLN 669–70). In a markedly similar way, the English hailed the English Astraea—most recently in the 1591 London pageant *Decensus Astraeae*. They celebrated Elizabeth's Accession Day as a public holiday; to commemorate the victory over the Armada, they were ordered to begin celebrating a new "saint's day" as well, St. Elizabeth's Day (November 19). All the popish rites with which the French surround their venerated martial maid eerily resemble the quasi-religious ritual that surrounded England's Virgin Queen, particularly in the 1580s and after, when the cult of Elizabeth became most prominent and elaborated.

At the same time, the spectacle of the "woman on top" in *1 Henry VI* evokes some of the same anxieties about female dominance, at least from those characters who are not immediately dependent on Joan's military prowess:

> *Bur.*   . . . But what's that *Puzell* whom they tearme so
> pure?
> *Tal.*   A Maid, they say.
> *Bed.*   A Maid? And be so martiall?
> *Bur.*   Pray God she proue not masculine ere long:
> If vnderneath the Standard of the French
> She carry Armour, as she hath begun.
> (TLN 698–703)

The interchange can, of course, be understood as a series of bawdy puns like so many of the English remarks about the "*Puzell.*"[34] But it can also be taken literally. Contemporary moralists expressed precisely the same fear about actual women who wore elements of male attire. If Joan persists in her violation of accepted sex roles, she may eventually turn male, perhaps through the same magic that allows her to triumph over men, or perhaps through some obscure physiological mechanism, like those catalogued by Stephen Greenblatt, by which a deviant male sexuality could be stimulated in an apparent female.[35] Joan's crossing of the gender boundaries marking men off from women threatens a whole set of cultural polarities by which the categories were kept distinct. The English forces in *1 Henry VI* are markedly less tolerant of cross-dressing for military purposes than the English had been at Tilbury. Joan provokes English skepticism and anxiety of a kind which could not be voiced openly in 1588 about Queen Elizabeth and the anomalous identities she claimed.

Yet even when Joan is unmasked as a sorceress, she continues to throw off echoes of Elizabeth. Almost incredibly, the two Frenchmen she confesses to have taken as lovers are the duke of Alençon and the duke of Anjou (Reignier)—precisely the names of the two French noblemen Elizabeth had come closest to marrying in the decades before: first the duke of Anjou, then his brother the duke of Alençon, later also called Anjou.

These highly charged details are not to be found in Shakespeare's sources.[36] There are too many of them and they form too insistent a pattern to be attributable to mere chance. Rather, we are dealing here with a deliberate strategy. But what the playwright sought to accomplish through such an insistent topical overlay is another and more complicated matter. It is possible, of course, that some or all of the potentially explosive details were omitted from at least some performances. We have the play only in the 1623 folio version. The early quartos of Parts 2 and 3 of *Henry VI* omit many of the classical references which exist in the folio texts, perhaps in order to simplify the plays for performance; the same excisions could have been made for performances of Part 1.[37] Yet even without the most explicit echoes, the similarities between French *Puzell* and English "Virgin Prince" are insistent enough to have registered on some level with 1591–92 audiences. Those were years in which war fever and the passion for topical decoding were both so intense that, as one dramatist complained, he had only to mention "bread" to be taken as referring to "Bredan in the low countries."[38] The image of Joan could not have been impervious to similar, probably covert, speculation.

The echoes have also registered on some level with more recent editors and critics, even though they have not been acknowledged. The unease generated by the play's impossible, insistent topicality gets expressed as something else—as vague irritation at the ungainliness of Shakespeare's language, for example, or at the incoherence of Joan's character. Despite his usual attention to historical detail, G. B. Harrison remarked of the phrase "Astrea's Daughter," "The excessive use of classical names in this passage is typical of Shakespeare's early work."[39] It is interesting that he singled out the particular passage he did to make the complaint. For the Disintegrators, similarly, the blatant but inadmissible echoing of attributes between the English Astraea and the French "Astrea's Daughter" has almost invariably registered as textual contamination. The scenes in which men fight heroically or engage in political maneuvering (as in the Temple Garden) are most likely to be "Shakespeare"; those containing the disturbing echoes of the language surrounding Elizabeth are "certainly not Shakespeare."[40] The play's topicality—even though unacknowledged—has been read as bad aesthetics, unsettling textual turbulence.

As local reading of *1 Henry VI* forces us to recognize, "Shakespeare" in this play is inextricable from something that looks suspiciously like political sacrilege. It is not the moderate image of the Bard of the chronicle plays that we have traditionally been offered, but it is just as much Shakespeare as other things we have felt more comfortable calling by that name. That is not to say that the issue of intentionality in the play is at all clear-cut. Even as the dramatist plants the specific details which could generate subversive thoughts about the queen, he makes them part of a structure so unstable that it refuses to

settle into a single set of political implications. The play's topical overlay sets in motion a broad, indefinite set of speculations about the extent to which the parallels between the two celebrated virgins can be
said to hold. There is not one topical interpretation of the play, but a
burgeoning, proliferating array of possible interpretations, any one or
more of which might have been seized on by members of a contemporary audience. The play sets off chains of local associations, but without the subtle shaping and end-capping which we might expect to
control them given the sensitivity of its subject matter. Instead, its
very unsettledness is its protection. What it does is create such an open
field for speculation that audience response is scattered as a prism scatters colors. What might have been taken even at this early date as the
Author's Intent is unreadable because it can be read in too many different ways.

In one area of the play, according to the testimony of Thomas
Nashe, audience response in 1591–92 was quite uniform: everyone (or
nearly everyone) thrilled over the deeds of "braue Talbot" and sor-
rowed over his death. To the extent that they admired English Talbot,
early audiences probably hated French Joan, who humiliates him in
combat and mocks his "Stinking and fly-blowne" corpse. But Joan's
odd resemblance to Elizabeth undercuts the appeals to patriotism, or
at least sets them apart from attributes and images associated with the
English queen. Let us survey, in rather scattershot fashion, some of the
areas of possible signification in which this rift can be observed.

Most obviously, perhaps, the play's vision of an outwardly immaculate virgin "ruler" who turns out to be a slut underneath brings
common gossip about Elizabeth to pungent dramatic life. Rumors
about the sexual appetites of her "mortal body" had plagued the queen
throughout her reign, but became particularly rife in the 1580s and
early 1590s. One Henry Hawkins claimed in 1581 that Elizabeth had
had five illegitimate children by Dudley—all of them delivered while
the queen was on one of her summer progresses, for "she never goethe
in progress but to be delievered." In 1587, as we have noted, a young
Englishman who was arrested in Spain on charges of espionage claimed
to be the queen's illegitimate child by Dudley: he provided inter-
rogators with an elaborate story about how he had been kept in England incognito and finally escaped to the Continent. In 1590, one
Dionisia Deryck declared that Elizabeth "hath already had as many
children as I, and that two of them were yet alive, one a man child and

the other a maiden child, and the others were burned." Leicester, their father, had "wrapped them up in the embers in the chimney which was in the chamber where they were born." According to another similar account from the same year, Leicester "had four children by the Queen's Majesty, whereof three were daughters and alive, and the fourth a son that was burnt."[41] These rumors were likeliest in places and times of extreme disaffection, but could be encountered almost anywhere. The queen's openly flirtatious, sometimes scandalous behavior with Leicester and other favorites did nothing to dispel them. Before 1588, such "slanderous words against Her Majesty" were often punished with imprisonment or worse; after the Armada threat had passed, perpetrators were likely to get off more lightly, perhaps by being sentenced to the pillory, where they would wear their seditious words on a paper attached to their foreheads for all passers-by to read.[42]

Joan of Arc's naming of her lovers is both a displacement and a display of rumors like those which dogged the English queen. If Elizabeth, according to persistent and seemingly independent accounts, had had secret liaisons with her favorites and made a practice of burning her unwanted offspring, the French *Puzell* confesses to very similar liaisons; she and the unborn child she claims to be carrying are both burned together. It is not entirely clear, however, that the image of the virgin-whore perishes along with Joan of Arc. The play can be viewed as "pillorying" scandals about Queen Elizabeth—airing them for public inspection and repudiation through the figure of Joan of Arc, who admits her scarlet past as she stands under guard in a situation rather like that of an Elizabethan doing penance for slander. But like the pillory, the play gives public visibility to the very scandals it brands as shameful. *Henry VI Part 1* can easily be viewed as *reinforcing* the illicit English passion for "slanderous words against Her Majesty," again through a process of displacement and display. Its endless bawdy punning about the fallen female appetites that can lurk beneath a public self-presentation of sacred, untouchable virginity would, for contemporary audiences, have been hard to dissociate from rumors about Elizabeth.

And what are we to make of Joan's specific choice of lovers? By the 1590s, the prospect of a French marriage was dead and the queen herself was past childbearing. Nevertheless, the spectacle of a "Pucelle" or "Puzzell" who confesses that she has taken Alençon and Anjou as lovers conjures up grim earlier fears about the queen's seeming appetite for Frenchmen. If she married Anjou, many of her Protestant subjects were convinced she would inevitably revert to Catholicism, since, as John Stubbs put it in *The Discoverie of a Gaping Gulf whereinto England is Like to be Swallowed* (1579), "If woman, that weaker vessel, be strong enough to drawe man through the aduantage whiche the deuill hath within our bosome, (I meane our naturall corruption and proonesse to Idolatry) how much more forcibly shall the stronger vessell pull weake woman considering that with the inequalitie of strength there is ioyned, as great or more readinesse to Idolatrye and superstition." The public spectacle of Elizabeth and Anjou together, as their miniatures appear together in her prayer book, enclosing between them the queen's own devotions (figure 13), aroused strong anxieties among the English about the future of Protestantism. Moreover, as Stubbs argued, since the wife is subject to the husband, Elizabeth through her marriage would in effect cede England to France. In Stubbs's horrific imaginings, marriage to Anjou would engulf Elizabeth—and the nation with her—in French duplicity and disease. England would become a playground for dread agents of the Catholic League like Catherine de' Medici, who had engineered the St. Bartholomew's Day Massacre and surrounded herself with "familiar spirits" who obeyed her every wish against the Protestants.[43]

This complex of fears involving Catholic superstition, female danger, and demonism was not Stubbs's isolated vision. Although he was sentenced to lose the hand with which he had written his seditious book, there were many who shared his feelings. The queen's attempt to suppress *The Discoverie of a Gaping Gulf* merely increased public agitation. According to Ambassador Mendoza, Elizabeth's proclamation calling in extant copies, "instead of mitigating the public indignation against the French, has irritated it and fanned the flame." William Camden recorded the silent "commiseration," the "apprehensions of strange doubts" and "secret inward repining" with which spectators witnessed Stubbs's punishment.[44]

After the Armada, the secret repinings began to be vented more openly—as though with a collective sigh of relief that finally the marriage issue was defunct. In 1591, for example, Edmund Spenser had published his *Mother Hubbard's Tale*. That work was so transparently an allegory of court intrigues surrounding the French match that it was immediately suppressed, to reappear in print only in 1611. Shakespeare's play was not, so far as we know, suppressed on stage, but un-

13. Queen Elizabeth's prayer book with twin miniatures, attributed to Nicholas Hilliard, of the duke
of Anjou (earlier Alençon) at the front and Elizabeth at the back. The prayer book itself disappeared sometime after 1893. Photo courtesy of the
British Library.

like the other two parts of *Henry VI*, it was never published in a quarto
edition—perhaps because it too, although far more fragmented and
piecemeal than Spenser's political allegory, could give rise to similar
associations. [45]

A common tactic during the crisis over Anjou had been to associate
the French match with a return of the Wars of the Roses. Elizabeth's
proclamation against Stubbs complained that whereas previously her
subjects had conjured up images of the English civil wars in order to
convince her to marry, "to avoid all such or greater civil wars and

bloodsheds as betwixt the houses of York and Lancaster," they now used the same historical argument to *dissuade* her, thereby claiming "contrary" effects of "one self Cause."[46] In *1 Henry VI*, which chronicles the opening skirmishes in the bloodshed "betwixt" York and Lancaster, many of the chauvinistic beliefs which had fueled opposition to the queen's match with Anjou circulate around "Astrea's Daughter." Despite the play's pre-Reformation setting, its Englishmen are sturdy, manly "Protestants" who mock at French Catholic credulity and cowardice. They keep their own Cardinal Winchester (the "Scarlet Hypocrite") at arm's length on account of his association with Rome and popish corruptions. From the first, they brand Joan of Arc as a witch. In fighting the French, they fend off the specter of what England itself could become if it were absorbed back into popery, and by destroying Joan, they banish the dread vision of a debased French Catholic Elizabeth, a queen become travesty of her Protestant self. Or at least, they evacuate it temporarily. No sooner is Joan condemned to the flames than another overbearing Frenchwoman, Margaret of Anjou, emerges to reign over England.

Shakespeare's treatment of Joan could have given rise to many other associations with French and "Popish" queens and claimants—with Elizabeth's half-sister Mary Tudor, for example, who had scourged English Protestants, or with Mary Queen of Scots, who had briefly been queen of France, who had plotted endlessly against Elizabeth and Protestantism until her execution in 1587, and who was much more openly (and justifiably) reviled as a whore than Elizabeth. But the play's reverberations between Joan and Elizabeth are by far the most insistent and most troublesome. By a perverse magnetism, the figure of Joan picks up not only contemporary fantasies about Elizabeth in her "mortal body" as a woman but also more covert and extraordinary fantasies about Elizabeth's self-presentation in her "immortal body" as a man. Reading John Stubbs's tract, we can sense that after the terrible fright caused by the French marriage negotiations of the 1560s and 1570s, the idea of Elizabeth as male in her "body politic" came to have a certain attractiveness. Stubbs calls her the "Eue" but also the "Adam" of the national Eden, "our Adam & soueraigne Lord or lordly Lady of this Land," as though to remind the queen in that way that her composite identity as ruler was incompatible with marriage.[47] And yet, as we have already noticed, the queen's *mascula vis* could give rise to its own set of anxieties, particularly after Tilbury, 1588.

Throughout the *Henry VI* cycle, female dominance is associated with bloody rites of violence and "misrule." But there is a particular concentration of such motifs in Part 1, which is presided over, as Renaissance riots frequently were, by a cross-dressed woman. In Part 1 carnivalesque inversions proliferate like Hydra heads, almost always at the expense of the English. There is, for example, the episode of the "Master Gunner of Orleance, and his Boy." Taught to spy out the enemy as they file through the secret gate, the boy is able to strike down two English heroes, one of them the great Salisbury, who had overcome in "thirteene Battailes."[48] Similarly, after the first English victory of the play, Alençon compares the victorious English to "*Samsons and Goliasses*" (TLN 230). What he intends is a reference to military might: in Edward III's time, England had bred Olivers and Rowlands; now she has given birth to a new race of heroes. But the names he chooses are both associated with the motif of destruction through inversion: Samson was defeated by Delilah, a woman; Goliath, by David, a young boy. Throughout the play, Talbot is a particular target for just such reversals. He is verbally humiliated in the episode with the countess of Auvergne, who is incredulous that such a "Child" and weak "shrimpe" can be the mighty warrior. His dealings with the young Henry VI have some of the same quality of topsy-turvydom: the hero must defer to the sovereign authority of a child. But the play's most flamboyant inversion is the figure of Joan triumphant. She is lethal to English manhood—on stage, she drives English troops like "Doues" and puppies before her without so much as a fight (TLN 618). Whenever she encounters Talbot, she bests or equals him. Even after her powers have been proved fallible by the English recovery of Orleans and Rouen, Joan maintains that Frenchmen will triumph so long as they keep her "on top":

> Let frantike *Talbot* triumph for a while,
> And like a Peacock sweepe along his tayle,
> Wee'le pull his Plumes, and take away his Trayne,
> If Dolphin and the rest will be but rul'd.
>   (TLN 1590–93)

And she does turn the tables once more. Talbot and his son die valiantly in battle against overwhelming odds, and Joan mockingly shatters the high-flown titles with which the English bear witness to his glory. Talbot the "Earle of Shrewsbury," and "Great Earle of *Washford, Waterford*, and *Valence*, / Lord *Talbot* of *Goodrig* and *Vrchinfield*, /

Lord *Strange* of *Blackmere*, Lord *Verdun* of *Alton*," and so on (TLN 2295–99), lies "fly-blowne" at her feet.

These reversals follow the pattern articulated by John Knox: when women turn Amazons and rule, men become like women, or at least lose the ability to show themselves in traditional cultural terms as men. Eventually, of course, some of the topsy-turvydom is righted. Joan's reign of "misrule" ends when she is captured and executed. But she leaves behind her a disquieting set of associations with another woman in authority. In *1 Henry VI*, the ability to tolerate female rule is exclusively (and risibly) French. The play offers two competing visions of a society with the "woman on top." Initially, Joan appears France's savior. The Dauphin and his nobles submit to her gladly because they are caught up in her mythos of holy virginity and believe she will bring them victory. It is a partially secularized version of the traditional festival message *Deposuit potentes et exaltavit humiles*, and reverberates with the kind of self-sacrificing veneration which the English queen was also able to inspire. But the overturn of sexual hierarchy in the service of more exalted patriotic goals is something for which the English in the play express nothing but scorn. They perceive it as the effect of French superstition and credulity, and label Joan's "monstrous regiment" over men as dangerous and deviant from the start. It is as though, in *1 Henry VI*, despising female dominance is a necessary part of being male, English, and "Protestant." How are we to read this pattern, given the strong topical associations between Joan and Elizabeth? The easiest response would be to take the figure of Joan as blatant and unambiguous travesty, a debased caricature of Elizabeth that is finally empty and demonic because it lacks an essential element of the queen's self-presentation, the sacred "immortal body" of kingship. Such an interpretation would smooth over some of the play's most potentially subversive edges, but would also close off interesting areas of possible signification which emerge when *1 Henry VI* is located in terms of the national situation in 1591–92. It is time we turned briefly to the play's other and less volatile area of topicality, its evocation of materials relating to England's French campaigns during the early 1590s.

After the Armada, the English were quite unaware that they had just passed over an important national watershed. Both before and after the brief period of euphoria following the news that the Spanish fleet had been destroyed, there was widespread restiveness and disappointment that no more had been accomplished. Part of this was let-down of the type that could be expected after such a stunning triumph, but part of it was frustration that the English had been (and were continuing to be) denied the chance to come face to face with the enemy and defeat them decisively in battle. Francis Walsingham himself had written gloomily from Tilbury, "Our half-doings doth breed dishonour and leaveth the disease uncured." After Tilbury, the "half-doings" had maddeningly continued.[49] In the three and a half years between the Armada and *1 Henry VI*, England had remained at war, but relatively little had happened. English troops had fought against elements of the Catholic League on the Continent, but with little to show for their efforts but yet more frustration. Moreover, some of the English commanders who had made the most brilliant showing at Tilbury were gone. The earl of Leicester, who had marched alongside the queen, had died only six weeks later; the earl of Shrewsbury, who together with his son, Lord Talbot, had made the most impressive display of troops at the camp, had died in 1590.[50]

The situation of England at the beginning of *1 Henry VI* —a time of depression and confusion after a major military triumph—closely parallels the situation of England in the early nineties. *Henry VI Part 1* begins shortly after Henry V's glorious victory at Agincourt, but the young warrior-king is dead and his French conquest is dissolving away; England in 1591–92 had experienced a similarly miraculous victory followed by a similar series of reversals and disappointments in France. Shakespeare massively rearranges fifteenth-century history in order to bring out the parallels between the two times of waning heroism. Even some of the names of heroes are the same, such as Talbot, created earl of Shrewsbury in one of the play's seemingly extraneous scenes, and his son, Lord Talbot. The obstacles that stand in the way of clear-cut victory are, in each case, the same: a "want of Men and Money," a desire to gain the fruits of success without the passionate force and unanimity required to bring it about. The messenger's critique of affairs in fifteenth-century France at the beginning of *1 Henry VI* precisely parallels English objections to the conduct of the French wars of the 1590s.

> Amongst the Souldiers this is muttered,
> That here you maintaine seuerall Factions:
> And whil'st a Field should be dispatcht and fought,
> You are disputing of your Generals.
> One would haue lingring Warres, with little cost;
> Another would flye swift, but wanteth Wings:
> A third thinkes, without expence at all,

By guilefull faire words, Peace may be obtayn'd.
Awake, awake, English Nobilitie,
Let not slouth dimme your Honors, new begot.
                                    (TLN 80–89)

After the assassination of Henry III of France in 1589–90, it seemed possible that France could be brought into the Protestant fold. Reformed Englishmen yearned for a commitment of money and men large enough to tilt the balance in favor of the Protestant king Henry IV and French Huguenots in their war against the Catholic Guise. Elizabeth did send some money and ammunition and promised troops, but because of severe factional feuding among the chief ministers and her own dislike for massive embroilment on the Continent, England offered French Protestants only feeble support—more "half-doing" of the kind that "bred dishonour." From the point of view of militant English Protestants, there was, once again, a burning need for the "English Nobilitie" to "Awake, awake."

Parallels between the French campaigns in Shakespeare's play and the earl of Essex's expedition to Rouen in 1591–92 have frequently been remarked. The expedition was intensely popular in England and volunteers flocked to join the effort. Those at home paid avid attention to the smallest scrap of information from the Continent. And Shakespeare's play gave them "information." Joan's signal of fire from a high tower, the English officers' surveys of fortifications and decisions about the placement of artillery, Talbot's challenge to "*Alanson*, and the rest" in Rouen, "Will ye, like Souldiors, come and fight it out?" (TLN 1501–2), and his visit to the countess of Auvergne, even the ribald jokes about the Dauphin and his "shriving" of Joan—all of these episodes resemble events of the Essex campaign, which were hot news in 1591–92. The parallels are not precise—and would not have had to be—in order to create a feeling of intense contemporaneity. When English audiences watched *1 Henry VI*, what they saw was a bustling, bloody palimpsest of past and present militarism.[51]

But let us not overemphasize Essex, as topical readings of Shakespeare generally do. In terms of its depiction of valor under impossible circumstances, *1 Henry VI* is even closer to a slightly earlier campaign, the French rescue mission undertaken by Baron Peregrine Bertie Willoughby and four thousand men in 1589–90. Queen Elizabeth had first authorized the expedition, then countermanded it at the last minute, too late to prevent the troops from sailing. Willoughby's men aided Henry IV's forces in the successful capture of Vendôme, "wading through the river and ditches and climbing over the walls in most valiant manner," and in the capture of Le Mans and Alençon. According to Willoughby himself, the Alençon garrison said "that they would not have surrendered if they had not been more afraid of the English behind them than of the French at the breach." Henry IV of France also praised the valor of the English troops. More than once, their presence appears to have made the difference between Huguenot victory and defeat.[52]

Elizabeth wrote Willoughby of her pride that his troops had given the lie to "such as have conceived an opinion either of our weakness or of the decay and want of courage or other defects of our English nation." Nevertheless, despite the continuing success of Willoughby's zealous Protestant warriors, Elizabeth failed to send them adequate money and supplies. As time wore on, they continued to fight bravely, but suffered increasingly from sickness and want of food and clothing. One of Willoughby's men was his cousin John Stubbs—the same John Stubbs who had sacrificed his right hand in 1579 to the cause of preventing Elizabeth's French match. He wrote back from France (left-handed) that it was "an honour to [have] been in this journey," but he included a pathetic description of the hardships suffered by the men. Stubbs and most of the rest of Willoughby's soldiers never made it back from France, despite all their "forward endeavours and valour," but perished of hunger and neglect. When Henry IV officially dismissed Willoughby's men (because he could not afford to pay them himself), some eighty of them stayed on to fight in the French king's army. Others straggled back to England at the beginning of 1590.[53] It is a tale very like the story of Talbot and other doughty Englishmen in *1 Henry VI,* a tale of English Protestant heroism against impossible odds and defeat as a result of a maddening and seemingly unnecessary "want of Men and Money." Essex's expedition, of course, renewed hopes, but it was quickly bogged down in factionalism and conflicting orders. In 1591–92, when "ten thousand spectators at least (at seuerall times)" beheld Talbot's "triumphe" on the stage and shed tears over his "bleeding," they were bewailing as well the cause of French Protestantism and the doomed heroism of many of the Englishmen who had fought for it. They were shedding, perhaps, tears of rage and frustration, as well as tears of sorrow.

The villain in the affair, or at least the government official easiest to cast in the role of villain, was Queen Elizabeth herself. She had, of course, good reasons for her reluctance to enter into prolonged wars on the Continent. Money was in very short supply; she may have perceived earlier than some others that Henry IV simply could not defeat the Catholics in France. By 1593, he had himself converted with the famous comment that Paris was well worth a mass. We are dealing here, however, with public passions, not measured, judicious assessments. During the brief period when victory in France seemed to be tantalizingly within England's grasp, Elizabeth's delay and endless vacillation brought ultra-Protestants to rage and despair. If what they saw in *1 Henry VI* was a palimpsest of fifteenth-century and contemporary martial adventures in France, then the part played by Queen Elizabeth herself in the present could easily enough be related to Joan's obstruction of proto-Protestant heroism in the past. We could put the matter in terms of our own language of psychodynamics. From the perspective of militant English Protestantism, the figure of Joan is a projection of hatred and pent-up resentments which it was impossible to vent directly in full vehemence against the English monarch.

Many of the xenophobic plays of 1588–91 restaged and reworked the Armada events. John Lyly's *Midas* (1589 or 1590) refers to the Armada defeat and satirizes Philip of Spain. In Robert Wilson's *The Three Lords and Three Ladies of London* (printed 1590), Londoners bravely face a "mighty host" of Spaniards and engineer a victory over the Armada that is "London's achievement alone." Wilson's *The Cobbler's Prophecy* also commemorates the Armada, focusing on treason at home.[54] Shakespeare's *1 Henry VI* follows the pattern of many of the post-Armada plays, identifying, as many of the others do, a foreign scapegoat for divisions at home, reenacting the events of the Great Year with an obsessive intensity. But Shakespeare's play is unusually explicit in its probing of the queen's part in the memorable events.

We are obviously entering a highly speculative area here, but let us press further. It is not only that Joan La Pucelle frustrates English heroism. She does so while at the same time being, in covert ways, dependent on it. Almost immediately after the death of Talbot, Joan is revealed as the witch he had all along argued her to be. With "charming Spelles and Periapts" she summons her "Familiar Spirits" as usual, but they refuse to do her bidding and slink away in silence (TLN 2427–39). Without them, Joan loses her ability to "rule" over men. It is as though her black magic loses its force once it no longer has Talbot's heroism to feed on. The link is reminiscent of the "strange wonders" of Elizabeth at Tilbury—inspired, according to contemporaries, by the martial valor of her troops, but simultaneously taking away from that valor by depriving them of the opportunity to fight. It is characteristic of the dynamics of witchcraft belief that what is attributed to divine influence in times of success can easily be reinterpreted as demonic in the case of failure. So long as Joan succeeds she and others on her side attribute her incredible victories to divine intervention. But in failure, she is associated instead with heretical traffic with demons. If we read this pattern back into the English situation at Tilbury and after, we uncover a set of covert associations between the uncanny image of Elizabeth in her *mascula vis* and ideas about witchcraft.

The witch was a particularly virulent subspecies of the Renaissance "disorderly woman." Witches were sexually ambiguous creatures who, according to widespread contemporary belief, often used their occult powers to prey upon male strength and sexual potency. So close was the cultural association between witchcraft and other forms of sexual reversal that individual instances of female domination were often considered evidence of witchcraft or demonic possession.[55] Queen Elizabeth faced the peculiar challenge of keeping the "white magic" of her sacred power as ruler separate from these strong cultural associations. Disaffected subjects attempted to use witchcraft against her—at various times during the 1580s and 1590s, officials found doll-sized replicas of the queen stuck through with pins and portraits which had been stabbed or otherwise defaced. But she was also suspected of witchcraft herself during the same years, usually by England's enemies. Scottish Catholics accused her of having been "cosenede by the devile" in the sentencing and execution of Mary Queen of Scots, and Mary herself had made similar insinuations. In fact, Elizabeth did keep up an interesting friendship with the astrologer and "cunning man" John Dee, but the precise nature of their relationship is unclear.[56]

After the Armada, especially on the Continent, there was occasional covert speculation that such a seemingly miraculous victory could only have been accomplished through witchcraft. Not only had the Spanish fleet been harried from the English coast after only brief naval skirmishes, but it had been almost completely destroyed by gales and mysterious naval disasters on the way home. The Armada portrait depicts just such storms in the vignette to the queen's upper right (figure 12); in *1 Henry VI*, Joan's first appearance against the English is marked by a similarly portentous "tumult," thunder, and lightning (TLN 569–70). Particularly in the aftermath of the Armada victory, the English, like their adversaries, may have had secret questions about the power behind the queen's androgynous "wonders" at Tilbury. In Shakespeare's play, the figure of the witch brings such anxieties into the open. The furthest limit of our speculations about Joan of Arc and Elizabeth is to suggest that Joan's demonism in the play evokes contemporary fears about Elizabeth's "strange" and unfathomable powers—in particular, a fear that the queen's anomalous self-display as a male warrior had in some mysterious fashion drained away the efficacy of the English forces. It is yet another version of Knox's formula by which the Amazon, by taking on male attributes, reduces men to women.

Witchcraft beliefs provide a language and explanatory system contemporaries would have been likely to invoke to account for the puzzling series of post-Armada failures and the feelings of military impotence that went along with them. We in the late twentieth century might invoke a different explanatory system. In addition to the more concrete reasons for failure, we can speculate, for example, that the queen's violation of sexual boundaries may have had a real (if temporary) psychological impact upon her male subjects' sense of sexual identity and military acumen. The mighty Talbot describes his state of mind after his first encounter with Joan triumphant as a temporary loss of identity:

> I know not where I am, nor what I doe:
> A Witch by feare, not force, like *Hannibal*,
> Driues back our troupes, and conquers as she lists.
> (TLN 615–18)

If we substitute the divine for the demonic, we have a reasonable approximation of James Aske's reaction in *Elizabetha Triumphans* to the dazzling sight of the queen marching at Tilbury. She is a mysterious force that amazes and scatters her own men as though they are the enemy.

There are, of course, other aspects of the queen's complex self-presentation which could easily be read out of the play: the matter of Joan's pastoralism, for example, which can easily enough be associated with the pastoral imagery surrounding "Eliza Queene of Shepheardes," or the matter of Joan's bastardy (Elizabeth had also been declared illegitimate by a father), or the play's handling of ideas about succession. Once the mind starts working on the parallels between Astraea and her "Daughter," there is no end to the tangled speculations which the play can set in motion. What needs to be emphasized, however, is their half-formed, equivocal nature. It is easy to interpret *1 Henry VI* as a blatant call to arms in the aftermath of the Armada: "Awake, awake, English Nobilitie, / Let not slouth dimme your Honors, new begot." But the play's many echoes of the language surrounding Elizabeth do not add up to a similarly uniform statement unless we lean hard on one possible line of interpretation while simultaneously suppressing others.

And yet, although they do not yield an interpretation, the echoes do seem to arrange themselves according to a repeated pattern—the pattern already referred to of airing through displacement. Various possibilities for meaning collect about the figure of "Astrea's Daughter" like a vast heap of cultural fragments. What must remain unspoken is spoken of somebody else who is either an alter ego of the queen or her debased image, but neither definitively, so that it is hard to judge whether the play would have registered with contemporaries as subversion or as containment of subversion. At this point, we can choose either to abandon the vexed search for topical meaning stimulated by the unstable figure of Joan, or to carry it forward on a different level. Let us look at the play's distinctive pattern in terms of its broader cultural functioning. *Henry VI Part 1* is virulent in its scorn for the claptrap of Catholic ritual, and yet it creates a quasi-ritual pattern of its own. It is a markedly iconoclastic play, a ceremony against ceremony.

RITUAL BURNING

There is a series of events from the height of the anti-Catholic persecutions of the late 1570s that curiously resembles the pattern of Shakespeare's *1 Henry VI* in that it exposes a demonized image of the queen. During Elizabeth's visit to Norwich in her progress through East Anglia in 1578, she was lodged at the house of a local Catholic gentleman named Edward Rookwood. When he appeared before Elizabeth to kiss her hand (she was, after all, borrowing his house) the Lord Chamberlain, finding that Rookwood had been excommunicated for popery, suddenly lashed out against him, demanding to know "how he durst presume to attempt her reall presence, he, unfytt to accumpany any

Chrystyan person." The phrase "reall presence" immediately suggests both the royal presence of the queen (with perhaps a slight echo of *real*, the Spanish for royal) and the doctrine of the "real presence" of the body and blood of Christ in the sacrament, a Catholic doctrine that no sixteenth-century Protestant accepted in its fullest Catholic form.[57]

There are several curious things about the Lord Chamberlain's accusation. One is his apparent surprise. It is highly unlikely that court officials were unaware of Rookwood's Catholicism or that he posed a genuine threat—he had apparently signed a declaration of loyalty to the queen. It is much more likely that the queen's visit was deliberately engineered as one of Richard Topcliffe's ingenious public dramatizations of the Catholic menace. There is also uncertainty about how the Lord Chamberlain's reference to the "reall presence" relates to the person of the queen. Is she, or is she not, a sacramental figure to the English in the same sense as the Eucharist is to Catholics? If she *is* a secularized version of the "real presence," then Rookwood's crime is that he, an excommunicate and therefore barred from the sacrament of the English Church, is attempting to approach her as only a lawful communicant dared to approach the altar. But it may be that the Lord Chamberlain uses the phrase "reall presence" sardonically to refer, not to an attribute of the queen, but to Rookwood's perverse Catholicism. By lodging the queen at his house, Rookwood would then be attempting to construct a sacramental presence within his gates which would validate his own religion over and against the established church. Even in this opening salvo of the Norwich events, there is uncertainty about the religious significance of the queen's sacred identity and her adoption of attributes associated with "Popish" superstition for her secularized mythos of rule. Either way the Lord Chamberlain's remarks are taken, Rookwood loses. He is trapped within an official ambiguity about the nature of the queen's "body politic."

Rookwood was thrown in jail for his unintentional crime against Elizabeth. Court officials conducted a thorough search of his estate, finally finding in a hayloft the image of idolatry they had been looking for—an icon of the Virgin Mary. The icon was another "reall presence" on the Rookwood estate which paralleled and rivaled that of the Virgin Queen herself:

> Suche an immaydge of O*ur* Lady was ther fownd, as for greatnes, for gaynes, and woorkmanshipp, I did never see a matche; and, after a sort

of cuntree daunces ended, in her Ma*jesty*'s sighte the Idoll was sett be-
hinde the people, who avoyded: She rather seemed a beast, raysed upon
a sudden from Hell by conjewring, than the Picture for whome it hadd
bene so often and longe abused. Her Ma*jesty* com*m*anded it to the fyer,
w*hich* in her sight by the cuntrie folks was quickly done, to her content,
and unspeakable joy of every one but some one or two who had sucked
of the idoll's poysoned mylke.[58]

The local villagers had been dancing before the queen in honor of her
visit. The Lord Chamberlain's agents stole up behind them with the
icon of the Virgin and thrust it up opposite the queen. The dancing
had ceased, yet the act of raising the image over the heads of the dancers
suggests a fleeting recreation of Old Testament worship before the
golden calf or Dagon. What the officials were doing was staging one
of the standard Protestant arguments against the Catholic veneration
of images—the complaint that it revived pagan idolatry. The sudden
appearance of the icon caused a terrible fright among the villagers,
who "avoyded" because they took it to be demonic: "She rather
seemed a beast, raysed upon a sudden from Hell by conjewring, than
the Picture for whome it hadd bene so often and longe abused." But
they may also have fled from the terror of apparent likeness between
the two competing versions of the "reall presence": the Virgin Queen
in a place of honor and the Virgin Mary from the hayloft, held up opposite the queen as though to provoke comparison.

In the written account, there are suggestions of contamination between one "presence" and the other. The "she" who seems a beast
lacks a clear antecedent and can easily on first reading be taken as a
reference to the queen herself. The dancing before the queen retro-
spectively takes on some of the taint of a dance before the idol. This
was a period during which, despite the anti-Catholic persecutions, the
queen appeared to be reviving her marriage plans with Anjou, and
that dread prospect was much on the mind of some of the court agents
at Norwich.[59] The image of the queen as flirtatious suitor to Anjou can
be glimpsed—furtively—in the great, "gay" image held up across
from her. There were also objections from the "hotter Protestants"
about the ritualism with which Elizabeth was increasingly surrounding her reign. Frances Yates has described the alternative cults: "The
bejewelled and painted images of the Virgin Mary had been cast out of
churches and monasteries, but another bejewelled and painted image
was set up at court, and went on progress through the land for her
worshippers to adore."[60] At Norwich, the resemblance between rival

images was immediately effaced through burning. The queen herself ordered that the idol be committed to the fire, and this was done before her and the villagers, to the satisfaction of all but confirmed Catholics who had sucked the idol's "poysoned mylke."

By ordering the burning, Elizabeth publicly severed herself from the image of Our Lady and the associations with popish ritualism. Moreover, after the event, several local ministers who had been silenced for Nonconformity were relicensed to preach.[61] These zealous Protestants could be counted on to impress the Rookwood affair upon their congregations as an object lesson in the evils of popery. What seemed to have been accomplished through this bizarre episode is that a dangerous resemblance was evoked in order to be disavowed and obliterated. The royal presence of the queen was cleansed of beliefs and practices which it was all too easy to associate with the cult of Elizabeth.

We do not know what the queen's underlying role was in this ritual of Protestant iconoclasm—whether she had helped to orchestrate it and was indeed "content" with Rookwood's persecution, or whether she was an unwilling participant in the Norwich events. In any event, they had a devastating impact on Rookwood's family. He eventually died in prison and they forfeited the estate. Someone of the same family name was later executed in connection with the Gunpowder Plot, perhaps turned from loyal subject to rebel as a result of the 1578 trap and its aftermath.[62] The Norwich events displayed a social mechanism—and one which the queen could be said to countenance—for separating the monarch's "reall presence" from the false and demonic. It is a mechanism which resembles the burning of the false Catholic "Elizabeth" in Shakespeare's *1 Henry VI*. If the play is understood in terms of such a ritual pattern, its potential for subversion is at least partially defused.

The burning of the Norwich idol parallels many earlier episodes of Protestant ritual burning. In a similar way, Catholic images had been collected and destroyed during the virulent iconoclastic phase of the Edwardian Reformation. In 1538, for example, the Rood of Grace from a Kentish monastery was paraded through the London streets and displayed at a sermon against idolatry delivered by the bishop of London; then it was publicly smashed and burned. Similar rituals erupted after the Marian interlude when Elizabeth became queen. In London, wooden rood images were burned in two huge bonfires in

1559, and comparable ceremonies took place elsewhere.[63] From time to time, even Maypoles were cut down and burned as "Idolls." Elizabeth's government did the same thing with subversive books and pictures. The hangman's public burning of copies of John Stubbs's book falls into this category. Even the firing of the Spanish ships at the time of the Armada echoes the pattern. The holy crusade of the Armada sailed under the flag of the Virgin Mary. Many of Philip's vessels bore the names of specific images of the Virgin (*Nuestra Señora de la Rosa, Maria Juan, Nuestra Señora de la Rosario*); a captured Spanish flag bearing the image of the Virgin was displayed in London after the victory. By sending out the fireships by which the Spanish "Virgins" were destroyed as they lay at anchor just off the English coast, the Virgin Elizabeth, who was popularly credited with masterminding the exploit, performed a naval version of Protestant ritual burning. One contemporary Armada medal bore the image of a ship in flames with the inscription *Dux Foemina Facti.*[64]

Later in the 1590s, Elizabeth's subjects could even witness the burning of images of the queen. At her own command, "false" portraits of Elizabeth were called in and publicly incinerated so that the queen's "true" portraits could be purified or preserved incontaminate. Through such rituals, false images were placed in the same category as false Christian doctrine. Public burning was still the ecclesiastical penalty for heresy: the secular government burned heretical books and images just as, when it was required by the church courts to do so, it would immolate heretics at the stake. In England, the last such public burning of a human victim took place in 1611.[65]

In the official records at least, Joan of Arc's chief crime was also heresy. The burning of Joan La Pucelle in *1 Henry VI* can be assimilated to the iconoclastic pattern of Protestant ritual burning. The play is full of broken ceremonies. The constant disruption of ceremonial structures has some of the quality of Protestant iconoclasm, a ritualized breaking of "superstitious" rite.[66] It can be argued that some of the emotional energy which accompanied the breaking of icons in the streets of London is defused by the play's status as a theatrical event. But not all of the energy is defused. In the early 1590s, more openly than at most other times, the theater functioned as a site where public tensions were aired and worked through. *Henry VI Part 1* exposes suppressed idolatries. False images and "heresies" about Elizabeth are routed out of their hidden places in her subjects' secret thoughts and assembled around the French witch so that they can be publicly anni-hilated. When public bonfires were lighted in Elizabethan times, indi-vidual citizens would often bring their own faggots to feed the fire. In a similar way, the play stimulates its viewers to spin out their various dark fantasies about Elizabeth so that all such speculations can be thrown in one vast heap and consumed together. Joan, like Rook-wood, is a sacrifice to tensions created by the queen's anomalous and "idolatrous" self-presentation. Variants of the same pattern are also common in more elevated literature—in *The Faerie Queene*, for ex-ample, where the encounter between Una and Duessa is only the first of a long series of encounters between true and false images of queen-ship and religious authority. In Shakespeare's play, as in such non-dramatic texts and in the official iconoclasm of the state, it is the like-ness between true and false images that gives the ritual burning its feverish intensity.

Yet the model of iconoclastic burning does not quite fit the play, which is unlike most other occurrences of the pattern in that it does not display a "true" image of Elizabeth in triumph over the false ones. All of the ritual burnings ordered by Elizabeth and her officials at least implicitly and sometimes explicitly offered such a "true" image in the person of the queen at whose behest the ritual was performed. *Henry VI Part 1* was never, we think, performed at court; nor was it an official act like the burnings performed by the common hangman, in which Elizabeth's implied presence as head of state was part of the event. The play does not portray anyone on the English side as a positive, re-deeming image of female authority to set up opposite its demonized travesty in Joan. The nearest candidate for such a function is Talbot himself, whose part is structurally parallel to Joan's throughout the play. But Joan presides over Talbot's death instead of the other way around, and he is too relentlessly masculinist to be easily associated with the composite image of Elizabeth. The closest the play comes to suggesting a connection between Talbot and Queen Elizabeth is the prophecy, spoken over the broken bodies of Talbot and his son, that "From their ashes shal be reard / A Phoenix that shall make all France affear'd" (TLN 2326–28).

When the phoenix burns, its replica rises from the ashes. The refer-ence to the phoenix is a positive, generative image of ritual burning which can be counterpoised against the horrific execution of Joan, in which she and the unborn child she claims to be carrying die together, or against the final moments of Talbot, who perishes with his dead son in his arms. The phoenix was a motif strongly associated with Queen Elizabeth; it appeared, for example, on the city gates at Norwich for the royal entry in 1578, at the time of the ritual burning on the Catholic Rookwood's estate.[67] If we read the prophecy as a reference to Elizabeth, we can establish numerous connections between the queen in her *mascula vis* and Talbot, between Elizabeth's campaigns in France and the play's images of patriotism and martial valor. But these connections are to some degree subverted by the insistent parallels between Elizabeth and Joan. As at Norwich, the perception of likeness creates contamination. And the prophecy can easily be read otherwise: as a reference to the earl of Essex and his ongoing siege, for example, or to the French king Henry of Navarre, who in 1591–92 was still expected to triumph over French Catholicism. Although staging could have given it more impact than it has in the printed text, the single equivocal reference to the phoenix rising out of Talbot ashes does not take on sufficient dominance to counterbalance the powerful image of Joan. Instead, almost at the end of *1 Henry VI*, there is another female figure who rises up like the immortal bird to take Joan's place after the witch is led off for execution.

At least initially, Margaret of Anjou appears to be a promising candidate for the role of positive counterpart to Joan. She was not always portrayed as demonic in Tudor times; indeed she was sometimes listed among the "Female Worthies." She was also, for better or for worse, associated with some of Elizabeth's attributes. Numerous chronicles, including Hall's and Grafton's, had noted Margaret's "stomacke and courage, more lyke to a man than a woman." The language is much like the habitual rhetoric of Elizabeth, so much so that in Holinshed's history, published under Elizabeth, references to Margaret's "manlike courage" were suppressed.[68] In Shakespeare's version, too, many potential links between Margaret and Elizabeth are effaced. When Margaret appears in *1 Henry VI*, she is described as valiantly courageous, with a strong "vndaunted spirit / (More then in women commonly is seene)," but this strength will, according to Suffolk's crafty version of the future, "answer our hope in issue of a King" (TLN 2892–94). She will show her strength only through her sons. There are, of course, intimations of disaster to come. Margaret is, symbolically at least, Joan's daughter (Astraea's granddaughter) in that she is child to Anjou, whom Joan has named among her lovers.[69] But it is not clear until

Parts 2 and 3 that she has succeeded Joan as the reigning "disorderly woman" upon Joan's death. The burning of Joan obliterates one set of idolatrous images of female rule, but facilitates the emergence of another figure at least potentially "monstrous," whose bent is as yet unknown.

Ritual burning in *1 Henry VI* is not staged, but imagined as happening offstage. Nevertheless, it seems to perform some of the cultural functions of Protestant ceremony against ceremony, cleansing the royal image from the superstitious veneration accorded popish Joan. But there is another model of ritual burning by which it can be understood—a model which is not so easy to assimilate to official Elizabethan orthodoxy. Shakespeare's play carries strong elements of much older forms of ritual immolation for the annihilation of public menace. At the beginning of the play, when Bedford has just heard the doleful news from France, the regent promises his comrades, "Bonfires in France forthwith I am to make, / To keepe our great Saint *Georges* Feast withall" (TLN 165–66). He and his fellow warriors leave Henry V's funeral rites unfinished and head off for France to repossess the territory they had won under Henry. Although Bedford himself does not live to see it, the burning of Joan in a sense fulfills his vow for a festival bonfire in honor of St. George and English patriotism. Motifs from St. George's Day appear elsewhere in the play—in the repeated battle cry "St. *George* and Victory"; in the skirmishes between the Protector's men and Cardinal Winchester's, "Blew Coats to Tawny Coats," in which the proto-Protestants wear the blue strongly associated with St. George against the "Popish" tawny.[70]

In Elizabethan times, particularly in rural areas, festival bonfires were still lighted sporadically in honor of St. George's Day (April 23), as well as the other spring and early summer festivals like May Day and Midsummer Eve. Sometimes these bonfires featured the burning of an effigy—a witch or a figure associated with Lent or winter, or, in the most strongly Protestant versions of the ritual, a straw image of the pope. English "need-fires" followed a similar pattern but without being attached to specific holidays. Making use of the idea that fire drives out witches and other demonic influences, country folk would light a need-fire, sometimes burning an effigy or symbols associated with witchcraft, in order to break the spells that were believed responsible for collective misfortune. Yves-Marie Bercé has aptly termed such curative rituals "psychodrame avant la lettre."[71] The English

"Bonfire" for St. George in *1 Henry VI* has some of the same quality of quasi-magical expiation. The English forces in the play manage to assimilate Joan of Arc's reign of "misrule" into a festival for the revival of English militarism. She is the scapegoated witch at the center, first leading the rites of violence, then sacrificed to the flames to precipitate a collective release from the powerlessness she has created.

Such public rites did not always function to preserve the *status quo ante*. They could be used to effect a transition out of discarded social forms or away from hated social institutions.[72] John Knox's *First Blast of the Trumpet* makes use of ritual burning's potential for communal cleansing in order to eradicate female rule altogether. The tract ends in a fiery symbolic immolation of the authority of women:

> For assuredlie her empire and reigne is a wall without foundation: I meane the same of the authoritie of all women. It hath bene vnder-propped this blind time that is past, with the foolishnes of people, and with the wicked lawes of ignorant and tyrannous princes. But the fier of Goddes worde is alredie laide to those rotten proppes . . . and presentlie they burn, albeit we espie not the flame : when they are consumed, (as shortlie they will be, for stuble and drie timbre can not long indure the fier) that rotten wall, the vsurped and vniust empire of women, shall fall by it self in despit of all man, to the destruction of so manie, as shall labor to vphold it.[73]

A similar incineration of the "wall" of "vniust empire" can be identified in *1 Henry VI*. The play equivocates between the two models of ritual burning. On one level, it enacts a Protestant ritual immolation, evacuating false icons of the queen, but on another and deeper level, it carries vestiges of the older scapegoating rituals out of which Knox's symbolic burning of the "straw" authority of women and other icono-clastic burning had evolved. The second model is more explosive in its implications for the play. In terms of the immediate demons which seemed to need banishing in 1591–92, the play can be seen as a mas-sive but futile attempt to slough off the "monstrous regiment of Women" and all the superstitions and inhibitions associated with fe-male rule, in favor of an aggressive and highly masculinist Protestant militarism like that of Talbot and the English, an expansionism which was being stymied by the French wars, but which would later have its glory days in connection with English imperialism and empire build-ing. In terms of these older ritual forms, it is Elizabeth herself, in her contemporary aspect as covert enemy to English manhood, intran-sigent obstacle to male conquest, who is immolated. Of course, in the play, the witch doesn't burn, or if she perishes in one incarnation, it is only to reemerge in another further on in the trilogy. One disturbing image of Elizabeth does die with Joan, however: the image of "Astrea's Daughter" in male battle attire, creating a cult around her mystique of virginity—the dazzling, enervating image of the queen at Tilbury. Other dominant women rise with Margaret to take Joan's place, but without the same intense level of topical identification with the reigning monarch.

The *Henry VI* cycle has some of the quality of repetition-compulsion which critics have noticed in other plays of the early and mid 1590s.[74] The same demons rise up over and over again without being definitively vanquished. Part 1 ends inconclusively, with Margaret and Suffolk poised to transfer the "misrule" associated with Joan of Arc and France to England itself. One of the things this ending does is create the need for a sequel—a good thing to have if a company of players wishes to keep its audience. English patriotism hangs in the balance: "brave Talbot" is dead and his tormenter, the French man-woman, has been extinguished. But she may be reborn. What impact will Joan's "progeny" have upon the nation? Shakespeare's trilogy repeatedly whets the contemporary appetite for patriotic triumph, but also dashes it repeatedly.

I do not intend to offer detailed "local" readings of *Henry VI* Parts 2 and 3 as I have for Part 1, although such readings could readily be constructed. Instead, I will content myself with suggesting some of the ways in which the topicality of Part 1 colors the rest of the cycle. In dealing with Parts 2 and 3, we have two texts to work with instead of one—the quarto editions of 1594 and 1595 in addition to the folio versions. The quarto and the folio texts differ in interesting ways that cry out for topical analysis, but they agree in the essentials that will be touched on here. The cycle in both versions is an unholy succession of dominant women: in Part 1, Joan, the countess of Auvergne, and Margaret; in Part 2, Margaret and Eleanor, duchess of Gloucester, who dabbles in black magic in hopes of attaining the crown and thereby destroys her husband, the Protector. Margaret's rise to power is also associated with a waning of male and English strength. Through her marriage to Henry, England is deprived of the territory of Anjou, which is recklessly ceded to her father. As "princely" Queen Margaret grows in *mascula vis*, Henry VI becomes weaker and more vacillating:

it is the "Amazon effect" all over again, except that in this case, the impotent ruler appears never to have had much potential for strength. In both the quarto and folio versions of Part 3, Margaret is more than once called an "Amazon." She herself sends word from France that she means to "put Armour on" in defense of the Lancastrian cause (TLN 2139)—again, as earlier with Joan of Arc, there is the prospect of a cross-dressed woman warrior on stage, and in performance Margaret may well have worn armor for the battle scenes in which she acted as "generall" over her troops. Although the motif of the monstrous woman persists, the echoes of Elizabeth are faint. Margaret takes on none of Elizabeth's explicit symbology of power. There is still a potential for identification between the two queens, but it is not forced upon the audience with anything approaching the immediacy and shock of Part 1.

As we noted earlier, contemporary interest in the internecine strife of the Wars of the Roses was bound up with fears about the Elizabethan succession. In the course of the *Henry VI* plays, male succession in England is increasingly disrupted until in Part 3, we are confronted with the ultimate horror of parricide and filicide: "Alarum. Enter a Sonne that hath kill'd his Father, at one doore : and a Father that hath kill'd his Sonne at another doore" (TLN 1189–91).[75] The extinction of male succession is linked with the continuing dominance of the "woman on top" and other forms of festival inversion. But the motifs of ritual burning which came together in such fierce concentration in Part 1 are splintered among different characters and factions in later plays of the trilogy.

The rebellion of Jack Cade in Part 2 is carried out in terms of a May Day celebration turned to riot, with Cade himself serving as Lord of Misrule, devising monopolies and overthrowing law and parliamentary privilege like an absolutist sovereign, leading his forays, according to the folio text, like a violent May Day morris: "I haue seene / Him capre vpright, like a wilde Morisco, / Shaking the bloody Darts, as he his Bells" (TLN 1670–72). Although these lines and some of the explicit allusions to forms of royal abuse are missing from the quarto version, the Cade episodes there have the same quality of holiday topsy-turvydom gone violent. Following immediately upon Cade's death in both the quarto and the folio there is a call for another celebratory bonfire like that which had consumed Joan, but the fires are ordered by York in honor of his own aspiring kingship, and therefore are not a collective expression of English patriotism like the St. George's Day fire in Part 1.[76]

In Part 3 Margaret herself leads a bloody feast of misrule, crowning York as carnival king on his molehill to make "sport" out of his suffering. In both the quarto and the folio texts, York, like the Talbots in Part 1, is associated with the phoenix. He prays that after his death, "My ashes, as the Phoenix, may bring forth / A Bird, that will reuenge vpon you all" (TLN 495–96). It is one of the very few classical references to be found in the quarto text, and was probably kept in performance.[77] At the end, Margaret is finally reined in, but never annihilated as her "mother" Joan had been; she lives on mysteriously into *Richard III*. Meanwhile, another strong woman has emerged to take her place in the monstrous succession—the Widow Gray, who succeeds in marrying the rising king Edward IV. The new queen, however, appears on stage in the final scene of *3 Henry VI* along with her newborn child—an image of devoted female domesticity in marked contrast to the vanquished Amazons.

Taken in the rough order of their composition and performance, Shakespeare's history plays from *Henry VI* to *Henry V* progressively marginalize the dominant woman. "Monstrous regiment" survives into *Richard III* in the person of Margaret, almost a disembodied spirit from the past, but is extinguished in the *Henry IV* plays. Falstaff, another incarnation of carnival misrule, professes himself a follower of the queen and huntress Diana: "Let not vs that are Squires of the Nights bodie, bee call'd Theeues of the Dayes beautie. Let vs be *Dianaes* Forresters, Gentlemen of the Shade, Minions of the Moone, and let men say wee be men of good Gouernement, being gouerned as the Sea is, by our noble and chast mistresse the Moone."[78] He is associated, in such speeches, with a principle of virgin power and disorder which could easily enough be linked up with images of Queen Elizabeth, but he and his lunar travesty of good government are banished at the end when Prince Hal emerges as Henry V. Again, a version of female "misrule" has been suppressed. In the final play of the sequence, patriotic triumph and aggressive expansionism finally have their day, and in terms which are strongly male and "Protestant." France is conquered once more, and a French princess with it; Henry's successful wooing of Katherine in *Henry V* is an assertion of male and English dominance over the wayward, the French, and the female.

Of course, the moment of supremacy is brief. We who read the plays in the order of their composition and staging can supply the ironic coda that the cycle is poised to begin all over again: after Henry triumphs at Agincourt, he dies, and with his death we are thrown back into the woman-dominated world of *Henry VI*. But audiences in the 1590s were spared that turn of the wheel. Although *Henry V* does allude to the death of the hero, it is unlikely that the earlier plays were restaged all over again in sequence after it was added to the repertoire. Instead, what audiences in the 1590s were offered was a gradual conquest over deviant female rule.

Reading the plays was another matter. The folio version of the histories creates a very different pattern for readers of 1623 and after. When the plays were arranged in the folio order, chronologically by reign, the pattern of slow but steady conquest over the "monstrous regiment" was completely effaced, and with it, some of the most disquieting topical resonances from the early histories. In the folio, readers were invited to move from *Richard II* through *Henry IV* and *Henry V* into the *Henry VI* plays and *Richard III*; and we have evidence that some readers, at least, did read the folio histories in chronological order by reign.[79] *Richard III* was immediately followed in the folio text by the much later play *Henry VIII*. Only *Richard III*, with its resounding pro-Tudor conclusion, stood between *Henry VI* and *Henry VIII*. The recurrent phoenix and ritual burning motifs of *Henry VI* therefore looked forward with much greater immediacy in the folio to the creation of the Tudor dynasty in *Richard III* and the moment of Elizabeth's birth in the belated history play *Henry VIII*, where she is brought on stage as an infant and hailed in the full glory of her cultic attributes as Elizabeth, the "Mayden Phoenix" whose "sacred Ashes" will bring forth James I (TLN 3411–20).

The folio arrangement denies Henry V some of his triumph, since his interrupted funeral rites come immediately after the victories of *Henry V*, but it also mitigates some of the topical virulence of *Henry VI*'s portrait of Joan of Arc. When read with *Henry VIII* as its terminus, the pattern of ritual burning in the *Henry VI* plays appears less virulent against queenship as an institution. With a positive image of Elizabeth held up just over the horizon, so to speak, it is easier at least in retrospect to identify the French "*Puzell*" and everything she is associated with as unequivocally demonic sacrilege against the sacred image of the queen. By 1623, of course, the specter of the woman ruler was distant enough from English experience to have lost some of its subterranean terrors. The "gentle" Bard of the First Folio presides over a Joan of Arc who has been tamed of her malevolent immediacy. That is not to suggest that the cross-dressed "disorderly" woman disappeared altogether from Shakespeare's dramatic output during the 1590s. The figure was progressively marginalized in the history plays, but given new centrality during the same period in Shakespearean comedy, where it carried many of its old associations with festival inversion, but without the old menace to male strength and collective well-being.

SPECULATIONS AND RAMIFICATIONS: RELOCATING "MONSTROUS REGIMENT"

In the early 1590s, Robert Greene had called Shakespeare a "tiger wrapt in a player's hide." The comment registers a high level of jealous bile, but also intimates a connection between the upstart playwright's violation of his proper place and the "disorderly" cruelty of Queen Margaret, whom the tormented York had called a "tiger wrapt in a woman's hide" in *3 Henry VI*.[80] It is a teasing and highly interesting potential kinship, but one which even Greene himself would probably not have carried over to the Shakespeare of the comedies—a Shakespeare who appears far closer to the idealized Bard we have all been taught to value. Here, we will take only a perfunctory look at other "local" versions of the woman on top—not enough to construct full topical readings of the plays, only enough to suggest a range of alternative constructions which our discussion thus far has not touched. The furies of female "regiment" unleashed in the early history plays are conspicuously absent in the high comedies, or at least considerably muted; they are reactivated in later plays like *Macbeth*.

There are four comedies, all of them usually assigned to the last years of the sixteenth century or the very beginning of the seventeenth, in which the sexually composite woman appears with particular prominence. In three of them, *As You Like It*, *The Merchant of Venice*, and *Twelfth Night*, the heroine adopts male disguise; in a fourth, *Much Ado*, she adopts no disguise, but is observed to be much like her "honorable father" and brings up the subject of cross-dressing in a series of "merry" observations. In these plays, the dominant manwoman is not burned, but she is nevertheless extinguished. She is allowed her time of preeminence and revelry, then she is married off. It is an alternative version of an old fantasy, long past the slightest possibility of fulfillment, about Elizabeth I.

As we have observed, Elizabeth herself regularly interpreted court comedies of the 1560s as advice about the succession: she, like the heroine, was expected to give up her "dislike of the woman's part" and marry. Later on, plays like John Lyly's *Galatea* trafficked in a similar association of ideas. During the period when there were actually "Two Queens in One Isle"—Mary Queen of Scots and Elizabeth of England—more than one loyal subject expressed the wish, as Nicholas Throckmorton had put it as early as 1559, "That one of these two Queens of the Isle of Britain were transformed into the shape of a man, to make so happy a marriage as thereby there might be an unity of the whole isle." Mary herself had joked that if only she or Elizabeth were a man, they could have married—the very fantasy on the brink of fulfillment in *Galatea.* The Scottish ambassador James Melville recalled that at one point, he had jokingly offered to spirit Elizabeth off disguised as a page boy so that she could meet Mary in person, and that Elizabeth had replied, "Alas! if I might do it!" The story is probably apocryphal, but it illustrates the kinds of things that got said—in jest or in earnest—about the queen of England. The same configuration can be found in discussions of other potential partners. Elizabeth queried the Spanish ambassador about Philip II's widowed sister Juana, "saying how much she should like to see her, and how well so young a widow and a maiden would get on together, and what a pleasant life they could lead. She [the queen] being the elder would be the husband, and her Highness the wife."[81] This matrix of odd, elusive fantasies about succession and the queen's *mascula vis* hovered about her person throughout much of the reign. Shakespeare's comedies throw off seemingly random echoes of such fantasy material along with a "delirious plenitude" of other "selves and meanings."[82] They offer a fecund, generative vision of the cross-dressed yet sexually available virgin—a vision which gains some of its nostalgic energies from the fact that it comes too late.

Historians tell us that there was a surge in the number of "masterless women" in late sixteenth-century England, with a crisis around 1600. "Masterless women" could be milkmaids or spinners or wealthy widows or vagrants—any woman who lived on her own outside the structure of the male-dominated household.[83] But they could also be heads of state. It is tempting to speculate that the presence of Elizabeth on the throne may have stimulated emulation of her independence on the part of women further down the social scale, as increasing numbers of them in fact separated themselves from the immediate authority of men. But such a contention would be impossible to prove. There are too many other factors that need to be taken into account— shifting economic conditions, changing perceptions of normative family structure. If Elizabeth's rule to some degree encouraged female "misrule," the queen also made it her business to put a firm cap on the phenomenon by insisting on her own male-identified patriarchy and using it to curb court ladies under her direct authority, by fostering the creation of new devices for curbing the waywardness of those who were "mere" women but claimed the prerogatives of men. During the 1590s there was a decided increase in institutionalized devices specifically for the curbing of women. For example, more and more villages invested in "cucking stools" for the punishment of domineering wives and scolds.[84]

What was depicted as a crisis for Tudor society is less threatening in Shakespearean comedy. The "masterless women" of the late comedies are renderings of a contemporary type, but also revisions of the menacing martial women of the early histories. After the Armada, the "woman on top" had been a focus for suppressed rage and fears of powerlessness; in the late 1590s, in Shakespeare at least, it becomes the generative center for more positive fantasies and idealizations. At least some of the comedies were staged at court. What was set up opposite the queen on the occasion of such performances was not a dangerous, demonized virgin like the Norwich icon burned in 1578, but a version of the royal composite in which the deviant and "popish" elements had to a considerable extent been emptied of their menace.

Given the Elizabethan passion for political lock-picking, we can imagine various ways in which Shakespeare's cross-dressed heroines could have registered with contemporary audiences as analogues of Elizabeth. In *The Merchant of Venice*, Portia offers a becoming speech of womanly submission to Bassanio, then heads off in male garb to do justice in a high court of law (to which, incidentally, she brings legal principles like the equity actually practiced in the queen's Court of Chancery).[85] "Man and woman both," Portia enacts over time Queen Elizabeth's standard rhetorical ploy of declaring her weakness as a woman, then successfully asserting her masculine prerogative over a resisting body of men. In *As You Like It*, Rosalind exerts almost complete control over the world of Arden, playing many parts male and female, using her disguise as Ganymede to get what she cannot as a woman, pairing couples off to suit her purposes as Elizabeth was notorious for doing at court. Rosalind's protean, free-form movement in and out of male and female identities is very much like the flirtatious games Elizabeth habitually played with her favorites, to their exasperation or delight. Unlike Portia and Rosalind, Beatrice in *Much Ado about Nothing* does not adopt male disguise, but she can be seen as mimicking some of Elizabeth's strategies with language and royal identity. Like the queen, she makes adamant protests against marriage; she comments that if she is saddled with too young a husband, she will "dresse him in my apparell, and make him my waiting gentlewoman" (TLN 446–47)—a muted echo of the "Amazon effect." Viola of *Twelfth Night* is less forceful, seemingly less content with her enforced self-sufficiency and only briefly "masterless," but caught up in the same intriguing games of oscillating sexual identities. Any of these possibilities for identification could easily have been intensified during performance through actual imitation of the inflection and mannerisms of Elizabeth. We know that strong-nerved actors were capable of such mimicry at other times, and at least one play from the end of the 1590s actually brought the figure of Elizabeth onto the public stage.[86] But by the same token, through staging, the potential for identification could have been diminished.

Some of the potential resemblances are negative. If Portia seems to carry justice too far against Shylock, for example, does that mean Shakespeare is accusing Queen Elizabeth of a similar deficiency—in the Lopez case of a few years earlier or more generally? Rustlings of the old, threatening "disorderly woman" can be heard on the edges of the comedies' festival inversions. The "horn music" and repeated references to cuckoldry in *As You Like It*, for example, evoke the shaming rituals of the Skimmington, in which the violation of sexual hierarchy was held up to public ridicule.[87] Readings which bring such motifs to the surface can easily be generated, but without much security of interpretation. It is time to move, once again, from the protean referentiality of topical reading to the level of "local" function. To the extent that parallels were (either consciously or subliminally) perceived by a contemporary audience, what might have been their effect, particularly given the sudden concentration of such images just at the end of Elizabeth's reign?

All of the "women's" parts in Shakespeare's plays were, of course, played by men or young boys. But only in certain cases was the sexual multivalence of the "woman" on stage overtly thematized. Joan of Arc is a partial example: when the duke of Burgundy jests, "Pray God she proue not masculine ere long: / If vnderneath the Standard of the French / She carry Armour, as she hath begun" (TLN 701–3), he can be understood on a metadramatic level as gesturing toward the actual sexual identity of the "woman" under the armor. But such a level of theatrical self-consciousness has to be read in from the outside; the play does not constantly gesture toward its own fabricated nature as Shakespearean comedy was to do later on. Indeed, the portrayal of Joan depends on the perception of a fundamental inauthenticity in her self-fashioning as a warrior. She dresses in male armor, but never presents herself as anything other than a woman. She is therefore an incomplete analogue of Queen Elizabeth. When Elizabeth donned elements of male battle dress at Tilbury to incite her troops to valor, she was—and her speech for the occasion made that clear—not merely taking on the dress appropriate to her role as military commander but gesturing toward her sacred identity as monarch. In a secularized epiphany, her masculine accoutrements unfolded her essential "Kinglike" nature. Or at least such was the intent. We have already considered the possibility that for the disaffected or skeptical among her subjects, the bold gesture may have aroused more uncertainties than it dampened—hence the subversive potential of Joan, a defective analogue of the queen, to suggest flaws in the royal composite itself.

In Shakespeare's comedies, the metadramatic "truth" of the stage woman's male identity is far closer to the surface, if only because the plays repeatedly assault the distinction between their own fictions and an external reality, repeatedly set the actors apart from their roles, male and female, then playfully merge them back into them. At the end of *As You Like It*, the heroine actually steps outside her female identity and confesses her maleness: "If I were a Woman, I would kisse as many of you as had beards that pleas'd me, complexions that lik'd me, and breaths that I defi'de not : And I am sure, as many as haue good beards, or good faces, or sweet breaths, will for my kind offer, when I make curt'sie, bid me farewell" (TLN 2791–96). This revelation, surprising, perhaps even shocking, yet "licensed" by the free-form interplay which has preceded it, establishes a layering of sexual identities which is congruent with the queen's anomalous self-presentation rather than subversive of it.[88]

The dramatic construct of a boy clothed as a woman, an altogether credible woman, who then expands her identity through male disguise in such a way as to mirror the activities which would be appropriate to her actual, hidden male identity—that construct precisely replicates visually the composite self-image Queen Elizabeth created over and over again through language. She showed herself a woman on the stage of public life—and she liked to call it that—but with a male identity, her princehood, underlying her obvious femininity and lending her authority, offering the subliminal promise of growth into kingship as a boy actor would grow into a man. She did not, except on highly unusual occasions like Tilbury, dress herself as a man, but performed so effectively the "male" responsibilities of government that in that sphere her subjects were invited to forget—and sometimes did forget—she was female. She called much more attention to her male "immortal body" than Shakespeare's heroines do to their latent maleness, but her emphasis was necessary to achieve the same perception of multivalence. She had to create a new convention which cut across accepted gender distinctions, build a conceptual model which seemed to belie the visual data offered by the "frail" female body that her subjects saw; the sexual identity of those playing female parts on stage was, by contrast, understood from the outset, a familiar theatrical device.

What is distinctive about the four Shakespearean comedies we are considering is not their use of boy actors to play female parts, as all plays before the 1620s in England did, but the fact that they call attention to the convention by acting it out in reverse in the person of the central character through a disguise which replicates the actor's underlying sexual identity. As they watched Shakespeare's heroines move in and out of their manhood, members of the Elizabethan audience witnessed the creation of sexual composites which resembled the "man and woman both" that Queen Elizabeth claimed to be. And her public rhetoric appears to supply the only full contemporary analogue. Shakespeare's comedies helped to validate the queen's anomalous identity by presenting the construct visually through witty and attractive characters who were easy to admire, full of charm and charisma, linked with disorder but also with images of festival regeneration. The heroine in these plays performs a normative function with regard to potentially deviant images of the queen. Her sexual multivalence on stage recapitulates, softens, and domesticates the claim of sexual duality which Elizabeth herself deployed to maintain her effectiveness as a ruler.

But the plays also limit the myth of Elizabeth's composite identity—undo it, insofar as they separate the idea of orderly succession from the actual person of the queen in her "mortal body." Quite unlike Elizabeth herself, Shakespeare's heroines all marry at the end; they all end up playing the part which the queen professed to dislike. The fundamental ambivalence of a boy actor playing a woman's part remains at the end of the play, but the audience is left with the unspoken assurance—or at least the strong culturally reinforced expectation—that the heroine will no longer act it out through the donning of male garb and male identity. Portia is the only one of the four comic heroines whose behavior we observe after marriage. When she goes to Venice as a stripling doctor of law, she is a wife but still a virgin. There are inklings that her *mascula vis* is not quelled—will not be quelled even in marriage. But she will at least cast off the virgin's immaculate isolation. Like the other heroines, she will accept wifehood and fertility—do the things Elizabethans had yearned for decades for their queen to do in the interest of stability and continuity. In the 1560s and 1570s, the wish had been at least potentially capable of fulfillment; by the 1590s, it was pure fantasy.

Shakespeare's androgynous comic heroines were created at an interesting point in English history, a time when the frustrations of the post-Armada period had become endemic and many considered the nation to have declined from its brilliance of a decade or two before. The grave old courtiers and advisers were gone, and the young were more impatient, more volatile; the moral tone of the court was perceived as more degenerate than before; the queen's financial problems were more serious. National fertility was no idle issue during the late 1590s: there had been a series of disastrous harvests and the usual concomitant dearth and starvation. And there were suggestive analogies (for those of a superstitious bent) between the apparent waning of the nation and the physical condition of the queen herself. Elizabeth was unmistakably aging, withdrawing from the close interaction with her subjects that had been one of the hallmarks of her rule. The old, ugly

rumors and anxieties about the succession again became very prominent in the late 1590s.[89] In her final years, the queen still dressed like a
young virgin despite her black teeth and wrinkled breast, still clung
tenaciously to the sustaining myths of her reign. But there was an increasing sense of strain, increasing distance between the sublime immortality of her "body politic" and her evident mortality as a "frail
woman."

At the end of her reign, Queen Elizabeth continued to portray herself as self-contained and self-perpetuating: she was husband and wife,
mother and firstborn son, encompassing within her own nature the
separate beings required for a genuine succession. Shakespeare's plays
reinforce the queen's rhetoric in that they enmesh the heroine's temporary masculinity with the search for and testing of an appropriate marriage partner. Rosalind and Viola use their male disguise at least in part
to be near the men they love and interact with them in a freedom
which would be impossible otherwise. Their playing-out of masculine
roles furthers their marriage and the creation of a succession—one of
the very fantasies Queen Elizabeth sought to perpetuate about her
own "body politic" through her assimilation of husband and prince
into her own identity. But simultaneously, the plays dismantle the fantasy by separating out the component beings. For some incandescent
moments on stage, the "white magic" of the royal myth is allowed
free play, and those moments have a peculiar power. But in the end,
the myth is undone. Rosalind and Viola cannot marry themselves,
cannot permanently sustain the self-sufficiency of their composite natures, but must go out and get themselves husbands—something it
was obviously too late for Elizabeth herself to do.

Shakespeare's comedies perpetuate the magic of the queen's rhetoric
by displacing it from her person, removing her language and strategies from Whitehall into the theater. It is there on stage, not at the
royal court of the late 1590s, that the dazzling, idealized images of
Elizabeth's sexual multivalence retain their full vibrancy. Of course art
cannot undo mortality. The widening cultural rift between the rich
matrix of fantasies surrounding the queen and the stark reality of her
physical finitude may help to account for the patina of melancholy that
burnishes and softens the mirth of the final comedies. The queen's language, her brilliant, protean talent for multiform self-presentation,
can succeed theatrically in comedy because it has been separated from
the danger and decay of the royal person. But the separation is not

complete. Shakespeare's plays depended for the power of their element of political wish-fulfillment on the continuing existence of the "mortal body" of the queen. The "local" version of the dominant woman we have identified here, with its joyous interplay among gender roles, its expansive optimism about the male-female heroine's capacity to revive and renew, died along with Queen Elizabeth I.

In the Jacobean theater, the figure of the sexually composite woman reemerges, but with significant variations. The most fascinating of these is the comic Roaring Girl in Dekker and Middleton's play by that name: Moll Frith in many ways perpetuates positive elements of the myth of Elizabeth, but several rungs down the social ladder. She is unruly, yet virginal, dressed in male clothing, an affront to male authority, yet for the most part salutary in her impact, associated with social restructuring rather than the maintenance of a preexisting equilibrium. She is therefore less conservative than Elizabeth had been in most of her public self-representations, but functions in some of the same ways that the image of the queen did for disgruntled Jacobeans. As reformers harked back to the glorious reign of Elizabeth in their impatience with the autocracy and ineptitude of her successor, James I, so Dekker and Middleton seem deliberately to have constructed an ambivalent, low-life variant upon the once-threatening Amazonian image, a self-sufficient yet isolated virgin figure whose virtue shows up the corruption of the times. Another play sometimes attributed to Dekker was explicitly about Elizabeth, her early tribulations, and her triumphs. It was entitled *If you know not me, You know no bodie* and appeared in many seventeenth-century quarto editions with a large woodcut of the queen on its title page. The cultural memory for Elizabeth's mannerisms and characteristic strategies was longer than we are likely to find credible, and continued to exert a subtle shaping on stage depictions of female dominance—particularly those with a reformist bent—even decades after her death.[90]

Shakespeare, however, did not tap into this vein of nostalgic Jacobean reconstruction after 1603. His most significant Jacobean transmutation of the Elizabethan composite merges her back into the monstrous "unruly woman." Lady Macbeth is a "woman on top" whose sexual ambivalence and dominance are allied with the demonic and mirror the obscure gender identifications of the bearded witches. Her "unnatural" dominance blasts orderly succession and unleashes a series of catastrophes which nearly destroy a kingdom. One possible reading of Lady Macbeth is as a revivified scapegoat figure who gathers up yet once more the residual power of the image of Elizabeth. There was at least one person in England—King James I—who would have been profoundly interested in the eradication of a symbology of female power which showed up his own royal impotence. If, as we hypothesize, *Macbeth* was performed at court in 1605 or 1606, we can read the figure of Lady Macbeth as a symbolic cancellation of the female dominance which had haunted James throughout his early life, and which he particularly associated with Queen Elizabeth, who had presided over the execution of his mother and had demonstrated her superior political skills to James's humiliation on many occasions. Such a "local" *Macbeth* would celebrate the Jacobean succession and blacken the barren female authority associated with the previous monarch—James I is one of the kings reflected in the play's prophetic glass, one of a long line of male monarchs with the promise of more to come. Ben Jonson's *Masque of Queens*, which was performed before James the year before the 1611 stage revival of *Macbeth*, enacts a similar ritual banishment of demonic "monstrous regiment," replacing the witches of the antimasque with a crew of Amazonian queens who place themselves reassuringly under James's kingly authority.[91]

But *Macbeth*, like some of the plays we have been discussing, also carries topical associations which work against such an "official" line of interpretation. A good local reading of the play would have to take some of those into account. I will leave the task to those who have already begun it[92] and turn instead to another play which seems even more insistently to demand "royal" reading, to marginalize the image of Elizabeth, and to promote the Stuart cause.

3

James

The First Folio's dedicatory epistle to the earls of Pembroke and Montgomery begins with a flourish of official titles and offices:

TO THE MOST NOBLE
AND
INCOMPARABLE PAIRE
OF BRETHREN.
WILLIAM
Earle of Pembroke, &c. Lord Chamberlaine to the
Kings most Excellent Maiesty.
AND
PHILIP
Earle of Montgomery, &c. Gentleman of his Maiesties
Bed-Chamber. Both Knights of the most Noble Order
of the Garter, and our singular good
LORDS.

This formal opening establishes clear links between the volume's patrons and the court milieu of King James I. Pembroke is addressed as "Lord Chamberlaine" to his "*most Excellent Maiesty*" and Montgomery, as "Gentleman of his Maiesties Bed-Chamber." But this is the last, except for the two-word reference to "our *Iames*" in Ben Jonson's dedicatory poem, that we hear in the First Folio of the "*Kings most Excellent Maiesty.*" The omission would not be particularly striking were it not for the name and associations of the theatrical company behind the volume. Nowhere in the First Folio is it mentioned that Shakespeare or Heminge or Condell or any of the others included in "The Names of the Principall Actors" belonged to a company called the King's Men. The omission of the name is probably not inadvertent. It follows the rhetorical pattern of the rest of the front matter, constructing Shakespeare not as the King's Man but as his own man, not "authored" by a higher power but Author in his own right.

Moreover, after the opening flourish, the dedicatory epistle aborts its incipient placement of Shakespeare's collected plays within an official Stuart context. The editors appeal to the earls of Pembroke and Montgomery not as servants of James I—Lord Chamberlain and Gentleman of the Bed-Chamber—but as patrons and surrogate parents who exact their own ceremonies of devotion. Heminge and Condell approach the two brothers humbly, "with a kind of religious addresse," to offer up the volume. In the same manner, they aver,

> Country hands reach foorth milke, creame, fruites, or what they haue : and many Nations (we haue heard) that had not gummes & incense, obtained their requests with a leauened Cake. It was no fault to approch their Gods, by what meanes they could: And the most, though meanest, of things are made more precious, when they are dedicated to Temples. In that name therefore, we most humbly consecrate to your H. H. these remaines of your seruant *Shakespeare*.   (A2v)

This ritualized language is worlds away from the iconoclastic violence of the early 1590s, from the blaring militarism of Shakespeare's *Henry VI*. It is the kind of language and gesture we might expect in a Jacobean court setting in the year 1623—a decorous Presentation at the Temple, at once classical and Hebraic, of the "first fruits" of Heminge and Condell's editorship, or of their firstborn literary "son." Similar ceremonialized offerings were made over and over again in the Jacobean court masque before the "divine" person of the monarch.

If we wished to carry forward the implicit Stuart analogy and read the First Folio dedication as part of the milieu of Stuart court ritual, we could regard the earls of Pembroke and Montgomery as high priests in the "Temple" of James I—a fitting enough role for men who served the king as Lord Chamberlain and Gentleman of the Bed-Chamber. The volume's patrons would then be priestly intermediaries who receive the offering of Shakespeare's "remaines" in the name of the supreme authority (both secular and "religious") in whose service they hold high "place." But there is a telling slippage. The earls are not priests *in* the temple, they themselves are the "Temples" *to* which the work is dedicated, the gods whom Heminge and Condell reverently approach with their offering of Shakespeare for consecration. Mean things are made worthy by being dedicated *to* temples; in the same spirit, Shakespeare's plays are dedicated to the Honorable Pembroke and Montgomery. It is unclear in whose "name" the offering is made. What name is "that name"? The name of the king, the name of God? The ceremony refuses to "make sense" in terms of its own nascent scheme of Stuart court allegory.

The slippage is particularly interesting in view of Pembroke's known sympathies for reformist and populist causes. The year after the publication of the First Folio, for example, he appears to have helped instigate the staging of Thomas Middleton's *A Game at Chess*, which caused a sensation because of its satire against the king's pro-Spanish policy. The play was suppressed after twelve days of performance.[1] Heminge and Condell's folio epistle dedicatory, in its apparent artlessness, indeed *through* its apparent artlessness—as though its abrogation of the hegemonic design of Stuart court ritual is no more than inadvertent bumbling—creates an independent edifice called Pembroke and Montgomery. Within that "Temple," the authority of the king is invoked, not as the Absolute toward whom the folio offering is ultimately directed, but as a name which lends luster to other names, the names of the two earls, the name of their "noble" stepchild Shakespeare. The King's Men evade the king as parent figure, as "author"; they can almost be said to restructure themselves in the company's pre-Jacobean form as the Lord Chamberlain's Men. The language of Stuart court ritual is recentered in a "religious" space constituted by the patrons themselves as independent agents, not intermediaries with the king.

The seemingly slight gesture would not have the significance it has if James had been a different kind of monarch. James was himself an Author who viewed both his own literary production and his "arts" of government in strongly proprietary terms. He had preceded Shakespeare as the author of a collected folio edition of *Workes*. So, of course, had Shakespeare's fellow dramatist Ben Jonson. But Jonson's folio *Workes*, published the same year as the king's, calls considerably more attention than the Shakespeare First Folio to the author's connections with James I. Not only does Jonson's *Workes* include numerous poems and court entertainments which celebrate the king and royal policy, but Jonson went out of his way to close the volume with an echo of James. He disrupted the performance order of the masques so that his *Workes* would culminate in *The Golden Age Restored*, an entertainment closely tied in terms of its "present occasions" to the king's Star Chamber speech about restoring the countryside, the speech which concludes *The Workes* of James I.[2] Shakespeare's First Folio shows at least some evidence of similar rearrangement. It ends, quite oddly, with *The Tragedie of Cymbeline*, a play which is clearly out of place among the tragedies, but deeply immersed in topical issues relating to James I. With its climactic scenes invoking the image of Emperor Augustus and the *Pax Romana*, *Cymbeline*, like the final entry in Jonson's *Workes*, resonates with Golden Age ideas as they surfaced in Jacobean political panegyric. The play's anomalous placement in the folio could have been engineered by Ben Jonson, who sometimes performed similar generic violations for rhetorical purposes in his own dramatic work, and who supplied the verses which structure the First Folio's opening pages. As our discussion later on will emphasize, however, there is more than one way in which the peculiar placement of *Cymbeline* can be understood. And in any case, as we have seen, the volume itself was put together in ways that discouraged topical reading. The folio's elevation of the Bard to a transcendent realm of Art, its refusal to subsume Shakespeare within a space dominated by royal authority, would have drained off some of *Cymbeline*'s intense Stuart referentiality for readers in 1623 and after.

We are talking in the case of *Cymbeline* about a different kind of topicality from that in earlier plays we have discussed—a topicality which does not scatter interpretation in a number of directions but collects it along a single axis of political allegory. "Local" interpretation in *Cymbeline* is therefore a more decorous and orderly activity than in *1 Henry VI* or the high comedies, but that fact has scarcely made *Cymbeline*'s embeddedness in contemporary affairs more palatable for most Shakespeareans. In *Cymbeline*, as quite regularly in Shakespeare, "local" meaning has registered with generations of editors and critics as intolerable textual turbulence. The play's most obviously topical passages have been rejected as "not Shakespeare." In particular, editors have branded the mysterious tablet left for Posthumus by Jupiter as spurious: its "ludicrous" heavy-handed message is all too easy to interpret in terms of the guiding myths of the Stuart monarchy. Forty years ago, G. Wilson Knight set out to rehabilitate the prophecy as "true" Shakespeare and his effort led him—uncharacteristically for Knight but not surprisingly, given the material he was dealing with—straight into a reading of the play as political allegory. Some editors still argue that the prophecy cannot be "Shakespeare." They base their claim partly on stylistic evidence, since the passage is awkwardly at odds with other portions of the text, but even more on the grounds that it represents a political "intrusion," links the universal Shakespeare far too closely with a specific and not altogether laudable seventeenth-century cause.[3] It is as though when Jacobean ideology is at issue,

Shakespeare cannot be allowed any stylistic heterogeneity, even though accepting the prophecy as Shakespeare opens up new possibilities for interpretation. It is the old mechanism of Disintegration again: textual palimpsest is preferable to the dangers of a deidealized, unpredictable local Shakespeare.

Like the First Folio epistle dedicatory, *Cymbeline* seems to demand that we read it as part of the milieu of the Stuart court, rather as we might interpret the exquisitely detailed and sustained political allegory of a masque by Ben Jonson. And in fact, if we immerse ourselves in the Jacobean materials to which it seems persistently to allude, we will discover that the play is far more deeply and pervasively topical than even its most avid political "lock-pickers" have found it to be. But in some of its episodes, rather like the First Folio epistle dedicatory, the play stubbornly refuses to make sense at the level of Stuart interpretation. Those episodes will be of particular interest to us here. If the most obviously topical materials appear intrusive in *Cymbeline*, that is in part because they are presented *as* intrusions—they are curiously static emblems or mysterious written texts which arrest the play's theatrical momentum. To undertake "local" reading of *Cymbeline* is to enter a labyrinth in which political meanings are simultaneously generated and stalemated, in which the political "authorship" of James I is put forward in a series of arresting, even jarring visitations which impose a relentless textuality upon the flow of events, and which, through their resistance to assimilation in the action, undermine the very political message they seem designed to communicate.

THE JACOBEAN LINE

When James I came down from Scotland to claim the English throne, he brought something not experienced in England since the time of Henry VIII: a royal family, two sons and a daughter, the beginnings of a Jacobean line, the promise of an orderly succession from father to firstborn male offspring. One panegyrist exclaimed in 1610, seven years after James's accession, "O happy English, that haue no more women and children for your King, but a King full of strength, a king participating the verdure of his youth, and ful ripeness of his age." In outward appearance at least, King James did fit the virile image of kingship and "continuance" far better than his predecessor.[4] There were important ways in which he tried to perpetuate the tactics and image of Elizabeth. He sometimes portrayed himself, for example, as similarly possessed of a composite sexual identity: he was a king, but also a "louing nourish-father to the Church" and people. He also imitated some of Elizabeth's strategies with Parliament.[5] But more regularly, James sought to present his reign as a marked departure from the queen's.

James I once demanded that a preacher at court make sense or step down. He consciously cultivated a "plain style" himself, and liked to portray his own language and policy, in implicit contrast to the labyrinthine tactics of Elizabeth, as always making sense. As he put it in his published 1604 speech before Parliament,

> It becommeth a King, in my opinion, to vse no other Eloquence then plainnesse and sinceritie. By plainenesse I meane, that his Speeches should be so cleare and voyd of all ambiguitie, that they may not be throwne, nor rent asunder in contrary sences like the old Oracles of the Pagan gods. And by sinceritie, I vnderstand that vprightnsse and honestie which ought to be in a Kings whole Speeches and actions: That as farre as a King is in Honour erected aboue any of his Subiects, so farre should he striue in sinceritie to be aboue them all, and that his tongue should be euer the trew Messenger of his heart: and this sort of Eloquence may you euer assuredly looke for at my hands.

The speech caused a sensation among the king's new English subjects, in part because of the utter contrast between its promise of directness and the subtle, multilayered inscrutability of Elizabeth. James's royal language was, in his own view at least, transparent, void of ambiguity, expressing inner sincerity, and (he seems to have thought) therefore directly translatable into outward political action. Even seeming opacity was—and had to be—ultimately "legible"; in subsequent speeches James acknowledged that his meaning might at times require seeking out, and invited his subjects to look into the transparent "Christall Mirror" of his heart to "read" there the limpid clarity of the royal purpose.[6]

Unlike Elizabeth, who usually made a point of mystifying political intent, James demanded that his policy utterances be "read" according to the constraints of an authored document. Royal texts, like the policy behind them, had to be self-consistent and "legible." When he came down from Scotland, he brought his most illustrious book with him. *Basilikon Doron* was hastily published in a London edition in 1603 so that it could be admired by his new subjects at the same time that the new king offered himself for their "reading." His other major books were published in England in 1604. Given James's predilection for authorship, it was perhaps not mere happenstance that some of his major policy declarations became known as *Books*—the *Book of Sports*, the *Book of Bounty*. He made a point of claiming personal proprietorship over the subject matter and style of his royal proclamations: "Most of them myself doth dictate every word. Never any proclamation of state and weight which I did not direct." In a similar way, through his sponsorship of the King James Bible, he established himself even as a "principle mover and author" behind Holy Writ, at least as it was promulgated in England. After the Hampton Court Conference of 1604, admiring bishops called him "a Liuing Library, and a walking Study."[7]

In Scotland, King James had actually composed court entertainments. In England, he also "authored" masques in that he promoted (or at least rewarded) a new attention to architectonics and to the laws of visual perspective, so that entertainments at court not devoted to celebrating some other member of the royal family regularly centered on the king himself and his most significant policy initiatives: all lines converged upon the Jacobean "line." For better or for worse, through his own authorship, James provided would-be panegyrists with a wealth of texts which could be mimetically recapitulated in entertainments at court. The masque licensed deviations from the Jacobean political "line" but typically ended up containing them within a broader assertion of royal power and authority.[8] In proclamations, speeches, and entertainments, even (at times, catastrophically) in his attempts at practical politics, James insisted on his own governing line of interpretation and political action, a line emanating from the royal wisdom, the clear "sincerity" of his heart.

The editor of *The Workes of the Most High and Mighty Prince, Iames* complained in his preface that James's subjects scattered words and jangling criticism of the king's métier of Author as fast as he could gather the royal texts together, as though "Since that Booke-writing is growen into a Trade; It is as dishonorable for a *King* to write bookes; as it is for him to be a Practitioner in a *Profession*."[9] Behind the complaint are some of the new assertions about authorship that we have already encountered: it provided a way for lowborn self-made people to aspire beyond their origins; it was associated with the setting of limits upon the uncontrolled proliferation of meaning. The frontispiece to his *Workes* (figure 3) could even be taken as preferring authorship over kingship as a way of achieving monumentality and immortality:

Crownes haue their compasse, length of dayes their date,
Triumphes their tombes, felicitie her fate,
Of more then earth, can earth make none partaker,
But knowledge makes the KING most like his maker.

But such glory exacted its price. Like his editorial assistants, King
James saw himself as performing the patient authorial task of collecting meaning, arranging it, beating back the political and moral chaos
of unregulated signification in order to forge diverse materials into
"one Body" (Preface, B2v). It is the paradigmatic situation of authorial prerogative, whether bookish or political: the "imposition of a
conclusive, self-identical meaning that transcends the seriality of displacement," and translates politically into the imposed order of absolutism.[10] James's kingship was an absolutism of the text.

The king encountered considerable resistance to his novel ideas
about royal authorship and authority. According to the editor of his
Workes, many of his subjects complained, "It had been better his
Maiestie had neuer written any Bookes at all; and being written, better
they had perished with the present like *Proclamations*, then haue re-
mayned to *Posterity:* For say these Men, Little it befitts the Maiesty of
a *King* to turne Clerke, and to make a warre with the penne, that were
fitter to be fought with the Pike; to spend the powers of his so ex-
quisite an vnderstanding upon papers, which had they beene spent on
powder, could not but have preuayled ere this for the conquest of a
Kingdome:" (Preface, B2v). When James scolded his own son Prince
Henry for his inattention to learning, threatening to disinherit him in
favor of his brother Charles, "who was far quicker at learning and
studied more earnestly," Henry answered back indirectly through his
tutor, "I know what becomes a Prince. It is not necessary for me to be
a professor, but a soldier and a man of the world. If my brother is as
learned as they say, we'll make him Archbishop of Canterbury." His
father took the retort "in no good part."[11]

Sir John Harington left an amusing account of his first private inter-
view with the author-king. After he had been kept waiting over an
hour in a "smale roome" containing "good order of paper, inke, and
pens, put on a boarde for the Prince's [James's] use," James himself entered and "enquyrede" in detail about Harington's learning. The hap-
less Harington thought he was back in school: the king "showede me
his owne [learning] in suche sorte, as made me remember my examiner
at Cambridge aforetyme." In the course of the long and uncomfortably
erudite conversation, James asked Harington, "what I thoughte pure

witte was made of; and whom it did best become? Whether a Kynge shoulde not be the beste clerke in his owne countrie; and, if this lande did not entertayne goode opinion of his lernynge and good wisdome?"[12] Harington chafed under the display of royal pedantry and insecurity. For one who had served in the court of Elizabeth I, such ostentatious clerkish erudition did not "become a Prince."

James I did not invent the new expectations about unity and consistency. He merely sought to apply them to an area of the national life which had previously been characterized by multiplicity and carefully cultivated ambiguity. His declared intent was to bring new clarity to public policy, but his insistence on personal "ownership" sometimes had the reverse effect, at least on the masques and entertainments which celebrated his rule. He demanded that the Jacobean symbology of power be elaborately specific to himself and his own most cherished projects in a way that it had not been under Elizabeth. That demand made it harder for his subjects to "read" his rituals of state. The shift toward greater complexity and political specificity did not, of course, arrive overnight along with the new monarch. It can be correlated with a broad set of social and cultural transformations. We have already examined one version of the change in our discussion of the rise of the "comely frontispiece." But the change in monarchs gave it particular visibility in terms of the public symbology of power. We can measure its impact in England by looking at some of the differences between Elizabeth's and James's coronation pageants—public displays which are not utterly remote from the emblematic world of *Cymbeline*.

Elizabeth's pageant consisted of fairly generalized tableaux designed to be plainly "legible" even to the ignorant as celebrations of Elizabeth Tudor and English unity. It included emblematic devices like the red rose and the white, the Tudor tree and the Triumph of Time, always with interpreter figures who explicated the devices for the spectators. Richard Mulcaster described his own contribution to the pageant in the following terms: "Unitie was the ende whereat the whole devise shotte." There was no space within it which was not literally part of that unity: all the "emptie places thereof were furnished with sentences concerning unitie." Both aesthetically and politically in this pageant (and the two categories were but one), unity was a matter of the aggregation of emblems and appropriate "sentences." Although the unity at which the pageant "shotte" was made possible by the accession of Elizabeth, the queen did not "author" it: she did not stand outside it, but participated in it and even made sure she understood it aright: she was part of a collective celebration that was larger than she.[13]

James's coronation pageant, by contrast, used elaborate architectonics, "arcane images" and "symbols" specific to the king and his hopes for a British empire, to build up more complex assertions about the nature and goals of the new monarch. Here is Ben Jonson's description of the political and artistic purpose behind his part in James's pageant:

> The nature and propertie of these Deuices being, to present alwaies some one entire bodie, or figure, consisting of distinct members, and each of those expressing it selfe, in the[ir] owne actiue sphaere, yet all, with that generall harmonie so connexed, and disposed, as no one little part can be missing to the illustration of the whole: where also is to be noted, that the *Symboles* vsed, are not, neither ought to be, simply *Hieroglyphickes*, *Emblemes*, or *Impreses*, but a mixed character, partaking somewhat of all, and peculiarly apted to these more magnificent Inuentions: wherein, the garments and ensignes deliuer the nature of the person, and the word the present office.[14]

The focus and origin of the unity in Jonson's formulation have become the person and office of the monarch, and the "self-sameness" of the pageant has become a matter of the perfect articulation of parts. The king does not so much participate in it, as it strives to participate in him. There are no blank spaces in which the pageant's meaning has to be written in order to guarantee against the subversive potential of vacancy. All perceptual entry points lead to the king as "author" of the whole.

In James's coronation pageant, the strong emphasis on James himself leads to an abandonment of the obvious—things so general as to be readily understood—in favor of "mixed" devices that partake of a common language of symbols yet simultaneously evoke particulars about the person and "offices" of the king. Some spectators will be able to interpret the pageant as they would have "read" the earlier pageant of Elizabeth, but the reading is necessarily more difficult. James's political symbols are presented, according to Jonson, so that "vpon the view, they might, without cloud, or obscuritie, declare themselues to the sharpe and learned: And for the multitude, no doubt but their grounded iudgements did gaze, said it was fine, and were satisfied."[15] One of James's roles as the "beste clerke in his owne countrie" was to educate his people out of the mere "gaze" of the multitude into a new sharpness and discernment, impress his ideas upon them in much the same spirit as he taught his court favorites Latin, so that the English could "read" the Jacobean political line—the plain truth of the monarch's intent—"without cloud, or obscuritie." According to James's optimistic assessment of the relationship between speech and action, assent would inevitably follow upon enlightenment. With the passing of the years, he lost much of his early optimism about his subjects' capacity for reading. In defensive reaction to the repeated failure of his strategy of "plainnesse," he increasingly withdrew from that vulnerable openness and veiled himself in ideas about the impenetrability of the royal arcana. But that retreat, for the most part, came later; during the early years of the reign he still strove for clarity and directness in terms of his public presentation of the royal intent.

In *Cymbeline*, Shakespeare can be seen as operating according to Jonsonian precept in the construction of a political allegory which presents "one entire bodie, or figure" devoted to a "present office" of the king. There have been fragmentary topical readings of the play, but none has pursued the "Jacobean line" with anything approaching the thoroughness that contemporary evidence permits. The play is by no means easy. But if allowances are made for the difference in form between a Jacobean pageant or court masque and a play in the public theater, *Cymbeline* will support a remarkably subtle, detailed reading as political allegory. Following the "Jacobean line" in *Cymbeline* will require us to perform some of the integrative and harmonizing functions dear to the project of traditional historicism—we can account for some notorious cruxes and arrive at a new perception of unity. The play's gathering of topical connections creates something of the same quality of concentration and distillation that classically minded writers in the Renaissance sought to achieve by adhering to the unities of time and place. But the local Shakespeare created by such reading may prove almost as distasteful to universalizers as the warmongering chauvinist of *1 Henry VI*. *Cymbeline*'s Shakespeare is at least more civilized and gentlemanly, but looks rather too much like an elitist who traffics in Stuart ideology and iconography out of a misguided belief that such a narrow, particularized vision can somehow be made compatible with exalted universals like the Ideal of Human Betterment.

The name of Shakespeare cannot be kept utterly separate from the world of emblem and impresa—not unless we suppress contemporary records. In 1613 we find a Shakespeare—the same Shakespeare—collecting forty-four shillings in gold for his work, along with Richard

Burbage, on the earl of Rutland's impresa for the anniversary of James's accession. The dramatist named Shakespeare also took considerable care over his own family coat of arms.[16] But *Cymbeline* is not, by Jacobean standards at least, a collection of arcana. It would have been (or should have been, if viewers ever came up to authors' expectations) at least partially politically "legible" to a reasonable segment of the public acquainted with the dominant symbols of the reign—more legible, probably, than James's coronation pageant or the usual Jonsonian masque. The Shakespeare of *Cymbeline* is at least in part a King's Man—an author who subsumes his own orderly creation under the Authorship of James I. As in the coronation pageants, so in *Cymbeline*, the search for artistic "unity" leads the spectator directly to a vision of political concord under the reigning monarch.

And yet, for all our efforts to follow the play's "Jacobean line," there are ways in which the play itself resists it. Shakespeare seems to evade the Authorized Version of *Cymbeline* with almost the same energy that he promotes it. In part, of course, we find such resistance because we want to find it—pursuing *différance* is usually more congenial for new historicists and other postmodernist critics than constructing idealized visions of harmony. And yet, there is reason to suppose that contemporary audiences might have felt a similar discomfort with the play's call for unity. Along with an array of relatively commonplace Stuart motifs, *Cymbeline* displays a number of specific mechanisms which work against the communication of its Stuart message, engendering an unease with topicality which is specific to this play. We might call it an unease with Jacobean textuality. Inevitably, our sense of the relative strength of the play's Stuart message as opposed to its modes of evasion will depend on our own critical (and political) stance. And yet, in the interpretation of *Cymbeline*, as very frequently in the decipherment of the Stuart masque, we have to follow the "authorized" line of political allegory in order to discover the gaps, the devices by which (to repeat King James's own language) the clear text is "rent asunder in contrary sences like the old Oracles of the Pagan gods." It is not enough (and is never enough in terms of our project for localization) to say that the play deconstructs its own dominant mode of signification. That can be said of every play we call Shakespeare. Instead, we need to look for the "local" meanings of the deconstruction, its particular cultural and political resonances, the specific moments in the dramatic action at which its energies burst forth.

To do topical reading of *Cymbeline*, we must begin by playing the pedant along with James I, explicating political allegory in a rather straightforward, linear fashion—according to principles of unity like those articulated by Ben Jonson.

I use the term *reading* quite deliberately. At least initially, we will be interpreting the play according to methods more closely associated with earlier humanist moralities or sermons or court entertainments than with seventeenth-century plays in the public theater. After we have "read" *Cymbeline* we will consider the tricky business of the play's contemporary performance. There are interesting problems raised by Simon Forman's description of *Cymbeline* as he saw it staged in 1610 or 1611. The text of *Cymbeline* we will read is the 1623 folio text—the only early text we have. It is close enough to the play as described by Forman that our local reading will not be built upon impossibly shifting sand, although all of our earlier caveats about variability in performance will continue to apply. Yet even considered as theater, *Cymbeline* asks to be interpreted, given the fixity of a written text. It is through the very conventions of authorship which the play appears to countenance that *Cymbeline* reveals signs of uneasiness with the Jacobean line.

TELLING RIDDLES

In the third year of his reign, James I more than once descended upon Parliament like Jove with his "thunderbolts" to chide its members for their sluggishness with a pet project of his, the creation of Great Britain through the union of England and Scotland. He had expected his coronation in England and the Union of the Kingdoms to "grow up together" as a matter of course; instead, he had encountered "many crossings, long disputations, strange questions, and nothing done." The image of James as Jove swooping down with his thunder became a leitmotif of the parliamentary session. If the king were at a distance from that legislative body, they would be safe from his blasts: "*Procull a Iove, procul a Fulmine.*" But the king was at hand, attending closely to the debates, threatening to loose his blasts against the lawmakers if his project were not expedited.[17]

Court entertainment followed the governing line. In the most important masque of the same year, Ben Jonson's *Hymenaei*, the Union of the Kingdoms was effected symbolically through the marriage of two

young aristocrats from very different backgrounds. At least some contemporaries took note of the political allegory: they were able to
"read" its essential elements. Juno presided over the masque's marriage ritual, her name IUNO anagrammatized as UNIO to represent the
union of England and Scotland. Far above in the heavens stood Jove,
her spouse, with his thunderbolts, again a representation of James,
who liked to describe himself as a Jove figure and as a loving husband
to the nation, with UNIO, a united Britain, as his wife.[18] Here, however, Jove appeared in milder aspect, his menacing thunder silenced,
because in the masque at least, the "marriage" of the kingdoms had
finally taken place.

In Shakespeare's *Cymbeline*, written and performed perhaps two
years later, at the very latest in 1610, Jove appears yet again in connection with the theme of the Union of the Kingdoms.[19] Jupiter descends
straddling an eagle, spouting fire, hurling his bolts, to castigate the
mourning ghosts who "Accuse the Thunderer" of faithlessness toward
the sleeping prisoner Posthumus. The god proclaims his continuing
favor, promises to "vplift" the unfortunate man, and leaves upon his
chest a riddling tablet that, when interpreted at the end of the play,
turns out to presage the Union of the Kingdoms.[20] In terms of the
play's contemporary context, Jove is clearly to be identified with King
James I, the creator of Great Britain, who had a similar habit of intrud-
ing upon his subjects to lecture them when his plans for the nation went
unheeded or misunderstood. And yet, paradoxically, to take Jupiter for
James weakens the "governing line" of political interpretation.

Cymbeline seductively courts topical reading by presenting its audience with a series of riddles and emblems which arouse a desire for
explication. Some of them are interpreted within the play; others are
not. The effect is to make the unsolved puzzles all the more teasingly
enticing.[21] Many of the play's riddles are clustered in its final scenes.
The soothsayer twice recounts his vision of the eagle winging its way
westward to vanish in the beams of the sun. First he misinterprets it to
forecast Roman defeat of Cymbeline and the Britons, then he rein-
terprets it correctly as a sign of new Roman-British amity,

> which fore-shew'd our Princely Eagle
> Th'Imperiall *Caesar*, should againe vnite
> His Fauour, with the Radiant *Cymbeline*,
> Which shines heere in the West.
>   (TLN 3805–8)

The cryptic tablet placed upon Posthumus's breast by Jupiter is another important riddle. It is read twice during the action—the only text so privileged in all of Shakespeare's plays—and in the folio it is printed exactly the same way both times like a properly "authored" document.[22] At the end of the play, it is finally deciphered as linking the reunion of Posthumus and Imogen to the discovery of Cymbeline's long-lost sons and the regeneration of Britain.

Even out in remote Wales, far from the world of the court, there are emblematic "texts" to be interpreted, natural lessons in morality imprinted upon the landscape. According to the teachings of Belarius, tutor to the king's exiled sons, a hill signifies dangerous eminence like that won and lost in the courts of princes; the low mouth of their cave teaches the virtue of humble devotion. When Imogen begins breathing the mountain air of Wales, she too starts creating emblems. Her assumed name Fidele is recognized by the end of the play as a sign of her abiding faith in Posthumus despite his rejection of her. When she awakens after her deathlike sleep, she reads the flowers beside her as signifying the false pleasures of the world; the body of Cloten signifies its cares (TLN 2618–19).

Shakespeare calls attention to some of the play's riddles through the device of repetition: appearing more than once, they become insistent, demand interpretation. Along with the riddles and emblems deciphered within the play, there are other repeated motifs carrying an aura of hidden significance. "Blessed Milford" Haven is a Welsh port named many times by many different characters in the course of the action; it attracts them from widely scattered places as though by magnetic force. But the almost incantatory power of "Milford" is never satisfactorily explained by any of the characters. The victory of Guiderius, Arviragus, and Belarius over the Roman forces in the narrow lane is another insistent motif which is never quite unraveled. The episode is first enacted on stage, then recounted no fewer than four times, the last in a derisive rhyme by Posthumus that casts scorn upon people who attend overmuch to riddles:

> Nay, do not wonder at it : you are made
> Rather to wonder at the things you heare,
> Then to worke any. Will you Rime vpon't,
> And vent it for a Mock'rie? Heere is one:
> "*Two Boyes, an Oldman (twice a Boy) a Lane,*
> "*Preseru'd the Britaines, was the Romanes bane.*
> (TLN 2982–87)

Posthumus distrusts such marveling, his facile rhyme appearing to parody the play's heavy-handed way with prophetic language. But he himself is the play's most interesting riddle. Not only does he, at the end, bear upon his breast a tablet that demands and receives interpretation, but the other characters refer to him as though he were a text in need of explication, the "Catalogue of his endowments . . . tabled by his side" and he, to be perused "by Items" (TLN 320–21). Posthumus is Shakespeare's creation. He does not occur in the historical sources.[23] His past contains some mystery. One bystander acknowledges, "I cannot delue him to the roote" (TLN 37). He is praised for his "fair Outward" and for virtuous "stuffe" within; he comes of noble stock and—apparently—prosperous estate, yet appears impoverished, without the power or influence he might be expected to have to combat his sudden banishment.

In the artistic economy of *Cymbeline*, riddles exist to be interpreted—interpreted, as riddles conventionally are, through the finding of a single answer which dissolves their ambiguity into clarity. In fact, all of the play's riddles can be interpreted by reference to the play's contemporary Stuart milieu—even the cryptic "text" that is Posthumus himself. It is a marvelous device for arresting the free proliferation of topical meaning and focusing interpretation upon a single set of motifs. What is accomplished by such revelation of meaning "without cloud or obscuritie" is another matter, however.

It is, by now, pretty generally accepted by Shakespeareans willing to consider a Stuart *Cymbeline* at all that the play's emphasis on the ideal of a united Britain and its vision of empire—the Roman eagle winging its way westward to vanish into the British sun—can be interpreted in terms of James I's cherished project for creating a new "empire" called Great Britain, a revival of the ancient kingdom of Britain which had, according to popular legend, been founded by Brute, son of Aeneas.[24] Almost as soon as James had arrived from Scotland to claim the English throne in 1603, he had issued his "Proclamation for the uniting of England and Scotland," which called upon the "Subjects of both the Realmes" to consider themselves "one people, brethren and members of one body"; the next year, by proclamation, he assumed the "Stile, of King of Great Britaine." His subjects were blanketed with propaganda for the Union. The royal project was lauded in poetry and public pageantry, an organizing motif of his coronation pageant in 1604 and the Lord Mayor's shows for 1605 and 1609 and of courtly entertainments like Jonson's *Hymenaei*; it was also publicized through treatises and pamphlets, even through the coin of the realm. One of the new gold pieces issued by James I bore the inscription *Faciamus eos in gentem unam*.[25]

However, his subjects on both sides of the Anglo–Scottish border were less than enthusiastic about the proposal, muttering patriotic slogans about their nation's safety in isolation, much like Cloten and the wicked queen in the play, displaying distrust, even open hatred toward their "brethren" across the border, or (on a higher level of discourse) stating serious reservations, on grounds of legal and religious principle, about James I's strong identification with Roman ideals and institutions. A visiting foreign dignitary observed, "The little sympathy between the two nations, the difference of their laws, the jealousy of their privileges, the regard of the succession, are the reasons they will never . . . join with another, as the King wishes."[26] But James persisted nonetheless. The political plot of *Cymbeline*, in marked contrast to the prevailing spirit of nationalism in Shakespeare's earlier history plays, culminates in a vision of harmonious internationalism and accommodation that mirrors James's own policy. The British and Roman ensigns wave "Friendly together," the fragmented kingdom of Britain is reunited, and the nation embarks on a new and fertile era of peace.

The romantic plot of *Cymbeline* can be related to the same set of goals. James was an indefatigable matchmaker among his individual subjects, as among nations and peoples. He took particular pride in state marriages which bridged political and religious differences like *Hymenaei*'s union between Lady Frances Howard, from a pro-Catholic, pro-Spanish family, and the earl of Essex, from a line of staunch Calvinists. From *Hymenaei* in 1606 to the masques for the palsgrave Frederick and the king's daughter, Elizabeth, in 1613, nearly every court marriage important enough to be celebrated with a wedding masque at all was celebrated as a particular instance of the king's wider project for uniting England and Scotland. One of the new coins he issued in honor of Great Britain even bore an inscription from the marriage service: *Quae Deus conjunxit nemo separet*, "Those whom God hath joined together let no man put asunder." A prefatory poem to one of the wedding masques asked, "Who can wonder then / If he, that marries kingdomes, marries men?"[27] The ruptured, then revitalized marriage of Imogen and Posthumus in *Cymbeline*, like the actual marriages engineered by James, can be linked to his higher policy of creating a united Britain out of nations in discord.

So can the barriers to union: the play's constant quibbling with matters of law and ceremony echoes the same milieu of controversy. Attending to some of the fine points of the debate will aid us in reading the "text" of Posthumus. When James I left Edinburgh for London in 1603, he left his original subjects without a resident monarch. An integral part of his project for the creation of Great Britain through the union of England and Scotland was the naturalization of the Scots. His motto for the project was *Unus Rex, unus Grex, & una Lex,* "one king, one flock, one law." But that last phrase posed unexpected difficulties, since England and Scotland operated under very different legal systems. England had its venerable common law and Scotland, the civil law, essentially a Roman code. Despite his disclaimers, it seems clear that James I preferred Scots law over the English system and hoped to mold Britain's "one law" in accordance with the Roman model, which he considered clearer, more succinct, and more hospitable to his views on royal absolutism. But that hope was dashed by English parliamentarians and common lawyers, who viewed the import of aliens and the imposition of an alien legal system as tantamount to national extinction. When James descended upon them like Jove with his thunderbolts, the immediate question at hand was the naturalization of the Scots. Despite the attempts of James's supporters to argue for the honor and reasonableness of their brethren to the north, members of Parliament conjured up horrific visions of beggarly Scotsmen swarming across the border and devouring England's prosperity. Parliament refused to naturalize the king's Scottish subjects until the question of law was settled, preferably by bringing Scotland into accordance with England.[28]

Meanwhile, the Scots had their own fears about the Union: like the English, Scottish parliamentarians were adamant about preserving their "ancient rights" and liberties. But the Scots were even more adamant about preserving their own reformed Kirk. James's Project for Union called for the creation of a single British church, a ceremonial church upon the Anglican model. When it came to this aspect of the Union, it was the Scots who were anti-Roman, worried that their pure Kirk would be corrupted by a union with "popish" Anglicanism and enforced conformity with English canon law, a system also based upon Roman civil law. In Jonson's *Hymenaei,* Anglican ritual is celebrated as a comely descendant of Roman ceremonial and Roman civil law; it is attacked by "untempered humors" and "affections," but successfully defended by Reason and Order.[29] In actuality, the "humors" of the Scots were less easily overcome. By 1607, James's project for Great Britain was foundering on the rocks of English and Scottish prejudice. He was willing to modify his original proposal for "one law" and create a union which preserved the distinctness of the two legal systems. But both Parliaments balked. In England the Scots were scorned as aliens, mercilessly pilloried in plays and satires. Numerous duels were fought between Englishmen and Scotsmen. Scots were barred from holding public office and denied the precedence of rank: on ceremonial occasions, English parvenus would elbow out Scots of the old nobility. Since Parliament refused to remedy the situation, James I went to the courts. Through the famous case of the Post Nati, decided in 1608, he sought to settle the question of the naturalization of the Scots and thereby clear the way for his beloved Project for Union. Never, his advisers warned the nation, would there be a real unity of kingdoms until the "mark of the stranger" had been removed from the Scots.[30]

The Post Nati were all those Scotsmen born after James had ascended the English throne, theoretically uniting the kingdoms. James had proclaimed them citizens of Britain and according to the Roman code they were already citizens, yet in England they were deprived of any recourse at law. The case of the Post Nati concerned a dispute over land titles and hinged on whether a Scotsman born since the proclamation of union had the right to defend his ownership of property held in England in a court of English law. But despite the narrowness of the immediate problem it posed, it was perhaps the most important case of the reign, argued at the King's Bench, then moved on account of its momentous implications into the Exchequer, pondered by every one of England's highest justices. The case established principles about the rights of alien peoples which became fundamental to all later treatments of the same issues, such as the constitutional arguments of the American colonists before 1776. The case of the Post Nati was widely publicized, a matter of alehouse conversation; several of its most important documents were published. By nearly unanimous decision of the judges involved, the Post Nati were declared citizens, entitled to recourse at English law despite their continuing ties to the alien Roman system.[31]

We cannot be sure whether Shakespeare's play was written before or after the case of the Post Nati was settled in 1608; *Cymbeline* is usually dated 1608 or 1609. In any event, the probable outcome of the case was well known in advance. But in the character of Posthumus, the one "born after," a man theoretically married to Imogen in the Temple of Jupiter and therefore "wedded" to her kingdom yet kept in isolation and suspension, deprived of his natural rights, Shakespeare creates a dramatic figure whose alienation and restoration symbolically parallel the fortunes of James's subjects "born after," the Post Nati. *Cymbeline* recasts the faltering national union as a beleaguered marriage between two individuals, Imogen and Posthumus, and thereby invests the legal and political issues bound up with the project for Great Britain with a troubling immediacy, an urgency that seems to quicken toward a concrete political goal—James I's goal of relieving the agony of exile and creating a genuine union.

A PARABLE OF EXILE

The divided Britain of *Cymbeline* is not to be equated with the wrangling Britain of James I. Rather, it is a partial analogue and prefiguration. In the Britain ruled by Cymbeline, as in the Britain of James I, a "marriage" has produced dislocation. The situation of Posthumus at the beginning of the play is in many ways like that of the Scots after 1603. His surname Leonatus—born of or under the lion—suggests James's well-known device of the Stuart lion; the king was fond of comparing the Scots to his own heraldic animal.[32] Posthumus is a nobly born beggar, like many of the Scottish aristocrats, at least as they appeared to the more prosperous English. To his humiliation, he cannot reciprocate Imogen's gift of the diamond with a love token of equal value (TLN 132–42). He is an altogether proper gentleman yet held in low esteem. He has until the marriage held the office of gentleman of the bedchamber, a position monopolized by Scotsmen even in James I's court at Whitehall during the early years of the reign. But through the marriage, Posthumus is deprived and exiled, just as the citizens of Scotland were distanced from their king and from the center of government when James assumed the English crown.

Posthumus has gained the respect of most of Cymbeline's courtiers. But like the Scots, he is divided between Britain and Rome and, as a result, held in suspicion, particularly after the outbreak of Cymbeline's war against Rome. His birth under a "Jovial star," his Latinate name, his close ancestral ties with the Continent, especially Rome and France, place him in an enemy camp. But in the Britain of the play, unlike the Britain of James I, he has no king to take his part against the local chauvinists. The similarities between James and Cymbeline have often been noted in topical readings of the play: both kings have two sons and a daughter; like James, Cymbeline is associated by the final scenes with a vision of the rebirth of empire. Unlike James, however, and unlike the Cymbeline of Shakespeare's historical sources, who was noted for unfaltering devotion to Rome, the Cymbeline of the play has abandoned his earlier allegiance to Augustus Caesar and is as stubbornly anti-Roman for most of the action as any of his subjects. He lends a sympathetic ear to the patriotic sloganeering of the wicked queen and Cloten, who, like members of the English House of Commons, plead against Roman influence and the "Roman yoke" on grounds of their ancient British liberties. Cloten, in particular, is a fanatic about law. His speech is peppered with idle legalisms: even his wooing of Imogen is a "case" in which her woman will be enlisted as his "Lawyer" (TLN 1040–41). King Cymbeline himself, like his wife and doltish stepson, is a fervent advocate of native British law—the law of Mulmutius mangled by Caesar's sword. Mulmutius and the "ancient liberties of the House" were similarly prominent in contemporary parliamentary speeches *against* James I and his notions of empire and royal prerogative.[33]

But Posthumus is not only a victim of such prejudice—he nurtures prejudices of his own. He is almost as devoted to legalistic language as Cloten.[34] A much more devastating flaw is his susceptibility to the insinuations of Iachimo, an Italian, who convinces him all too easily that Imogen, his wife, is unchaste. Shakespeare ingeniously (albeit anachronistically) separates two levels of Roman influence in the play—that of the ancient Rome of Caesar Augustus, associated with the ideals of James I, with peace and a benevolent code of law, and that of the Renaissance Rome of the degenerate Italians, associated rather with perversion, bawdry, and amorality. It is probably not mere happenstance that Shakespeare modeled the romantic plot in accordance with a tale out of the bawdy Italian Boccaccio. Posthumus's easily aroused distrust of the virtuous Imogen recasts into personal terms the Scottish prejudice against the Church of England, that sluttish "Whore of Babylon." He displays a paranoid willingness to doubt Imogen even before the bargain with Iachimo is concluded—a trait which the wily Italian attributes to "some Religion" in him (TLN 452).

Imogen is far too full and complete a character to be reduced to the level of allegory, but she is associated with images of ceremonial worship throughout the play. Her chamber is likened to a chapel and resembles an elaborately decorated sanctuary, its roof "fretted" with "golden Cherubins" (TLN 1254). She is several times referred to as a "temple": by a lord of the court ("That Temple thy faire mind" TLN 900), by Arviragus ("so diuine a Temple" TLN 2316), and, finally, by the repentant Posthumus ("The Temple / Of Vertue was she; yea, and she her selfe" TLN 3502–3). She is also associated with the enactment of due ceremony. It is Imogen who observes in Wales that the "breach of Custome, / Is breach of all" (TLN 2257–58) and Guiderius reiterates her attention to decorum when he hears his brother's "*Solemn Musick*" in lament of her seeming death: "All solemne things / Should answer solemne Accidents" (TLN 2490–91). In the First Folio dedicatory epistle, as we have seen, just such attention to ceremony is diverted out of its courtly Stuart context and made independent of the monarch. In the play, it is much more closely bound up with members of the royal family, whether or not they are aware of its intrinsic connection with their birth and heritage.

In Wales, Imogen does not recognize her long-lost brothers, nor they her; yet there is an immediate bond of sympathy among them which is given outward expression through acts of religious propriety. The two princes in exile are, in fact, remarkably liturgically minded for a couple of untutored savages. Their pagan ceremonies curiously resemble the ceremonial Anglicanism advocated by James I and Archbishop Bancroft but distrusted by Puritan elements in the church. They greet the sun with a "mornings holy office," like matins; their dirge over the "dead" Imogen, her body laid toward the east, is spoken antiphonally to music, much like an Anglican liturgy. They have, of course, been guided by Belarius, but he comments on their "inuisible instinct" for civility as for valor (TLN 2470–75). Their innate respect for ritual and due ceremony is charged with political significance. It suggests, as James I and his churchmen often argued in defense of the Anglican church against English Puritans and Scotch Presbyterians, that liturgical worship is not some popish import but a native cultural form, as natural to the British as their valor. Their ceremonialism is pagan, to be sure, but a precursor of Anglican worship, like Cymbeline's thankful feasts and rituals in the Temple of Jove at the end of the play or like the Roman rituals of *Hymenaei*. It would be easy to make too much of the play's frequent allusions to questions of law and ceremony: such passages can be interpreted on many different levels. But taken in the aggregate, they shape a subtle pattern of reference which links the various factions in the Britain of King Cymbeline to analogues in the renascent Britain of King James I, the "parliamentary" xenophobia of Cloten and his mother balanced against Posthumus's hysterical willingness to heed rumors of "popish" Italian defilement.

In terms of the play's "Jacobean line," the wicked queen—who dominates her husband and other men, who operates politically through the possession of dark secrets, who speaks for the continuing insularity of Britain and incites the advocates of "ancient" law against the ideal of empire—can be seen as a demonized version of Queen Elizabeth I. More precisely, perhaps, the wicked queen is a dark rendering of the image of Elizabeth as it functioned in Stuart England as a symbol for civic and parliamentary opponents of James's absolutism. The queen's impassioned speech before the ambassadors and court dignitaries, with its arguments against the "shame" of invasion and conquest by sea, has even been taken by some readers as an echo of the political rhetoric surrounding the Armada victory.[35] Through the wicked queen, Shakespeare marginalizes the image of Elizabeth and its association with the valorization of England's "virginal" isolate intactness, in favor of the Stuart vision of internationalism and political accommodation.

The one central character who is always true to the Union is Imogen herself. She, too, is a kind of Elizabeth figure, carrying some of the former queen's attributes split off from their association with dangerous female dominance: she is heir presumptive to the throne; she is associated with the emblem of the phoenix, the "Arabian Bird"; like the heroines of the high comedies, she adopts "a Princes Courage"— male attire and identity—as part of her quest for her mate.[36] But for Imogen, being "male" is never more than a painful necessity, an exterior disguise with which she is markedly uncomfortable. She, unlike the earlier heroines, is already married and dedicated to wifely submission, despite her titular supremacy. She would relinquish her kingdom . if she could in order to be Posthumus's equal, and in fact, she never does become queen. Her devotion to her husband always comes first.

It does not falter even in the face of compelling evidence that he has "forgot Britain."

Imogen is not responsible for her enforced separation from Post-humus or for his neglect of her, yet even she is subject to error and has something to learn about the nature of prejudice. At the beginning of the play, she scornfully rejects Cloten on the grounds that he and Posthumus have nothing at all in common: "I chose an Eagle, / And did auoyd a Puttocke" (TLN 169–70). Cloten is not worth her hus-band's "mean'st garment." Even her scornful term "Puttocke" may appear too kind to Cloten, that dreadful "mass of unhingement." Yet Posthumus is also less than perfect. He and Cloten undergo parallel experiences, like a man and his distorted shadow. Both are step or fos-ter sons to the king, both woo Imogen, they fight one another, both gamble with Iachimo and lose. As Cloten sets off to rape Imogen, he assumes Posthumus's garments. By act 4, both men have literally or figuratively "lost their heads." [37] When Imogen mistakes the decapi-tated body of one for the other, their identities are temporarily super-imposed. She weeps over the puttock, thinking him an eagle; clothes become the man.

The scene of Imogen's desolate but misguided grief over Cloten is difficult to read without an uncomfortable admixture of levity; it is also difficult to stage effectively. Stephen Booth's suggestion that the two roles be played by a single actor removes the most obvious in-congruity. [38] But there remain awkward moments, perilously close to low comedy, like Imogen's reaching out toward what she takes to be Posthumus's "Ioviall face" only to find the head unfortunately miss-ing. And yet the scene makes excellent sense as illustration of the "Jacobean line." Imogen's error demonstrates the interchangeability of the two men, considered only in terms of their outward endowments, and therefore serves as a forceful argument against blind prejudice of either the English or the Scottish variety. The political fragmentation of a divided Britain deprived of its Jove-like or "Ioviall" head is associated with bizarre images of physical and psychic dissolution.

Throughout the play, prejudice is associated with extinction and dismemberment—a vision of a part, not the whole. When Posthumus is convinced of Imogen's falseness, he vows to "teare her Limb-meale"; yet without her, he is "speechless," his name at "last gasp"; he has "forgot himself" and his identity becomes increasingly problematic. Imogen unknowingly echoes her husband's wish to destroy her when she discovers his failed trust: "I must be ript. To peeces with me" (TLN 1724); "I am nothing," she declares as she embraces the dismembered body of her "Master" (TLN 2696). Cloten's actual mutilation parallels Posthumus's loss of identity as a result of his own and others' prejudice. When the seemingly lifeless body of Imogen is laid beside the headless corpse, both partners to the union appear to have become the "nothing" each is without the other. Of course, the extinction is apparent, not real: Posthumus is still alive. But Imogen does not know that. She awakens, mourns her slain "Master," and embraces him, only to swoon again like one dead upon the lifeless body as on a "bloody pillow."

Discovering this grisly mockery of the ideal of union, Lucius comments on its unnaturalness: "For Nature doth abhorre to make his bed / With the defunct, or sleepe vpon the dead" (TLN 2684–85). As a sequence of events, *Cymbeline*'s grotesque tableaux of dismemberment are improbable, even ludicrous. But they can be read as emblems of the political effects of prejudice. Genuine union is organic: one part of it cannot exist without the other. Cloten is a body without a head; so Posthumus has been a subject unnaturally deprived of his "head" the king. In his published speeches and proclamations, James I frequently used similar images of dismemberment—a body without a head—to convince his English and Scotch subjects of the bizarre indecorousness of continuing to thwart the Union of the Kingdoms, a "marriage" suspended as a result of needless exile and alienation like the marriage of Posthumus and Imogen.[39]

Imogen clings faithfully to the ideal of union, achieving a certain pathos despite the horror of her symbiotic attachment to the mutilated body. But that lowest point in her fortunes is soon transcended. The Roman soothsayer and Lucius, the Roman commander, encounter Imogen and the corpse just as the soothsayer has interpreted his vision of the eagle winging its way westward into the sun. On stage, the visual image of a union in extinction is counterpoised against the soothsayer's words of prophecy, promising vigor and prosperity to come. Imogen quickly returns to consciousness. It is almost as though she is roused by the soothsayer's vision from the "nothing" she has felt herself to be in symbiotic identification with the corpse. She buries the body and attaches herself as a page to Lucius, the honorable Roman: the heiress to Britain's crown adopts the cause of its opposite in war.

As Imogen and the other characters gradually converge upon

"blessed" Milford Haven the dismembered and alienated fragments of the kingdom are slowly gathered back together and the riddles gradually resolved. Milford Haven, as numerous commentators have noted, was the Welsh port where James I's ancestor Henry VII had landed when he came to claim the kingdom in the name of the Tudors. James's descent from Henry gave him his right to the English throne; his identification with the first Tudor was so intense that when he died he was, at his own wish, buried in Henry VII's tomb.[40] As Henry's claim formed the basis of James I's project for a reunited Britain, so Henry's landing place becomes the locus for the reunion of the lovers and a healing of the fragmentary vision that has kept the two apart. All of the play's tangled lines converge upon the point at which the "Jacobean line" originated. Imogen is more right than she knows when she exclaims, "Accessible is none but Milford way" (TLN 1552).

Imogen and Posthumus become unknowing precursors of a new era of peace and accommodation between the warring Rome and Britain when each of them changes sides. As Imogen becomes "Roman," so Posthumus, who has been living in Rome and arrives back in Britain among the "Italian Gentry," assumes instead the guise of a British peasant to fight alongside another group of exiles, Belarius and the king's long-lost sons. The riddle of the man and two boys in the narrow lane who save the Britons from the Romans is taken from Scots history and was an exploit actually performed by three Scotsmen named Hay—the ancestors of James I's favorite Lord Hay, one of the Scots who, like Posthumus in the play, had to contend with insular British prejudice.[41] The three heroes in the lane, like Posthumus himself, are associated with the heraldic animal of James: they "grin like Lyons" as they repel the attack. The joining of the two lines of "Lyons" to uphold Britain is a common motif in contemporary materials supporting the idea of Great Britain. The emblem of James I in Henry Peacham's popular collection *Minerva Britanna: Or, A Garden of Heroical Devices* (London, 1612), for example, is addressed "To the High and mightie *IAMES*, King of great Britaine" (figure 14), and depicts the English and Scottish lions uniting (as they did in the royal person of the king) to hold up the crown of "famous Britaine."

Through the battle in the narrow lane, Posthumus proves himself the equal of the sons of Cymbeline. Even the most narrow-minded of James I's English subjects admitted that the Scots were excellent fighters. By his valorous part in the action Posthumus demonstrates his

To the High and mightie *I A M E S*, King of greate Britaine,

Scilicet Anglicus T WOO Lions ftout the Diadem vphold,
et Scoticus.   Of famous Britaine, in their armed pawes:
                    The one is Red, the other is of Gold,
                    And one their Prince, their fea, their land and lawes;
                        Their loue, their league: whereby they ftill agree,
                        In concord firme, and friendly amitie.

BELLONA henceforth bounde in Iron bandes,
Shall kiffe the foote of mild triumphant PEACE,
Nor Trumpets fterne, be heard within their landes;
Envie fhall pine, and all old grudges ceafe:
    Braue Lions, fince, your quarrell's lai'd afide,
    On common foe, let now your force be tri 'de.

Vnum fuftentant gemini Diadema Leones,   Fœdere iunguntur fimili, cœloque, faloque,
Concordes vno Principe, mente, fide.   Nata quibus Pax hæc inviolanda manet.

14.   Emblem of James I from Henry Peacham, *Minerva Britanna* (1612).

possession of the proverbial "strength o' th' *Leonati*" and its value to Cymbeline's side. His association with things Roman and French is no barrier to his ability to act for the good of Britain. But no one recognizes that yet because no one knows who he is. Indeed, he is practically invisible, effaced from accounts of the glorious victory in the lane. Just as James I and his advisers had claimed that there could be no act of union until the "mark of the stranger" had been removed from the Scots, so the vision of a united Britain that concludes the play depends on the discovery and reading of the "text" of Posthumus.

Even without a disguise, Posthumus has been an unsolved enigma for others and "to himselfe vnknown." He shifts his garments and allegiance with protean speed—he is Italian, then British, then Roman. Ironically, he makes the final shift out of a suicidal wish to "spend his breath" to aid the cause of his dead Imogen, unaware that she is still alive and has also changed sides. His frantic oscillation between the two warring nations must give way to the recognition that his marriage is still intact. Through it, the two nations have already begun to dissolve into a new composite entity. To rediscover who he is and what his experiences mean, Posthumus must go through a symbolic union-in-death with Imogen just as Imogen had earlier with him. In the British prison he hopes only for reunion beyond the grave; he falls asleep communing silently with the wife he believes he has destroyed. But as in Imogen's encounter with Lucius and the soothsayer, Posthumus's embracing of death is lifted and transformed by a vision of renewed life. His seeming extinction is like the political extinction feared by English and Scottish patriots who opposed the Project for Union—more apparent than real. His noble ancestors appear "as in an Apparation" to offer him back his identity and plead for his restoration to the esteem, prosperity, and marriage befitting his noble worth. His mother demands,

> With Marriage wherefore was he mockt
>   to be exil'd, and throwne
> From *Leonati* Seate, and cast from her,
>   his deerest one:
> Sweete *Imogen?*
>
> (TLN 3099–103)

In pleading for Posthumus, his forebears plead for a restoration of the Union of the Kingdoms. Posthumus's continuing deprivation is a "harsh and potent" injury upon a "valiant Race," the race of the

Leonati, or the Scots. But Posthumus is not only an analogue of the exiled Scots; he is a more generalized figure whose exile, trial, and restoration take on theological dimensions and assume the pattern of spiritual rejuvenation. Jove descends and announces, in answer to the prayer of the Leonati,

> Whom best I loue, I crosse; to make my guift,
> The more delay'd, delighted. Be content,
> Your low-laide Sonne, our Godhead will vplift:
> His Comforts thriue, his Trials well are spent.
>   (TLN 3137–40)

Exaltavit humiles: as Britain has been saved and ennobled by the valorous deeds of its "low-laide" exiles, so Jove will "vplift" the exiles themselves. The god assents to the prayers of the Leonati, leaving upon Posthumus's breast the riddling tablet that ties the restoration of the kingdom of Britain to the end of his "miseries" and banishment.

The new era of empire, of peace, harmony, and fertility, commences, appropriately enough, with the public reading of Posthumus's "rare" book:

> When as a Lyons whelpe, shall to himselfe vnknown, without seeking finde, and bee embrac'd by a peece of tender Ayre: And when from a stately Cedar shall be lopt branches, which being dead many yeares, shall after reuiue, bee ioynted to the old Stocke, and freshly grow, then shall Posthumus end his miseries, Britaine be fortunate, and flourish in Peace and Plentie.
>   (TLN 3766–72)

No sooner is the text explicated by the soothsayer, now called Philarmonus, than Cymbeline announces, "My Peace we will begin." And reading the text of Posthumus provides the necessary keys for the correct interpretation of the vision of the soothsayer. The eagle of empire will pass from the Rome of Augustus Caesar to a reunited Britain. As King Cymbeline's reconciliation with Posthumus, the "Lyons whelpe" presages English acceptance of union with the "alien" Scots, so the king's recovery of his long-lost sons restores another lost limb of his kingdom, the alien territory of Wales. The explication of the riddle of the tablet might almost serve as a model for the reading of the play's "Stuart line."

In the Britain of *Cymbeline*, unlike the Britain of James I, Wales, or Cambria, is a separate country. The Roman ambassador to the court of Cymbeline is escorted only as far as its border at the river Severn; British law is not applicable beyond that point. Belarius, like Posthumus, is a man unfairly cast into exile, accused of overfriendliness toward Rome, reacting to his disentitlement by developing prejudices of his own. But the renewal of peace with Rome rejoins Wales to Britain in the persons of Cymbeline's sons. Shakespeare may have intended a reference to Prince Henry, whose creation as Prince of Wales was imminent and would symbolically reaffirm Wales's part in Great Britain. Entertainments written for the investiture like Samuel Daniel's *Tethys' Festival* include references to Milford Haven and the Tudor conquest— some of the same political material evoked in *Cymbeline*.[42]

Through the discovery of the lost children, the ancient kingdom of Brute is finally reunited: England and Scotland at last all under one head, branches of a single tree, as Cymbeline, Posthumus, Imogen, Arviragus, and Guiderius all constitute one line. Imogen has lost her title to the kingdom, but gained "two worlds" in exchange. With the exposure of Iachimo, the last vestiges of Posthumus's suspicion of Imogen are dispelled and the corruption of Italianate Rome is clearly separated from the virtue of its Augustan antecedent. Earlier on, Posthumus's war-weary jailor had exclaimed, "I would we were all of one minde, and one minde good" (TLN 2242–43). That wish is answered in the play's long final scene of *polyanagnorisis* when all the characters gather to disentangle the remaining riddles, piece together a common history, and forge one nation out of a heterogeneous mass of individual "liberties" and customs, Roman and British laws.[43] Similar resolutions of the conflicts impeding the creation of Britain were common in contemporary pageants. Peacham's emblem of James also provides a striking analogue: according to the ideal of the Union of the Kingdoms, England and Scotland both uphold the crown of Britain,

> And one their Prince, their sea, their land and lawes;
> Their loue, their league: whereby they still agree,
> In concord firme, and friendly amitie.
> (figure 14)

The most important action occurring in *Cymbeline* as the peace of Augustus descends upon Britain may well be what happens offstage and unmentioned within the play: the birth of Christ, which took place during the reigns of Cymbeline and Augustus Caesar, bringing a new "gracious season" of love and reconciliation among humankind. But another event associated with the golden reign of Augustus was the redescent of Astraea, Goddess of Justice, and the birth of the Roman law. Cymbeline freely offers Augustus Caesar the disputed Roman tribute which earlier he had scornfully refused—a sign of amity between nations which demonstrates his new receptivity to the Roman law, the *jus gentium* that governs the relations among nations, a branch of the same law by which the Post Nati would have been granted automatic citizenship in Britain.[44] In the new alliance, the "justice" of Roman tribute and the mercy of peace and reconciliation are not opposed to one another, but work together for harmony, just as James I envisioned an Empire of Great Britain in which tolerance and respect for the "alien" Roman law would cement, not cancel, union. At the end of the play, legal niceties about whose law and what kind drop out of sight along with the factional interests that had given them such spurious importance. The play ends as James I's reign had begun, with a proclamation of union.

Cymbeline orders that his peace be "published" to all his subjects. But in his Britain, unlike the Britain of 1608, the prejudice and malice which have hindered the Project for Union have either consumed themselves, like the wicked queen who "concluded / Most cruell to her selfe," or been conquered through inward transformation. Posthumus and King Cymbeline have undergone a "conversion" to the cause of union. In terms of standard humanist theory and James's own cherished belief about the relationship between texts and actions, reading and "application," Shakespeare can be interpreted as calling for a similar self-searching and self-transformation on the part of his audience. Everyone who kept abreast of Jacobean politics in 1608 and 1609 was aware of the king's Project for Union, acquainted with its proposed benefits for the nation. By coming to know themselves and their own prejudice, the audience would learn to grow beyond the xenophobia of disreputable characters like the queen and Cloten, for whom "defect of iudgment" is the "cause of Feare" (TLN 2392–93). They would overcome their partial vision and learn to "read" Posthumus aright as the essentially noble figure he is beneath his own equivalent prejudice. One of the chief barriers to the Project for Union would thereby be removed. The play ends in an openness to the winds of change, a zest for expansion and renewal, as though to intimate that such a transformation is possible. Whether the space between texts and action is so readily negotiable is another matter, however. And so, finally, we return to the vision of Jupiter, which is curiously absent from the one contemporary description we have of the play in performance.

THEATRICAL DECONSTRUCTION AND
CRYPTONYMY

Cymbeline demands political interpretation. It displays various characters in the act of finding political meaning in cryptic emblems; it offers its audience an expanded set of verbal texts and symbolic visions that cry out for similar explication. But our reading thus far has left one "text" uninterpreted, the image of descending Jupiter. For anyone immersed in the contemporary milieu, an initial identification would be obvious and almost unavoidable: Jupiter is James, who had swooped down upon his Parliament in similar fashion to announce his continuing protection of his despised countrymen the Scots, who was frequently depicted as Jove with his thunderbolts in connection with the Project for Union ("Procull a Iove, procul a Fulmine"), or as Jove with his emblematic animal the Roman eagle. In the coronation pageant, for example, James and his "empire" appeared as a Roman eagle who had flown westward to London.[45] The dreamlike interlude over which Jupiter presides in *Cymbeline*—rather as the figure of Jupiter had presided over Ben Jonson's *Hymenaei* a little earlier—has some of the quasi-liturgical patterning to "Solemne Musicke" of a masque at court. And like a Stuart masque or pageant, *Cymbeline*'s Vision of Jupiter shows forth the royal will "clear" and "without obscuritie." The Leonati beg Jove to open his "Christall window" upon them in much the same way that James I himself had volunteered to open the transparent crystal of his heart to his subjects in several of his published speeches and in his admonitions to the 1606–7 Parliament. According to the folio stage directions, "Iupiter descends in Thunder and Lightning, sitting vppon an Eagle. hee throwes a Thunder-bolt. The Ghostes fall on their knees" (TLN 3126–28). Perhaps the members of Parliament upon whom James had descended with his "thunder" in 1606 and 1607 had reacted with a similar shocked obeisance.

After chiding the Leonati for their lack of trust, Jupiter reveals his plan, foreordained all along, for relieving the sufferings of the deprived Leonati. Posthumus's birthright and marriage will be restored. Like James as he portrayed himself before the 1606–7 Parliament, Jove will allow no impediment to come between his will and its execution: "I will not say anything which I will not promise, nor promise any thing which I will not sweare; What I sweare I will signe, and what I signe, I shall with GODS grace euer performe."[46] Jupiter departs, leaving behind him, almost exactly as the bustling pedant-king James I might have done, a written text for his thunderstruck subjects to ponder until they achieve enlightenment. It is a rather stupendous set of images, or at least it can be with the right staging, as several twentieth-century productions have demonstrated. But the Descent of Jupiter can also be awkward, intrusive, like James I's sudden, "divine" visitations upon Parliament—as much fulmination as *fulmen*. Either way the vision is performed, it is hard to imagine how it could have been missed by anyone in a contemporary audience who was paying even minimal attention to what was happening on stage.

Simon Forman's 1610 or 1611 summary of *Cymbeline* shows considerable attention to intricacies of plot but lamentably little interest in political motifs that "might, without cloud, or obscuritie, declare themselves to the sharpe and learned." Both what Forman includes and what he omits are interesting in light of the play's "local" meaning. He picked up some of the incantatory power of "Milford," repeating the name several times, but conflated Posthumus and Cloten for part of the action, or so his confusion of pronouns seems to indicate. It is perhaps evidence that the two roles were performed by a single actor, but also evidence that the play's bizarre emblems of prejudice could easily be misread. In his account, Forman failed to include minor bits like the queen's attempted poisoning, but also major episodes like the Vision of Jupiter, unless we are to imagine such a potentially stunning *coup de théâtre* as subsumed under his final "&c." Here is the *Cymbeline* Forman recorded:

> Remember also the storri of Cymbalin king of England, in Lucius tyme, howe Lucius Cam from Octauus Cesar for Tribut, and being denied, after sent Lucius with a greate Arme of Souldiars who landed at Milford hauen, and Affter wer vanquished by Cimbalin, and Lucius taken prisoner, and all by means of 3 outlawes, of the which 2 of them were the sonns of Cimbalim, stolen from him when they were but 2 yers old by an old man whom Cymbalin banished, and he kept them as his own sonns 20 yers with him in A cave. And howe [one] of them slewe Clotan, that was the quens sonn, going to Milford hauen to seek the loue of Innogen, the kinges daughter, whom he had banished also for louinge his daughter, and how the Italian that cam from her loue conveied him selfe into A Cheste, and said yt was a chest of plate sent from her loue & others, to be presented to the kinge. And in the depest of the night, she being aslepe, he opened the cheste, & cam forth of yt, And vewed her in her bed, and the markes of her body, & toke awai her braselet, & after Accused her of adultery to her loue, &c. And in thend howe he came with the Romains into England & was taken prisoner,

and after Reueled to Innogen, Who had turned her self into mans apparrell & fled to mete her loue at Milford hauen, & chanchsed to fall on the
Caue in the wodes wher her 2 brothers were, & howe by eating a slep-
ing Dram they thought she had bin deed, & laid her in the wodes, & the
body of Cloten by her, in her loues apparrell that he left behind him, &
howe she was found by Lucius, &c.[47]

Beyond his repeated mention of the insistent name Milford Haven,
Forman shows no evidence that he grasped the play's Jacobean "line."
It would perhaps be utopian to expect to find such evidence. Forman
took his notes for purposes connected with his medical and magical
practice as a London cunning man. The explication of political allegory was not, perhaps, germane to his professional needs, whatever
those might have been. To the extent that contemporaries *did* under-
stand topical materials in masques or plays or pamphlets as conveying
some specific political message, they tended to note it only fleetingly
and in passing, in conversational or epistolary gossip.

Yet there may have been other factors contributing to Forman's
seeming oblivion. It is altogether possible that the Descent of Jupiter
was not performed in the version he saw, or that it was so massively
deemphasized that it became less than memorable.[48] Jupiter could have
walked on, for example, instead of descending by means of a machine,
and the lines describing his descent could have been cut. Or the descent could have been staged in such a problematic way that it was
easier to "forget" than to assimilate into a summary of the action. If,
to take only one possibility, Jupiter sat awkwardly on his emblematic
bird—hardly the usual mount for a being of human form—the gran-
deur of his visitation could have been massively undercut. Like the
episode of Imogen's misguided grief over Cloten's headless body, the
Descent of Jupiter is perilously balanced between the compelling and
the ludicrous. It is "double written" or overwritten in a way that calls
special attention to it and invites political decipherment but also provides a mechanism by which the "authorized" political reading can be
dispersed or ridiculed. To use James I's own complaining language for
such abuse of the clear royal intent, the Descent of Jupiter is contrived
in such a way that it can easily be "throwne" or "rent asunder in contrary sences like the old Oracles of the Pagan gods." In London, 1610,
before an audience for whom the play's political meaning was at least
potentially legible, how and whether the episode got "read" according
to the Jacobean line would depend in large part on how it was brought
to life in the theater.

The same is true of the play as a whole. By embedding *Cymbeline*'s "Jacobean line" within various structures which at least potentially call it into question, Shakespeare partially separates the play from the realm of authorship and "Authority," reinfuses its topicality with some of the evanescence and protean, shifting referentiality that were still characteristic of the Renaissance theater as opposed to authored collections of printed *Workes*. If King James I made a practice of beating off the subversive proliferation of meaning in order to communicate his "clear" political intent, Shakespeare in *Cymbeline* can be seen as one of those jangling subjects who scatter language and signification, dispersing the king's painstaking crafting of a unified whole nearly as fast as the royal author can put it together.

Cymbeline repeatedly invites its audience to "reading" and decipherment. If they follow its Jacobean line, they are invited to "apply" the play's message to their personal lives in much the same way that characters within the play repeatedly read moral maxims out of the landscape and events around them. And yet, the play's most important texts never operate according to such an orderly, rational agenda for interpretation. Reading in *Cymbeline* may be enticing, but it is also directly and repeatedly thematized as fraught with dangers, almost inevitably "misreading." Posthumus has to be "read," yet in the play character is seldom legible. "Who is't can read a Woman?" Cymbeline complains (TLN 3308), and Imogen and the others experience similar difficulties. Since the "Scriptures" of Posthumus have "turn'd to Heresie," she declares all reading suspect: "To write, and read, / Be henceforth treacherous" (TLN 2638–39); all interpretation is hopelessly "perplex'd." By the end, of course, such misreadings are disentangled and "unperplexed," but not before reading itself—the very integrative process by which the play's Stuart meaning can be collected by its audience—has been shown to be highly fallible.[49]

Cymbeline appears to posit a causal connection between the correct "reading" of its cryptic Stuart riddles and inner and outward transformation. Yet the translation of interpretation into action is not once effected within the play itself. Symbolic visions are often followed by salutary and revitalizing events. After the soothsayer's speech, Imogen awakens and attaches herself to the Romans; after Posthumus's dream, the prisoner is freed; after the interpretation of the riddling tablet, King Cymbeline proclaims the *Pax Britannica*. But in each case the relationship between the emblematic visions which demand reading and the acts which follow them is indecipherable. It is not clear whether or not Imogen is moved to action by the soothsayer. If so, she is inspired by false divining, since his interpretation is partially mistaken. Posthumus's dream is followed by his release from prison, but there is no clear causal relationship between one thing and the other beyond Jupiter's declaration that he has been controlling events all along. Posthumus himself has understood neither his vision nor the mysterious tablet. As often as not in *Cymbeline*, the riddling follows upon events instead of inspiring them, as in the maxim about the man, two boys, and the lane, and in Cymbeline's declaration of peace, which does not arise out of the reading and interpretation of the "text" of Posthumus, but has already been effected through the British military victory and the restoration of the exiles. Even as *Cymbeline* seems to argue for political action—the effacing of the "mark of the stranger" from the exiled Scots—the play calls into question the relationship between texts and action and therefore renders problematic its own status as a text which can be "read" according to the Jacobean line as a call for political unity and national renewal.

If *Cymbeline*'s riddling texts fail as pragmatic agents for change through acts of interpretation, the play leaves open the possibility that they may still serve, almost sacramentally, as vehicles for irresistible power, like the soothsayer's vision of the eagle of empire winging its way steadily westward—on high, remote, serenely indifferent to the human unraveling of riddles. That is the way Jupiter portrays himself as operating upon the world of human events. Everything has happened according to his master plan for Britain. He has allowed the "divorce" of Imogen and Posthumus in order to test and renew them both ("Whom best I loue, I crosse"); he also claims credit for the sudden reversal of fortune which reinstates the Union. The fact that characters in the play so frequently evoke "Jove" or "Jupiter" in their oaths and supplications adds to the sense of the deity's overriding presence in Britain.

Cymbeline's politics is embedded in a form which is less than hospitable to the potential for rational human action. In this play, as in Renaissance tragicomedy generally, human agency regularly dissolves; human beings are swept along by forces apparently incalculable. The dramatic form is, however, quite hospitable to the claims of Stuart absolutism, in that the wondrous energies which secretly govern the action can be identified with the "sacred" power of the monarch in his "body politic." Tragicomedy as a distinct, defined dramatic genre in England appeared shortly before the accession of James, and King James associated himself closely with it. He used the generic term himself to describe his marvelous deliverance (as a result of his own astute "reading" of an enigmatic plot) after the Gunpowder Treason in 1605. One of the purposes of that conspiracy had been, according to a chief perpetrator, to destroy the Union of the Kingdoms and blow the Scots back across the border. The deliverance of the nation was, in the king's own formulation, a "Tragedie" for the plotters, a "Tragicomedie" for himself and his "Trew Subiects."[50] Stuart court masques often celebrate a similar overriding destiny which grows out of the royal will and the king's special prescience. In the masque, royal proclamations were often portrayed as transforming the nation as though effortlessly, through the irresistible, divine power of James I—in much the same way that Jupiter claims hidden but absolute "Authority" over all the turnings of *Cymbeline*.

In *Cymbeline*, Stuart texts do sometimes evoke wonder among at least some of the characters. Reading, if it works at all in the play, works by inspiring the reader to marvel at the truth he or she has managed, with difficulty, to decipher. And yet, here again, discomfort with the interpretive process is overtly thematized. Posthumus ridicules the inane gawking of those who stand marveling at riddles and symbolic visions: "Nay, do not wonder at it: you are made / Rather to wonder at the things you heare, / Then to worke any" (TLN 2982–84). His taunt sounds very much like contemporary complaints against King James himself that he devoted himself too completely to the marvels of the book when he could accomplish far more by the sword. Yet Posthumus is describing a structural mechanism of the play he inhabits. *Cymbeline* plants seeds of impatience with the very riddles out of which it is constructed, an irritation like that expressed by Posthumus as he mockingly dissolves his own heroism into doggerel after his defeat of the Romans.

A prime example is the text offered by the great god Jupiter himself: it is written in very colorless prose (by Shakespearean standards at least)—only slightly more compelling than the doggerel produced by Posthumus. It is so inferior as a text to the marvel Jupiter seemed to promise that many editors have been convinced that it cannot be Shakespeare. And its Neoscholastic interpretation by the soothsayer is heavy-handed in the extreme. Asked, like an oracle, to "Read, and declare the meaning," the soothsayer infelicitously interprets "The peece of tender Ayre, thy vertuous Daughter, / Which we call *Mollis Aer,* and *Mollis Aer* / We term it *Mulier;* which *Mulier* I diuine / Is this most constant Wife" (TLN 3776–79). This niggling, labored mode of interpretation sounds rather too much like the pedant-king James himself, and can easily be understood as mockery of the play's own process of "wondering" decipherment of riddles and emblems of state. The play's major texts are awkward, apart—they produce disjunction, resist assimilation into the flow of events. Again we may be reminded of King James. Like Jupiter in the play, James was forever disconcerting his subjects by producing oracular documents, long speeches or proclamations which he liked to think of as *Books,* divine, arbitrary texts that heralded magnificent transformations for the nation, but were too often relied on by the scholar-king as though they could substitute for the painstaking political maneuvering that actually got things done. Jupiter's texts in *Cymbeline* are equally magical, or purposeless—perhaps evoking wonder, perhaps exposing the ineptitude of their "Author." If Jupiter is indeed, as he claims, all-powerful, why does he need texts at all? Similar questions could be asked about James I and his vast claims for his own prerogative.

If *Cymbeline* follows the Jacobean line, it also reproduces some of the incongruities in the actual working of Stuart policy that undermined royal claims about the mystical organic "union" of all James's subjects—like members of a single animate body—under his authority as head. In fact, James's political doctrine of essences was one of the major points of contention in the parliamentary debates over the Project for Union. Contemporaries "sharpe and learned" enough to read *Cymbeline's* Jacobean message at all were perhaps also capable of reading its portrayal of disjunctions between James's theory and his political practice. Upon such a contemporary audience, *Cymbeline* might well have produced dissatisfaction with the "Jacobean line." Or at least, through its critique of the wonders of the almighty Authored text, it may have intensified existing dissatisfaction with James, his clerkish political blundering, and his odd notions of kingship.

Much would depend on how the play was staged. To fall back time and again upon the range of political meaning which could have been elicited through different modes of staging is, perhaps, to abrogate the Duty of the Critic to determine the Author's Intent. But I would argue that it was part of Shakespeare's intent in *Cymbeline* to be able to sidestep the "self-sameness" and internal coherence growing out of emerging conventions of authorship. There was no way that he could "author" the play and its political message himself, even if he had wished to (and we have no particular evidence that he did). Following the play's invitation to linear interpretation would lead inevitably to the Jacobean line, to the Jacobean vision of organic political unity, and to James as "Author"—"Accessible is none but Milford way." By interweaving the play's "authorized reading" with a subtle critique of ideas about textual authority, Shakespeare gave the play back to the institution of the theater, created a potential for multiplicity and diversity in performance that the Stuart *Cymbeline* did not—by definition, could not—have.

The play may well have taken markedly different forms at different times and in different places. If it was performed at court, it could well have communicated the "Jacobean line" with almost the same stupendous glorification of James in his "immortal body" as monarch that was characteristic of the Stuart masque. In such a setting or in a theater capable of sophisticated theatrical effects, the play's overlay of uncertainties and questioning could have been overcome through spectacular staging of scenes like the Descent of Jupiter—through the creation of visual and auditory wonders marvelous enough to silence all but the most intransigent distrust of theatrical "magic." On the other hand, in a different setting or even in the same setting (since we should not be overly wooden and formulaic about the predictability of performance) the play could have been staged in ways that subtly highlighted its own deconstruction of reading and royal Authorship. Forman perhaps saw such a *Cymbeline* in the public theater—a *Cymbeline* in which the play's political symbols were muted or problematized to the point that they became indecipherable.

I have headed this section of the argument "Theatrical Deconstruction and Cryptonymy." Theatrical "deconstruction" of *Cymbeline* could have fragmented the Jacobean line by placing special emphasis on the play's barriers to reading, by undercutting its "wonders," and by giving strong credibility to characters like Posthumus who distrust such things. With the right balancing (or, in Stuart terms, the *wrong* balancing) of energies on stage, the play's perceptual and volitional gaps could easily have been made to appear unbridgeable. But given the play's contemporary milieu, there was also a potential for theatrical "cryptonymy" on the far side of deconstruction—for a mode of performance that read beneath and across the play's seemingly unbridgeable fissures and implanted a sense of underlying unity by uncovering an essence called Union identical with the person and power of the monarch. I am using the term *cryptonymy* much as it has been used in recent post-Freudian interpretation to describe the process by which a kind of "speech" can be given to gaps and splits which divide one area of the self from other areas and make it unavailable to the same discursive space. The fissures in question are not the same as those created by repression in that materials on both sides of the split are almost equally available to the self, but not at the same time or along the same perceptual continuum. Naming the word or constellation of words and events which underlies the fissure and constitutes it at least potentially allows a structural transformation that permits the two discursive spaces, the split-off areas of self, to flow together.[51] The same "healing" process can be invoked for political and artistic discontinuities to the extent that such splits follow a similar morphology, and to the extent that they are perceived as pathological, insufferable, urgently requiring repair.

Cryptonymy can, of course, be deconstructed itself, become part of an endless series of displacements, replacements, new displacements. But cryptonymy can also be invoked as a terminus upon the fragmenting process of deconstruction. A theatrical cryptonymy of *Cymbeline* would call attention to the play's disjunctions and difficulties in order to beckon beyond them toward an idealized realm of political essence which can be said to have helped create them in the sense that it induces a sense of human inadequacy, but which also heals them by giving access to the very realm of essence from which they are revealed as mere ephemera, surface turbulence upon a political and artistic entity which is indissolubly organic, at one with itself at the level of deep structure. *Mutatis mutandis* the play would then, for all its surface questioning, reaffirm the royal line not so much through King James as in spite of him; it would disperse the pedantic, orderly rituals of reading in order to "decrypt" the sacred immanence of royal power.

In the Renaissance, the two mutually reversing operations were equally possible and available (under different labels from those I have been using here) as counters in political debate. Legal and parliamentary "deconstructionists" challenged the doctrine of essences in its particular Jacobean form of official state organicism associated with the body of the monarch by pointing toward those elements of the national life which the Jacobean vision of unity had to disallow in order to constitute itself. Cryptonymy—"Platonic Politics" might be a more fitting label for it in its English Renaissance form—was a reading of underlying essences which "healed" social rifts and political fragmentation by pointing toward deeper unities already invisibly in place through the fact of James I's kingship. Part of the fascination of considering James I's Project for Union and *Cymbeline*'s fragile "unity" together is that both the play and the seething political debate mobilize similar strategies for defending and circumventing the Jacobean line.[52]

In *Cymbeline*, as in Shakespeare's earlier festive comedies, much of the power of the drive toward idealization is generated from the fact that the idealization comes too late. By the time *Cymbeline* was staged in 1608 or 1609 or 1610, James's Project for the Union of the Kingdoms and the creation of Great Britain had reached political stalemate. Parliament was no longer willing to consider the matter. The courts had indirectly endorsed the royal project, but without any way of enforcing it. James continued to rant and bluster, but gradually turned his attention to less intractable goals. The mistrust and prejudice continued on both sides of the border. Indeed, on the level of "local" function, *Cymbeline*'s discomfort with its own "governing line" can be seen as a symptom of continuing English and Scottish prejudice, continuing refusal to "read" the alien aright. For there was to be no ratification of the Project for Union during that century.

It is tempting to interpret the First Folio's placement of *Cymbeline* last among the tragedies and last in the folio volume—like the Golden Age materials which end *The Workes* of James and of Ben Jonson—as a comment on the failure of the royal project. If so, however, the play's political "tragedy" is extratextual and can be read in several senses. Is *Cymbeline*'s classification as tragedy to be read as a lament for the continuing intransigence of James's subjects to the enlightened project he offers them, or is it to be read instead as a comment on the king's failure, for all his claims of absolute authority, to heal the "divorce" between England and Scotland? Other readings of the generic label are also possible. For critics of James I's ecclesiastical and foreign policy like the First Folio dedicatee the earl of Pembroke, the "tragedy" of *Cymbeline* could have been the very success of its culminating vision of unity under empire. In the play, the enemies of Rome are all silenced; in England, they were vocal and prominent. In the eyes of such dissidents, the "happy" resolution of the play, which gives the Romans and Roman "superstition" a seemingly permanent foothold in Britain, might well have appeared less than fortunate. By the same token, for an enemy of the Project for Union, the tragedy of *Cymbeline* could have been the Union's success. All of these heavy-handed explanations of *Cymbeline*'s anomalous labeling are so highly speculative that it is impossible to choose definitively among them, impossible to entirely dismiss them. Even after the publication of the folio in 1623, however, we have circumstantial evidence that *Cymbeline* continued to be associated, in court circles at least, with the Stuart Project for Union.

Despite James I's victory in the case of the Post Nati, the "marriage" of England and Scotland was still hanging in "unnatural" suspension in 1633–34, when *Cymbeline* found favor with Charles I in a performance at court. It seems fair to assume that in this performance, the play's "Stuart line" was allowed to shine forth in its full flush of idealism and promise. The revival was almost certainly prompted by Charles I's celebrated progress to Scotland earlier that year to receive the Scottish crown: the head of the Scottish state had been fleetingly restored to his "exiles." It was his first visit as king of England to the northern kingdom. The public ceremony of his coronation as king of Scotland gave renewed visibility to the idea of the Union of the Kingdoms in the person of Charles, their mutual head. Not only that, but Charles's visit was designed to implement one part of his father's program for Britain, the creation of a unified British church by bringing Scotland into accordance with the Anglican liturgy and Anglican church government.[53] Given the immediate context, *Cymbeline*'s promulgation of official Anglican ideology about the indigenous nature of proper "liturgical" reverence and ceremony would have taken on particular prominence. But despite the renewed efforts on the part of crown and church, the stalemating of efforts for the Union continued. Charles I's attempt at matchmaking between kingdoms was even less successful than his father's. It led eventually to a destructive war with the Scots, a conflict that helped to precipitate the civil war and the execution of the king. Such cataclysmic divisions do not heal overnight. Great Britain was finally created only in 1707. And as recurrent, sometimes violent separatist movements since then have borne witness, the Union of the Kingdoms has never quite achieved the luminous harmony presaged in the final moments of *Cymbeline*.

RETROSPECTIVE:
KING LEAR ON ST. STEPHEN'S
NIGHT, 1606

During the early years of Stuart rule, the Project for Union was so prominent in public discourse that it provided an uncommonly rich matrix for theatrical topicality. Local reading of several of Shakespeare's plays would yield interesting results in terms of James I's project for Great Britain— *The Winter's Tale* most notably, perhaps, but also *King Lear*. *King Lear* is a play for which we have more than one early text. It therefore allows us to observe some of the subtle local differences about which we can only speculate in the case of *Cymbeline*. As a very brief exploratory coda to our discussion of the Jacobean line, I would like to consider one specific *King Lear*—the *King Lear* published in the Pied Bull quarto (1608) as having been "*played before the Kings Maiestie at Whitehall vpon S. Stephans night in Christmas Hollidayes*" in the year 1606.[54] The title page claims fidelity to that performance and sets forth its special institutional and liturgical context: *King Lear* was played at court before King James I; it was played on the night of the Feast of St. Stephen. We can supply the additional information that St. Stephen's Day was one of the official "red letter" days of the Anglican church, which had King James himself as its head. What might that particular localization mean in terms of the contemporary meaning of the play?

Several recent critics have pointed out *King Lear's* immersion in contemporary materials relating to the Union of the Kingdoms.[55] Like the much earlier tragedy *Gorboduc* performed before Queen Elizabeth in the 1560s, *King Lear* in both the quarto and folio versions can easily be interpreted as a dramatization of the perils of division. Both texts of *King Lear* portray a series of catastrophes unleashed by an aging monarch's decision to segment Britain into three parts, and those three parts can easily enough be identified with England, Scotland, and Wales. But neither text of the play offers a straightforward identification of either King Lear or his enemies with the "Jacobean line." Of the two versions of the play, the quarto is more permeated with local details relating to the Project for Union. In the 1608 version of Gloucester's initial speech, for example, he refers to the recent "diuision of the kingdomes" (664); the plural "kingdomes" is puzzling in terms of the Britain of King Lear, extremely evocative in terms of the divided Britain of James I. The folio reads instead "diuision of the Kingdome," muting some of the contemporary resonance of the phrase by altering the plural to a singular. But if the 1608 quarto version is richer in topical details evoking the royal Project for Union, it is also richer in particularized materials which can easily be interpreted as criticism of King James I.

The quarto *King Lear* includes several fleeting references to issues of royal prerogative which are not to be found in the folio. The "abuse" of royal monopolies had come up repeatedly in connection with James's high notions of his own prerogative. His Project for Union and his wholesale granting of monopolies to royal favorites were, for his critics, but two aspects of the same broad encroachment upon traditional "liberties." Both royal programs were contested during the first decade of his reign in terms of the same set of legal principles about the limitation of royal authority. In the quarto *King Lear* the fool brings up the monopoly system, taunting his royal master for giving away his land and rents to his daughters. The fool is a royal favorite who might be considered a prime candidate for monopoly, but he cannot claim sole right to his folly: "No faith, Lords and great men will not let me, if I had a monopolie out, they would haue part an't, and lodes too, they will not let me haue all the foole to my selfe, they'l be snatching" (672). That speech, with its implication that the whole royal system of monopolies is built upon (royal) folly, is omitted from the folio and its immediate context is altered.

There are similar differences later on. In the quarto *King Lear*, the stage directions for Lear's appearance during the battle between Albany and Cordelia's forces read "Enter Lear mad." His first words are, "No they cannot touch mee for coyning, I am the king himselfe" (695). In terms of Jacobean theory, the mad king speaks the truth. The king's absolute authority to coin money came up many times in contemporary debate in connection with James's more controversial assertions of royal prerogative.[56] In the folio version, the speech is subtly different. The stage direction does not call for Lear to enter "mad" and the key word "coining" is altered to the more general and neutral word "crying":

Enter Lear.

[*Edgar*]   But who comes heere?
             The safer sense will ne're accommodate
             His Master thus.
    Lear.   No, they cannot touch me for crying. I am the King himselfe.

                                                    (TLN 2526–31)

An attribute associating King Lear specifically with King James I is neutralized into a trait Lear shares with all humanity.

The most flamboyant difference between the quarto and the folio *King Lears* is that the mock trial in the hovel is entirely missing from the folio version. That scene, too, is full of pregnant references to issues of royal prerogative. By 1606, when *King Lear* was performed at court, James I had already encountered severe opposition to his highhanded notions about the power of royal prerogative to override legal and legislative curbs upon it. He regularly used the Court of Chancery, which operated as a court of equity according to his beloved civil law, to circumvent challenges to royal authority which emanated from the courts of common law. By 1606, Chancery had already demonstrated its receptivity to James's ideas about absolutism.[57] In the quarto *King Lear*, the wronged king attempts to create a commission of judges very much like a Chancery commission to pronounce on the justice of his daughters' behavior. In the eye of the storm and in the height of his madness, he appoints Edgar in disguise as Tom o' Bedlam as his first "robbed man of Iustice" and the fool as his second: "& thou his yokefellow of equity, bench by his side, you are ot'h commission, sit you too" (687). In contemporary England, "yokefellows of equity" were judges in the Court of Chancery.

When *King Lear* was performed at court during the Christmas holidays of 1606, the Parliament over which James I stormed like Jove with his thunderbolts was in session albeit recessed for the holidays; the Union of the Kingdoms and the naturalization of the Scots were at the center of parliamentary debate. James had ordered English and Scottish parliamentary commissions to meet jointly under Lord Chancellor Ellesmere (head of Chancery) to weigh the impediments to union and he was already proposing to submit the project to the courts.[58] In 1608, when the quarto *King Lear* was published, the case of the Post Nati had been tried in the Court of Chancery and the Lord Chancellor himself had issued a lengthy opinion on the Post Nati's right to citizenship on the basis of civil law and equity. The "royal commission" of the hovel Lear appoints to "arraign" and try those daughters who have stripped him of his authority and exacerbated the "diuision of the Kingdomes" is a madman's eerie echo of James I's actual tactics—in the matter of Great Britain and on numerous other occasions—for attempting to work his will upon recalcitrant subjects who committed more minor versions of the same infractions. By omitting the trial scene entirely, the folio version of the play skirts the interesting and uncomfortable problem of its insistent Stuart referentiality.

The pattern of alteration between quarto and folio is too regular to be a matter of mere chance. If we gauge authorial intent by collecting textual instances that appear to push meaning in a single direction, then what is at issue here is a matter of intent. It is not, however, clear whose intent is in question. Sometimes—to my mind implausibly, given the quarto's association with the court of James—the "intent" behind the alterations has been taken to be that of the official censor. We have no date for the composition of the folio *King Lear*, but editorial opinion is now inclined to place it later than the quarto version. If the revisions were made by Shakespeare, 1609–10 appears one likely period.[59] That would place the folio *Lear* in much the same contemporary milieu as the *Cymbeline* seen by Simon Forman, and create the interesting possibility that the two plays were "cleansed" of their intense Stuart topicality at about the same time. But the fact is that we do not know certainly when, why, or by whom the alterations were made, or even whether the folio version was revised from the quarto. I would be loath to insist that the quarto had to come first, or that it is a more authentic *King Lear* because it is "the Originall." There is no reason to regard one text as more "Shakespeare" than the other, or to assume that the alterations can be accounted for solely on the basis of either censorship or aesthetic considerations. By 1623, when the First Folio was published, many of the topical details evoking the king's Project for Union—details which provide such a striking localization of the quarto version—would in any case have lost some of their urgency. By 1623, James I had also taken strong steps to reform the monopoly system and the quarto reference to abuse would therefore have lost some of its heat.[60] What we have in the 1608 quarto and the 1623 folio are two "local" versions of *King Lear* among other possible versions which may have existed in manuscript, promptbook, or performance without achieving the fixity of print. One of our two *King Lears* is more closely tied than the other to a particular contemporary occasion.

What are we to make of the fact that the *Lear* most closely identified with the court of James I is also the *Lear* with the most potentially damaging references to specific royal policies? It is possible, of course, that some of the phrases we read in the printed quarto text were discreetly omitted from the performance before James. But we have no reason to suppose that they were. The common assumption that Stuart kings would never have suffered flouting before their face is not borne out by the evidence: there are many other instances of open criticism of the monarch and royal policies in masques and sermons at court. At Whitehall, as in the public playhouses, censorship was local and sporadic. Whether potentially damaging comments were suppressed or tolerated or even welcomed in royal entertainments was in large part a function of the specific conditions that surrounded each case.[61] We have no compelling grounds for contesting the quarto's claim to be the *King Lear* performed at court. The editorial tendency in recent years has been to elevate the status of the quartos, to give them far more textual credibility than Heminge and Condell's dark innuendo in the First Folio about "stolne and surreptitious copies" would suggest they deserve. I will work on the assumption that the play performed at court on St. Stephen's Night, 1606, followed the playtext we have reasonably closely. Even if there were significant alterations for performance, the title-page advertisement made it likely that 1608 readers, at least, would have bought and perused the quarto in the expectation that they were getting the court version of *King Lear*.

Steven Urkowitz, Michael Warren, and others have made valuable observations about differences in large structure between the quarto and the folio *Lear*s. The quarto version is slower-moving and more meditative, with frequent "cameo" speeches of moral reflection which arrest the progress of the plot; it is also less ambiguous in its portrayal of the moral nature of characters like the duke of Albany—closer, in short, to the structure of a traditional morality play.[62] It was performed at court at a time when the nation was blanketed in propaganda for the Union and Parliament was heatedly arguing the matter. Many of its strongest and most evocative ideas take on special local significance within the almost inescapable context of the contemporary debate.

Like pamphlets and speeches in support of the Union of the Kingdoms, *King Lear*'s major protagonists argue vehemently for a doctrine of essences—a set of knots "too intrinse t'unloose" between members of a family, a nation.[63] By assuming that he can divide up his kingdoms, shed his "body politic" while keeping the "name and all the additions to a King" (666), Lear has performed just the kind of hideous dismemberment of his sacred royal identity that King James and his advisers warned the nation so vehemently against. As in pro-Union arguments growing out of the contemporary debate, the division of the kingdoms in *King Lear* is associated with cosmic portents of chaos, the disruption of families and larger political alliances: it is a fragmentation at once psychic (expressed through Lear's madness) and political. All of these related catastrophes can be associated with the familiar set of interconnected paradigms which we used to call the Elizabethan "world picture." But considering the play in terms of the parliamentary and public debate shows how fragile such ideals were in terms of contemporary credence—how easily assimilated to the "Jacobean line," how easily contested by those who sought a less unitary, less authoritarian model of the state under the monarch. In *King Lear*, James I's notions about the organicism of Britain under the king as head are themselves placed on trial.

There are other ways in which the play's dominant ideas can be linked to the climate of contemporary debate. Let us take, for example, the parliamentary leitmotif from 1606–7 of James I as Jove the Thunderer, who would rain down his terrible punishments if the Project for Union were not expedited. The image of Jove—the storm, the implacable justice of his bolts from heaven—is extremely prominent in the play, as variations of the same topical motif were in masques and other court iconography associated with the Union. The chief victim of the "sulpherous and / Thought executing fires, vaunt-currers to / Oke-cleauing thunderboults" that shake the divided Britain of *King Lear* is the monarch who has initiated the "diuision of the Kingdomes." King Lear opens himself willingly to the bolts of Jove as though to acknowledge that he has deserved the god's "all shaking thunder" (683) for his crime against Great Britain.

The play's repeated motif of the casting off of good, "legitimate" offspring also reverberates with ideas about the Union. In England in 1606, the king's supporters were arguing that the "mark of the stranger" be effaced from the Scots, that they be received as legitimate subjects, elevated from their outcast beggary and given the kind of welcome in England that King James himself had received. The duke of Albany, who bears a Scottish title, is more sympathetically presented in the quarto than in the folio.[64] At a time when parliamentarians and others were venting strong prejudice against the king's northern subjects, expecting them to swarm across the border and engulf English prosperity if allowed the slightest favor, *King Lear* could easily be interpreted as an extended political exemplum promoting charity toward the Scots. A king becomes a beggar, looks for succor and is denied it, as a result of the "unnatural" division he has earlier unleashed: he becomes, in contemporary terms, an outcast "Scot" himself, suffering the same scanted courtesy to which King James's northern subjects had been unjustly treated in England.

At court in 1606, the play's moral message about hospitality toward the poor and the castoff would have been immeasurably strengthened by the announced liturgical context—at least for those viewers who reverenced the teachings of the church. St. Stephen's Day (December 26) was, of all the days of the year, the holiday most associated with the granting of traditional hospitality; it later became known as Boxing Day. On the Feast of St. Stephen, as in the more recent carol of King Wenceslaus, the high were to look out in pity upon the tribulations of the low. On that day, poor boxes in which cash donations had been collected all year would be broken open and the money distributed. Poor people would gather in groups and proceed from house to house asking for a charity which could be denied only at the peril of those within. Wealthy individuals who participated in the spirit of the day took pride in having an estate on St. Stephen's filled with as many guests as the "howse wolld holld."

In some places, "Stephening"—the demanding of holiday charity—took on a highly aggressive cast. One parish in the seventeenth and early eighteenth centuries preserved records of Stephening and its demise. At Drayton Beauchamp, Buckinghamshire, on the Feast of St. Stephen, all the parishioners were traditionally treated to "open house" by the local rector at his own expense. When one parsimonious rector tried to evade his traditional responsibility on the feast day by shutting his doors and hiding inside his house, angry parishioners scaled the walls, broke through the roof, and emptied out his larder, claiming their traditional privilege of hospitality in honor of St. Stephen. The parish custom was quickly reinstated and continued sporadically until 1834, when government commissioners appointed to inquire "concerning charities" investigated Drayton Beauchamp and ruled that there was no "legal proof" requiring the tradition's continuance.[65]

According to a popular saying, "Blessed be St. Stephen / There's no fast upon his even."[66] Shakespeare's play depicts the inconceivable. On the night of St. Stephen, 1606, *King Lear* enacted repeated violations of the festival "law" against fasting. In the liturgical lessons proper for the Feast of St. Stephen, the idea of bending to succor the less fortunate, of shedding "pompe" to "take physicke" and "feele what wretches feele" (685) occurs again and again. "He that by usurie and uniust gaynes geathereth ryches: he shal lay them in stoare for a man that wyl pitie the poore." "He that wyl be ryche al to soone, hath an euyl eye: and consydereth not that pouertie shal comme upon hym." "He that giveth unto the poore, shall not lacke; but he that hideth his eyes from them, shall have many a curse." [67]

It is easy to see how such a liturgical context—inescapable for anyone who went to church on the holiday as English subjects were required to—would frame the play itself, "solve" and disentangle some of its interpretive cruxes. King Lear and his retainers have been rich but have become poor, and like the poor on Stephen's Night, they boisterously demand hospitality of the daughters who have suddenly "gathered riches" through the king's abdication. Both their need and even a measure of aggression in demanding that it be met are "licensed" by the liturgy and customs of the day. But Goneril and Regan repeatedly shut them out, advising Gloucester as well to "shut vp your doores" against the king and his "desperate traine" (682). Gloucester passively allows the holiday violation to be perpetrated; one of the consequences of his act (at least in terms of the play's festival context in performance) is that he himself is blinded by the very guests he preferred above the needy. Denied hospitality by the "hard house, more hard then is the stone whereof tis rais'd," Kent resolves to "returne and force their scanted curtesie," according to the traditional liberty of Stephening (684). But the doors of the great ones remain shut. Only a hovel is open. In the quarto, the pattern of scanted Stephening receives particular emphasis if only because King Lear is given more extended contact with the company of outcasts who have, like him, been shut out of the hospitality of the night. He is shown physically supported by the lowly. [68] He reduces himself more, calling himself in one famous speech a "poore old fellow," which is far more shockingly base than the folio version—"You see me heere (you Gods) a poore old man"—but also more evocative of the holiday theme of kinship with the unfortunate. In the "friendship" of the hovel in the quarto version, King Lear actually puts "cold" hospitality on trial in accordance with liturgical precept and the doctrine of due reverence: "He that giveth unto the poore, shall not lacke; but he that hideth his eyes from them, shall have many a curse."

It is also easy to see how the play's lesson about succor for the needy and downtrodden could be given moral "application," according to the Jacobean line, as reproof against those in the English Parliament and elsewhere who, like Goneril and Regan in the play, were hardheartedly denying the nation's obligatory hospitality to the needy Scots. The preservation of old holiday customs was a very important policy matter for King James I. He had already issued royal proclamations calling for the keeping of open house during the Christmas season according to the traditional "laws" of hospitality; a decade or so later, he would codify his position in the *Book of Sports*.[69] And yet, in his own kingdom, in the matter of the Post Nati, the poor continued to be kept out; his parliamentary supporters argued in vain that it is better to give than to receive.[70] *Cymbeline*'s worthy, legitimate, outcast figure of Posthumus would have recognized the hostile moral world of *King Lear*. The 1606 *King Lear* performed before King James I was, in contemporary political terms, a demand for what had not been offered generously and freely, a morality play enforcing the king's arguments for naturalization and acceptance of the alien on the basis of liturgical and customary holiday injunctions.

What are we to make of the elements of the quarto *King Lear* that appear to criticize King James I and his notions of prerogative—the very notions which stood behind such arbitrary gestures as his attempt to enforce holiday hospitality by royal decree? To a degree, these elements take on an aura of ritual humiliation on the part of one of the powerful in connection with the holiday's strong message of *Deposuit potentes*. The liturgy for the day calls for just such self-abasement in kinship with the lowly on grounds that, as one verse of the lesson proper for St. Stephen's puts it, "Somme one commeth out of prison, and is made a king; and another which is borne in the kingdome, commeth unto pouertie."[71] The wheel of fortune repeatedly referred to in the playtext can turn, then turn again. By watching a play that made rather obvious references to his political failings, James could be interpreted as "taking physic" himself, displaying a comely willingness to enter into the charitable spirit of the day, which he was imposing on everyone else.

There was also local potential for the transmission of a stronger political message through the play's associations between festival folly and the dispersal of legal authority. St. Stephen, the first martyr, was condemned to death by Judaic legalists for his arguments that the Mosaic code had to give way to the new Christian dispensation. His story from the Book of Acts was read as part of the liturgy for the day. In a parallel with St. Stephen himself, *King Lear* displays a monarch martyred for his faith in extralegal charity and brotherhood. According to such a line of interpretation, King Lear would be less a negative antitype than an analogue of James I. As our discussion of *Cymbeline* has already noted, in early Stuart England ideas about transcending the strictures of law (particularly the common law) and appeals to larger notions of brotherhood, equity, and charity were strongly associated with King James in his various battles with Parliament and the courts. The play undermines the rule of law in accordance with traditional holiday ideas about Christmas "misrule" and the overthrow of all manner of legal hegemonies. Through his presence at the performance of *King Lear*, James I provided a "perspective" on the play from which it could be read as both a royal acknowledgment of the king's "sins of state" and a dispersal of just the type of legal authority which sought to undercut his absolutism. In keeping with the example of St. Stephen, James I could be interpreted, through his very tolerance of the play's critique, as forgiving his enemies—at least to the extent that public acknowledgment of hostile criticism can be taken as a kind of forgiveness.

There are, of course, other possibilities for interpretation set in motion by the quarto's liturgical and political context. As commentators have noted, the play can easily be taken as glancing at James's more personal foibles: his immoderate love of hunting, boisterous conviviality, and indulgence of his favorites; his sudden attacks of rage and recurrent fits of the "mother." [72] To the extent that James himself in his "body natural" replicated the flaws of King Lear, it could be argued that he, too, had been subjected to intolerable affronts, rendered unnaturally impotent and divided from himself, by his subjects' continuing fragmentation of his very essence through their inhospitality toward the Union. The continuing suspension of the royal project, from such a perspective, could be taken as an explanation of all manner of royal failings. The king could not show himself in the full glory and perfection of his "body politic" because his subjects would not allow him to be fully whole as himself—at one in "body natural," "body politic," and nation.

At court on St. Stephen's Night, 1606, the presence of the king presiding over the performance and the play's many resonances with the liturgy for the day to some extent dampened *King Lear*'s potential for undoing the royal "line." In the public theater and on a more neutral date, a similar performance might well appear seditious, or at least highly volatile in terms of its topical associations. For readers of the 1608 quarto, the play's lessons in Stuart political morality would have been less visible and clear-cut than in performance at court, since readers would not, in all likelihood, encounter the play on St. Stephen's Night itself. But some of the holiday "message" would have lingered about that particular playtext because of the elaborate specificity of its title page. For anyone who remembered what St. Stephen's Day was about (and who could possibly forget?) the quarto *Lear* was framed within a markedly conservative ceremonial context.

It would, of course, have been perfectly possible to reject the holiday message. There were many well-to-do Jacobeans who made a point of scanting their "obligatory" holiday hospitality on the basis of economic and religious principle. If anything, James's insistence on imposing the old forms made some people more hostile to them. The extent to which either readers or viewers "applied" the holiday lesson correctly in terms of the Stuart line would depend, in large measure, on their preexisting predilection for reverence toward the authority of church and state. Liturgical framing always carries with it an element of tautology. The Stuart line in *King Lear* would carry special credence only for those dutiful subjects who were already receptive to it. For those who were not, the play potentially opened itself to all manner of dissonant interpretation, even (as in Stephen Greenblatt's reading of the play) to the evacuation of the very traditions and unities that the court *King Lear* reinforced.[73]

The "official" *Lear* of the quarto is not the only possible *Lear*, or even the only *Lear* that could have been read out of that specific festival occasion. Like *Cymbeline* and many other plays we call Shakespeare, it was generically unstable—labeled a "Chronicle Historie" in the quarto, a tragedy, along with *Cymbeline*, in the folio. My purpose in focusing on the royal *Lear* as opposed to others is not to declare a preference for it but to stress, yet once more, the importance of localization for defining parameters of meaning. A play which was orthodox in one setting could have been unorthodox in another. Shakespeare's "double writing" of key scenes gave the theater the "high prerogative" of subtly altering a play's meaning in performance. The fact that there existed an "authorized" court version of *King Lear* in print after 1608 might have helped contain the play's obvious potential for interrogating Stuart orthodoxy. And yet, depending on the performance and the circumstances surrounding it, the play's energies could easily be opened out into a field of freer signification which, by its very scattering of the "authorized" liturgical reading, would weaken the Jacobean line. The *King Lear* of most modern editions is a different *King Lear* still. By interlayering the quarto and folio versions, editors have established "authoritative" versions of the playtext but also created new areas of ambivalence and instability which do not exist in either text considered separately. To which *King Lear* can we assign the Man Himself? Whether or not Shakespeare was a "King's Man" is a question which cannot be answered for All Time and in broadly general terms.

4

London

> To treat of the great and notable franchises, liberties, and customs of the City of London, would require a whole volume of itself.
>
> Edward Coke's *Fourth Institute*

Modern editions of Shakespeare obligingly provide readers with labels at the head of each play specifying the locus of the action. The First Folio was less solicitous. What sense of place it does offer generally comes via internal stage directions or dialogue, or through the play's title— *The Merchant of Venice, The Merry Wives of Windsor, Timon of Athens, The Two Gentlemen of Verona.* We may be tempted to include the folio's reticence about place among the devices by which it sloughs off particularizing details—details which might subvert its claim to universality by anchoring a given play too obviously in a specific milieu. Unlike the First Folio, Ben Jonson's folio *Workes* gives the place of the action for all but one of his plays in large block capitals preceding the text. But Jonson's meticulous labeling can scarcely be said to have established an ironclad precedent. The word *localization* dates, we will recall, only from the nineteenth century. We cannot assume that a Renaissance audience of readers or viewers would have felt the same disorientation we are likely to feel, conditioned as we are by more recent classificatory procedures and their reflection in editorial practice, over a failure to specify place.

In Shakespeare, place is often left mysterious, or at least undefined, until well into the play. If we are reading a text like *Twelfth Night, or What You Will* in the 1623 folio version, we can locate the action immediately because the first speaker is announced by title in the initial stage direction: "Enter Orsino Duke of Illyria" (TLN 2). But if we miss that written cue, it is not until scene 2—after we have been introduced to the lovesick duke and his court, then to a completely different set of characters—that Illyria is designated as the locus of the action. In per-

formance, before that point, a theatrical audience not provided with
the modern amenity of a printed program might well have been in fecund limbo—not knowing where the stage events were taking place
or whether that information was important. Would such an audience
have listened in wary uncertainty to hear the place named, asking, along
with Viola in scene 2, "What Country (Friends) is this?" Or would the
naming of the locale have been a matter of indifference?

In either case, Illyria was scarcely familiar territory, more significant, perhaps, for its evocation of like-sounding exotica—Elysium,
delirium—than for concrete geopolitical associations. But place in
other plays can operate in more topographically specific ways. Our
project for localization in the larger sense of the term needs to take into
account the matter of internal "localization"—the degree to which and
the means by which a given play sets itself apart from its contemporary London audience through an evocation of place which is clearly
alien, somewhere else, with its own idiosyncratic geographic and cultural features. Given the Renaissance penchant for topical speculation,
no locus could be said to be inviolate; no amount of topographical dis-
tancing could insulate a play entirely from the contemporary rage for
finding homologies with events and people about London. But the
kinds of topical speculation which a given play was able to provoke
could be strongly influenced by its particular locus of action. Place in
Shakespeare is more highly charged, more elusive, sometimes more
downright deceptive than the reassuring advance labels provided by
modern editors allow us to perceive.

There are two plays in the First Folio for which extratextual place
names *are* provided—not helpfully at the top of a text as they are in
Jonson's *Workes* and would be in a modern edition, but at the end of
the text, just before "The names of all the Actors." The fact that the
folio does not usually offer such information makes more curious and
provocative the two cases in which it does: for *The Tempest*, "The
Scene, an vn-inhabited Island"; and for *Measure for Measure*, "The
Scene Vienna." This uncharacteristic specificity has been accounted
for as the idiosyncrasy of the copyist Ralph Crane, who seems to have
liked to add such information when it had not already been supplied.[1]
But that explanation leaves interesting questions unasked. What effect
might the anomalous specificity as to place have had on folio readers
of these particular plays? "An vn-inhabited Island" is a rather odd description given that Prospero's domain is never quite unpopulated, at

least in the audience's experience of it. But the label which will concern us here is the one affixed to *Measure for Measure*: "The Scene Vienna." An unidentified island is potentially neutral territory; Vienna, most emphatically, was not. It was one of the capitals of the Holy Roman Empire, much in the news in the year 1604 as the traditional seat of the Hapsburg dynasty, the administrative hub of a vast and shifting Catholic alliance with which the English had been on hostile terms for decades.

There is, to be sure, little specific evocation of Vienna as a city in *Measure for Measure*, only a handful of references to people and places surrounding it—to the Hapsburg "Dukes," to Bohemia, and to "the King of Hungaries" peace (TLN 100–101). But those are precisely the local references that contemporary Londoners, unacquainted with Viennese topography but avid for the latest news about the fate of continental Protestantism, would have been most likely to pick up. In near-contemporary plays like Shakespeare's *King John* or Anthony Munday's *Downfall* and *Death of Robert, Earl of Huntington* "Vienna" and "Austria" are clearly enemy territory. (And in *Hamlet* the "Murder of Gonzago" takes place in Vienna.) How are we to interpret the folio's uncharacteristic insistence upon place in the case of *Measure for Measure*? And why is "The Scene Vienna"? That is only one of several interesting irregularities in the folio presentation of the playtext that we will want to consider.

The easiest answer to the question Why Vienna? has been to take the name as nothing but smokescreen. Vienna is not actually Vienna; it is London, or at least a place which can easily be taken for London. As numerous historical treatments of the play have pointed out, there are extremely close connections between the Vienna of Duke Vincentio and the London of James I. Mistress Overdone complains about conditions in Vienna, "Thus, what with the war, what with the sweat, what with the gallowes, and what with pouerty, I am Custom-shrunke" (TLN 172–74). All of these local misfortunes can be correlated with matters of public concern in the disease-ridden London of 1604: "The continuance of the war with Spain; the plague in London; the treason trials and executions at Winchester in connection with the plots of Raleigh and others; the slackness of trade in the deserted capital."[2] There are other resemblances as well. In London of 1604, as in Vienna, the "howses in the Suburbs" had been ordered to be "pluck'd downe" by a 1603 proclamation. In London, as in Shakespeare's Vienna, there had been a recent heating-up of efforts to stamp out prostitution. According to one contemporary, "the Lord Cheife Justice . . . hath plaide rex of late among whoores and bawdes and persecutes poore pretty wenches out of all pittie and mercy." Notorious brothel owners and employees from the suburbs were ostentatiously carted and whipped about London, then thrown into Newgate Prison, where they could form a reconstituted "house" like the one Pompey discovers in the Viennese jail, teeming with all his old customers.[3] London, unlike Shakespeare's Vienna, did not punish sexual incontinence with death, but there were numerous "precise" and vocal Londoners who argued, like Angelo, that it should. They made their case for more rigorous laws on the basis of Mosaic precept (in Old Testament law, the penalty for fornication *was* death) and the example of "reformed" cities on the Continent.[4] In London, finally, as in Vienna, there was an overriding "imperial" presence—that of King James I— whose coronation pageant earlier in that same year (1604) had been orchestrated as a Roman triumph over the city very much in the manner of the Holy Roman Empire, of the public pageantry of a Maximilian I or a Charles V.[5] Like Shakespeare's duke of Vienna and like the actual Holy Roman emperors, whose mythos of power James I adopted for himself, the English king frequently provoked, but also tested and challenged, sudden eruptions of local judicial severity within the "empire" of Great Britain.

The only early version of *Measure for Measure* we have is the text of 1623—nearly two decades after the period of its composition and performance. According to the Revels accounts, a play called "Mesur for Mesur" by "Shaxberd" was acted in the Banqueting Hall at Whitehall on St. Stephen's Night, 1604.[6] This may have been the play's inaugural performance and King James was almost certainly present. Again, as in *Cymbeline*, we are confronted with a text which can easily be understood as setting forth a "Jacobean line"—mirroring the king and his most cherished principles by displaying his ideas about equitable government (familiar to contemporaries through the just published *Basilikon Doron*, which was selling like hotcakes in London, and through other royal pronouncements) in triumph over harsher, more limited codes. According to what Richard Levin has derisively termed the "King James Version" of *Measure for Measure*, Shakespeare's intent in writing the play was to appeal to a courtly audience and curry favor with James I in the halcyon aftermath of the new monarch's accession. The purest and least equivocal form of the "authorized" *Measure for Measure* takes the play's local meaning for King James I as the whole meaning of the play.[7] Discordant elements are automatically excluded from the field of interpretation on grounds that King James would not have allowed them, nor would Shakespeare himself have been so fool-hardy as to perpetrate them. Small wonder, perhaps, that the King James Version of *Measure for Measure* so often gets dismissed as impossibly reductive.

But there is a deeper intolerance lurking beneath the charge of reductiveness—the old bugaboo of a Shakespeare tainted with ideology. We can accept Levin's rejection of the King James Version as the only "true" meaning of the play without following him in his efforts to cleanse it (and the name of Shakespeare more generally) from all taint of topical meaning. Like *Cymbeline*, *Measure for Measure* promulgates a Jacobean line, but is "double written" in a way that allows for other meanings, opens the play out to a range of audience reaction and potential signification. Except that in *Measure for Measure*, the devices which undermine the official line are far more flamboyant and ingeniously disruptive than the equivalent devices in *Cymbeline*. In *Measure for Measure*, there are many parallels between the play's locale and London, between its duke and James I. But there is also the problem of Vienna. If the play was designed to compliment King James I, it seems rather odd that it is set in a place associated for most of its 1604 viewers with fears of Catholic invasion and repression, with the dread specter of Hapsburg rule, a return to the Inquisition and to the bloody persecutions of Philip and Mary.

In local reading of *Measure for Measure*, nearly everything depends upon place. If Vienna is taken to be London, then the play goes a fair distance toward the Jacobean line, displaying a ruler who succeeds in establishing equity and a semblance of social order when his deputy has spectacularly failed. But if Vienna is Vienna, or (worse yet) a London *become* Vienna, then the play's topical resonances turn completely inside out: all of the gestures which seem to praise James in his triumphant mastery over London can become elements in a dark fantasy of alien Catholic domination. The play is like a Möbius strip—a single twist of the fabric in the process of construction, and every surface, every seemingly level plane, is at the same time its own volte-face.

WITHIN THE WALL

Let us start with the topicality closest to home—the striking likenesses between Shakespeare's Vienna and Shakespearean London. My heading is not meant to suggest that the burgeoning City of London in 1604, or the wide-ranging issues of concern to it, could be contained within its ancient walls. The city had experienced phenomenal growth in population, trade, and commerce during Elizabethan times, and it was to experience far more. In the half century after 1600 it was to double in size; by 1666, in John Dryden's *Annus Mirabilis*, it was, for the first time in English, called a "metropolis"—no longer to be mistaken for the large town it had been in the late medieval period.[8] London in 1604 was bursting out of its traditional topographical limits. There were city wards outside the old walls and the authority of the London Corporation spilled out in various ways into the populous suburbs beyond. The city, for example, had the right to appoint justices of the peace for surrounding areas like Middlesex.[9] Londoners tended to view the areas outside their jurisdiction as hotbeds of vice and disorder. To some extent, that perception was grounded in actual conditions: the suburbs were expanding faster than the City of London itself, and so were suburban problems. But to some extent, Londoners' perception of the lawlessness all around them registered an inability to conceptualize the changing character of the place they considered home. Seemingly chaotic alterations which could not be comprehended in terms of the London they were accustomed to got projected onto the areas outside it, areas which were more obviously outside their control and therefore more available in psychological terms as repositories for that which was new and alien, incapable of immediate assimilation.

Even within the walls, London was scarcely monolithic, more a patchwork of local differences than a single, uniform political and geographical entity. Within its boundaries there were areas outside the jurisdiction of the Lord Mayor and aldermen—pockets of special privilege like Blackfriars, Whitefriars, the Savoy, and the Liberty of the Minories which enjoyed their own "freedoms" apart from the customs and liberties of London. These areas were a constant thorn in the side of city government because they could serve as havens for all sorts of "lawless" activities—as sanctuaries for those seeking to escape military conscription, for example, or for Nonconformist preachers and congregations who sought to evade some of the pre- scribed ceremonial practices of the Anglican church, or for the com- panies of players who perpetrated that particularly "notorious abuse," the London theater.[10] But in the areas directly under the control of the London Corporation, there were also frequent conflicts over ju- risdiction between the Lord Mayor and aldermen on the one hand and the organs of national government on the other—the Privy Coun- cil and the Crown, the church and ecclesiastical courts. London offi- cials stood on their right to assert the customary privileges and juris- dictions which the city had enjoyed "time out of mind" by Magna Carta, a series of royal charters, and customary law; the Crown and church found ways of imposing their own "higher" authority on Lon- don by circumventing or running roughshod over the traditional free- doms of the city.

We are all familiar with the battles over the drama in the 1580s and 1590s both within London and in the liberties, a tug of war between the Lord Mayor and Privy Council which sometimes hinged as much on who was to control the theaters as on how that control would be exercised. The year 1599 provides a provocative illustration. For years, city authorities had been sending the Privy Council a stream of com- plaints against the "disorder" of the theaters without getting much satisfaction. Finally in 1599, *mirabile dictu*, the royal government fi- nally seemed to lend an ear. The Privy Council ordered that the Lon- don theaters be shut down. But then, the tables turned, city officials were reluctant to comply and the theaters were not shut down. There may have been numerous factors in this tug of war of which we are now unaware, but one element of the conflict was clearly the issue of whose authority would dominate London.[11] Similar battles took place over the use of the royal "dispensing power" in other fields of activity: the monarch would issue a proclamation or patent that exempted an individual or group from customary city regulations and barred Lon- don justices of the peace from enforcing local ordinances against the holder of the privilege, London authorities would then protest that their laws and jurisdiction had been flouted, sometimes there would be an actual physical clash between the agents of the Crown and local jus- tices of the peace, and the jurisdictional conflict would be joined anew. In the long-term dispute over control of the lands surrounding the Crown Liberty of the Tower of London, for example, Tower officials

actually removed the boundary stone that marked the limit of city jurisdiction and encouraged their adherents to repeatedly "invade" the
territory claimed by the citizens as a way of demonstrating royal jurisdiction. Debtors claiming the "privilege of the Tower" would take ref-
uge within the liberty; when London justices of the peace tried to ap-
prehend them, the justices themselves were arrested and held in the
Tower.[12] In many of these disputes, preserving local liberties "within
the wall," preserving local autonomy, was as important to London
officials as the relief of the particular "abuse."

To say that London valued its areas of autonomy is not to say that
the city was by any means autonomous. There were many ways in
which it was firmly and even comfortably under royal control. London was the most important source of revenue for the Crown and of
financing for the government and aristocracy. It was the Crown's
major supplier of goods and services in peacetime, a prime resource
for soldiers and matériel in wartime. The nation could not have functioned without a bedrock of cooperation between the city and the
Crown. But in terms of its traditional "liberties," London was proudly
and sometimes defiantly its own place, jealously guarding its particular customs and freedoms as a bulwark against engulfment in a larger
political and cultural entity. As Richard Helgerson has demonstrated,
London, like other areas of the realm, was beginning to display a new
interest in chorography—in mapping out its particular topographical
features in a way that declared an unprecedented involvement with individual "place" and a concomitant concern with individual identity
and autonomy.[13]

This emerging pride in local place is evident in John Stow's *Survay
of London* (London, 1603), which traverses the whole city, ward by
ward and street by street, in order to commemorate its chief worthies
and topographical features, the layers of history preserved in its ancient edifices and monuments. The *Survay* is much more than the
creation of a collective city heritage, however. At the end of it Stow
includes "An Appendix contayning the examination of such causes as
haue heretofore moued the Princes, either to fine and ransome the
Citizens of London, or to seize the Liberties of the Citty itself." The
appendix is a discreet but spirited celebration of London liberties, arguing that London had never really deserved the indignity of royal encroachment, never been seditious on her own, but only when led on
by others: she "neuer led the dance, but euer followed the pipe of the

Nobilitie" (565–68). Stow's defense of London argues, in effect, that
the deprivation of London's traditional freedoms had usually been the
result of royal tyranny. It is a most interesting display of civic pride in
which the delineation of London boundaries is inextricable from the
assertion of local autonomy.

With the coming of the new monarch in 1603, there was a new opportunity for the city to reaffirm its liberties. A petition from the
"Mayor, Aldermen, and Commonalty of the City of London" which
was probably initiated that year or in early 1604 complained to James I
of "certain persons endeavouring to get a grant from His Majesty of
privileges always enjoyed by this City both by Charter and usage."[14] It
was the first of a number of protests against Jacobean encroachments.
James was to be a far worse offender than Elizabeth had been, if only
because he lacked her tact and skillful indirection, when it came to the
assertion of royal prerogative against the privileges of the city. When
he entered London in triumphant domination as the new Augustus in
his coronation pageant in 1604, he was engaged in a different kind of
mapping from that practiced by Stow. The city and its multiplicity of
local "places" gave way to the single presence of the king. He tra-
versed the streets of London not in order to admire them, but to take
possession of them, display his dominance over them. The whole pageant was orchestrated as a symbolic conquest—a "pacification" of the
city as the *camera regis*, the submissive bride of the monarch, part of
the vast, organic body of empire which James wanted to call Great
Britain.[15]

Rival images of the city can be identified through different modes
of visual presentation. In John Norden's *Specvlvm Britanniae* (1593),
London's streets and buildings are framed by the insignia of her illustrious guilds (figure 15). The honor of the city is proclaimed through
reference to its structuring commercial institutions and their members. In the Londinium Arch of James's coronation pageant, by contrast, the city is upheld by the triumphal arch (inscribed with the message of royal dominance) through which the king passed as he entered
the city (figure 16). The city and its institutions are depicted as less
than the king, his mere dwelling chamber or *camera regis*. The prospect
of such royal domination and the loss of local authority and identity
did not necessarily sit well with Londoners. They were already beginning to suspect that James I's dream of empire allowed scant place for
the traditional freedoms of the city.

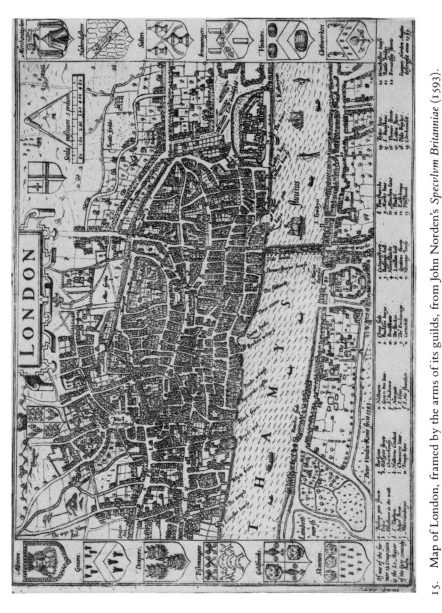

15. Map of London, framed by the arms of its guilds, from John Norden's *Speculum Britanniae* (1593).

16. The Londinium Arch from James I's coronation pageant as reproduced in Stephen Harrison's *Arches of Triumph* (1604). Photo courtesy
of the Huntington Library, San Marino, California.

For a contemporary theatrical audience, I would suggest, part of
the fascination of *Measure for Measure* was its engagement of a markedly similar conflict in a place called Vienna. Just as the king of
England had ceded his right to govern London directly to the Lord
Mayor and aldermen, allowing them by royal charter the privilege of
choosing their own Lord Mayor, so the duke of Vienna, acknowledg-
ing his inability to govern Vienna himself, confers his "absolute power"
by special commission on the new deputy Angelo: he has "Lent him
our terror, drest him with our loue, / And giuen his Deputation all the
Organs / Of our owne powre" (TLN 22–24). The parallel is not precise: in one case the king's surrogate is elected and in the other he is
appointed. But the basic mechanism of delegation is the same in both

cases, and sets in motion a set of conflicts over who will maintain public order and what form that order will take. The language of prerogative asserts itself: the duke has stamped Angelo with his own great and noble "figure" much as he would coin new money (as only a ruler was empowered to do). What remains to be seen is whether Angelo will prove true "mettle" (TLN 55). In both Shakespeare's London and Shakespeare's "Vienna," the ruler, having delegated his power, proves unwilling to let it remain securely with those to whom he has entrusted it. He hovers upon the scene incognito, covertly and then overtly asserting his own priorities for government over a city which is paradoxically enslaved both by too much "libertie" and by too much trust in the rigidities of law.

Much has been written about law in *Measure for Measure*. But law in the play is not one single thing, an absolute against which various forms of illicit "liberty" and transgression are played off. In terms of the play's meaning for London, we need to distinguish between different kinds of law: between "local" law, which is inscribed in specific places and bound within their limits, and "unlocalized" law, which operates, sometimes with apparent willfulness, across boundaries, outside the limits of place. London and its environs were a crazy quilt of different legal jurisdictions, some inextricable from topography, others more global, independent of topographical boundaries. The former would include city ordinances and customary laws. London's liberties and franchises were jealously guarded by her citizens and, in general, protected by English common law. But there was another system of law interlayered with the "local" law of the city and increasingly in competition with it during the early Jacobean period: that was the amorphous, pervasive, "unlocalized" jurisdiction associated with ecclesiastical law and the canons of the church, with royal prerogative (increasingly questioned by the advocates of common law, but buttressed by the civil law) and with the royal "dispensing power" to exempt individuals from the provisions of statute law. Common law and the liberties it guaranteed were specific to England, embedded in its particular "places" and history; civil and canon law were outgrowths of the Roman law, which was international, operating across boundaries between peoples and places.

The chief area of jurisdictional conflict in the "Vienna" of *Measure for Measure* is the matter of sexual incontinence—how it is to be defined and how it should be punished. The same matter was also a well-known battle ground between competing legal systems in the London of 1604. Twentieth-century interpreters have taken pains to establish whether, in terms of Renaissance perceptions, the play's various irregular unions would have been understood as fornication or as lawful marriage. But critical consensus on that thorny interpretive issue cannot possibly be reached if only because there *was* no single Renaissance understanding of what constituted valid marriage—at least not in England. Even in terms of the canon law, the line between illegal sexual incontinence and true marriage was very flexible in practice. The ecclesiastical courts did not always operate according to a clear-cut set of invariable principles out of medieval canonists or Justinian. And if their tolerance for exceptions was not complicated enough, there was also the problem that canon law itself had just altered. As a result of the Hampton Court Conference between James I, key bishops, and selected Puritan divines, a new canon revising the definition of lawful marriage took effect in 1604, the same year as *Measure for Measure*.[16]

Moreover, canon law was by no means the only legal code by which contemporaries could measure the validity of marriages. What constituted "true" marriage was a more nebulous matter in the London of 1604 than it had been for decades because of new and competing initiatives on the part of Crown, church, Nonconformist divines, and agents of city government to impose consistency upon an area of human conduct which had traditionally been subject only to sporadic regulation. In *Measure for Measure*, as in London of 1604, the question of whose authority will dominate in an area of uncertainty and conflicting jurisdiction is a question which is at least as important— probably more important—than the actual punishments meted out for incontinence.

In late Elizabethan and early Jacobean England, marriage was a long, drawn-out process with a number of steps—from the first private promise of marriage *de futuro* between the two parties themselves, to a public contract and the establishment of a property settlement, to the actual church wedding (if that step was even taken at all), and, finally, to sexual consummation (if that step had not been taken already). Before the new 1604 canon took effect, the point in the process at which the couple could be said to be married was largely a matter of local custom, varying from one place to another. In some areas, particularly rural communities, sexual familiarity before the finalization of marriage was tolerated. Couples, in effect, married themselves through the mutual promise of marriage followed by copulation. If, as in the case of Claudio and Juliet in the play, they became parents be-

fore their union was publicly acknowledged, they might get hauled
before the local "bawdy court" and required to do perfunctory penance before the congregation or, if they could afford it, charged a fine
to commute the punishment.[17]

If they were unlucky, however, such a couple might come to the
attention of local justices of the peace, who also had jurisdiction according to a parliamentary statute of 18 Elizabeth over any case of sexual incontinence which produced a child as well as customary jurisdiction over various other sexual offenses. According to the canon law
before 1604, clandestine marriage was legal but irregular; in common
law, it had no legal status at all. Property settlements under the common law required proof of open, public marriage. By the provisions
of the parliamentary statute, two justices of the peace acting together
could determine the disposition of a bastardy case and impose "by
their discretion" what seemed to them appropriate punishment of the
guilty parties.[18] It is easy to see that, given zealous officials, the statute
could create a much more severe climate for sexual offenders than the
church courts usually did. That, no doubt, was the intent behind the
parliamentary initiative. In some areas, justices of the peace and con-
stables actually conducted house-to-house midnight bed checks to
scout out illicit sexuality. Offenders could be handed over for trial either to the ecclesiastical or to the secular courts. Some cases of sexual
incontinence got bounced from the ecclesiastical to the common law
courts and back again, as each legal system tried to assert its jurisdictional predominance over the other.[19]

In addition to that possible double jeopardy, there were other quarters from which correction could come. Puritan ministers often took
upon themselves the revelation and punishment of fornicators within
their congregations. Their doing so was, strictly speaking, unlawful,
since it preempted the jurisdiction of the ecclesiastical courts. But the
divines who took such measures were usually markedly hostile toward
the church courts to begin with, regarding the whole canon law system as a lamentable survival of pre-Reformation "papal filth" that
made "but a jest" of vice. The public shaming Puritan divines imposed upon wayward members of the congregation might be similar
to the sentence which would have been imposed by the church courts,
but it would probably not involve the exacting of fines, it would be
imposed in an atmosphere of greater severity toward individual transgression, and it would proceed from a competing source of spiritual
jurisdiction.[20]

Some Puritan divines were also prone (like Oliver Martext in *As You Like It*) to conduct what the official church condemned as invalid marriages outside the parish church and without banns or license. Again, part of the point of creating such unions was to circumvent the official system, which would have required "superstitious ceremonies" like the use of a wedding ring. London liberties with substantial Puritan congregations also tended to be havens for irregular marriage.[21] The new ecclesiastical canons which took effect in 1604 were designed to stamp out such practices by specifying that marriage had to be performed by a duly licensed cleric in the parish church of one of the partners between the hours of eight in the morning and noon, after either the announcement of banns on three consecutive Sundays or festival days, or the procurement of a valid license from the bishop.[22] Since the new regulations had been passed by convocation as early as 1584, people had had the time to become familiar with them. Even before they were formally adopted as ecclesiastical law, several ministers who had conducted irregular marriages had been censured by the church.[23] With formal ratification, many more prosecutions were impending.

As it transpired, however, clandestine marriage between the parties themselves, without the use of a minister, remained a gray area of the ecclesiastical law. England did not go as far as Catholic Europe had after the Council of Trent, banning clandestine marriage entirely. But the continuing tolerance in practice was not specifically allowed by the canon. In 1604, with the new canons in place and new, stricter plans for forcing conformity upon resisting ministers, there was considerable uncertainty about whether clandestine marriages would have any continuing validity. Certainly they were now further from official acceptability in England than they had ever been before. The pattern of empire, by which "unlocalized" canon and civil law reached out to encompass and erase local difference, was brought closer than ever to realization in the area of marriage litigation through the canons of 1604.

In London, as we have noted, there was agitation in some reformist circles for the adoption of the Mosaic code as a basis for civic ordinance. That, if put into practice, would have brought London almost into line with the statutes of Shakespeare's "Vienna." Something very much like the Viennese ordinance was in fact put in place some forty years later, during the Interregnum. Under the Commonwealth government, a second offense of incontinence could be punished by death.

In addition, church marriage was abolished and justices of the peace were empowered both to conduct marriages and to dissolve them.[24] But such "root and branch" upheaval of the traditional system was only a theoretical model in the London of 1604. As it was, London's own customary penalties against sexual offenders—whipping, shaving the head, public carting, and jail—were far more draconian than the punishment prescribed in most other places and in the ecclesiastical courts. The City of London also claimed the "freedom" of overriding the ecclesiastical laws regulating sexuality with its own customary restraints. For example, London sometimes punished clerics for incontinence according to its own system of penalties, even though that function was in theory reserved to the ecclesiastical courts.[25] As the crackdown against bawds and whores had made evident, reform was very much in the air in London, 1604. The city was taking on a reputation for exceptional vigor against vice. And this was happening at a time when the Crown and Anglican church were exerting their own competing effort to surmount the crazy quilt of local jurisdictions with one overarching standard governing marriage and sexuality.

If Shakespeare's "Vienna" is a jittery and confused place when it comes to questions of sexual morality, Shakespeare's London could be said to suffer from a similar insecurity. What constituted valid marriage was not some idle legal nicety: it was an issue people had to confront in the most personal terms possible unless they remained totally celibate. Amid the nervous welter of conflicting jurisdictions over the crime of sexual incontinence, contemporaries would have differed sharply in their assessment of the validity of *Measure for Measure*'s clandestine marriages. Their opinions—if they were able to come to a clear-cut opinion at all—would vary according to their degree of familiarity with recent changes in secular and canon law, and according to their general ideological bent. At a time when the Anglican church itself had launched a new offensive against the problem of clandestine marriage, intolerance for the practice did not necessarily make one overbearingly "precise." Despite the range of different opinions, however, there was one area in which there would have been substantial unanimity in London, 1604. To anyone who lived from day to day amid the open jurisdictional skirmishes among competing authorities in London, the styles of legal authority played off against each other in Shakespeare's "Vienna" would have been immediately identifiable in terms of the local conflict.

Angelo, as chief governor of Vienna, is in effect the city's Lord Mayor, and as a London Lord Mayor would, he acts with the powers of a justice of the peace to defend and strengthen the city's local ordinances, in this case, the "biting" written statute that requires fornicators to be put to death. The duke initially claims that his own goal is also to restore the integrity of the statute—put teeth back into a local code which has fallen into disregard like "threatning twigs of birch" long unused and therefore "More mock'd, then fear'd" (TLN 314–17). But the duke's secret motive is instead to test Angelo—to probe into the workings of city government and the significance of his own delegation of authority by trying the virtue of a "precise" man whose whole demeanor and life seem dedicated to the rigor of law, specifically to civic government and to the common law. The duke praises Escalus for his knowledge of the "*Cities Institutions*, and the Termes / For Common Iustice" (TLN 13–14). In contemporary parlance, the "Termes for Common Iustice" is a phrase specifically associating Escalus and city government with expertise in the common law.[26] This is the realm of legal discourse within which Angelo, too, will function.

In *Measure for Measure*, Angelo and Escalus follow the basic pattern of London civic authorities or justices of the peace, conducting open, informal interrogations and, in accordance with the parliamentary statute of 18 Elizabeth but unlike any of Shakespeare's sources and analogues, working together as a pair to inquire into cases of sexual incontinence and bastardy. The obscure offense committed in Pompey's unsavory "house" against Elbow's pregnant wife at least potentially falls within the statute, since she is with child by someone, but the exact nature of the allegation Elbow wishes to make is hopelessly lost in tangles of lexical confusion. He, a constable and therefore an agent of city law and order, is an "elbow" indeed, incessantly turning the law and language back upon themselves until all possibility for stable meaning is lost. The fact that such an engine for the decomposition of system can hold public office bodes ill for public order in "Vienna." Angelo to some extent abrogates his role as a justice in dealing with Elbow's case, at least by the standard of the English parliamentary statute, in that he eventually loses patience with the constable's obscurities and leaves Escalus to deal with the matter alone. Usually he is more punctilious. In the bastardy case of Juliet and Claudio, the two justices also confer together to determine appropriate punishment and this time Angelo is the more persistent of the two in following through on the case and applying the full rigor of the law. His insistence on the exact letter of the statute makes him close kin to actual London reformers who grounded their campaigns against vice similarly in the powers of surveillance mandated by the "*Cities Institutions*" and "the Termes for Common Iustice."

Angelo, of course, proves corrupt in office, counterfeit "mettle" rather than true coin. For London theater audiences, part of the game of topicality in "Vienna" would have been the titillating pleasure of measuring the hypocrisy of Angelo against their own civic authorities. One obvious candidate for resemblance would have been Chief Justice Popham, probably the most prominent common law justice of the time, who had spearheaded the initiative against brothels about London and was called "bloody Popham" by his enemies. He was known to be so "precise" in his personal habits that he kept the Sabbath Day meticulously even when he was riding circuit for the provincial assizes. He was also widely suspected of hypocrisy. Another prime candidate might have been Sir Edward Coke, who was already known for his defense of the common law and city "liberties" and for his interest in reviving the rigor of old statutes, but who had recently entered into a scandalously irregular marriage himself despite his ostensible veneration of the law. As usual, the game of topical identification was juicy and potentially endless: other ripe candidates were available from among the ranks of pompous London authorities—aldermen, recent Lord Mayors, sheriffs, and zealous justices of the peace. The city's crackdown on vice was bound to create friction and resistance, even perhaps among those who advocated London "liberties" in theory. Other plays of the period make similar capital out of the unveiling of the secret vices of staid, bourgeois officialdom.[27]

But the figure of the duke was just as vulnerable to the game of topical identification. His various personal likenesses to King James I do not require recapitulation here—they are obvious enough to have struck editors and readers of *Measure for Measure* since at least the eighteenth century.[28] As we will note later on, there are several other contemporary figures whom Shakespeare's duke of Vienna could also be said to resemble. What could perhaps bear more attention at this point, however, is the remarkably Jacobean *style* of the duke's activities in the play in terms of the contemporary conflicts over law. He, like the new king of England, begins by asserting his reverence for local customs and ordinances: they are, he claims, *his* laws, "our Decrees"

(TLN 317), and he commits himself to giving them more authority. As it transpires, however, the duke is not at all interested in restoring the rigor of the statute against fornication. Instead, he acts in various ways to mitigate it with flexible principles drawn from the civil law and equity. Like James I in London, he acts indirectly and through intermediaries to assert his own ultimate jurisdiction over the city's customary privilege of policing its territory within the walls.

At the end of the play, despite all the initial talk about the rigid enforcement of law, the Viennese statute punishing fornication with death is forgotten. It disappears almost unnoticed amid the splendid theatrics of the public trial before the city gates. Nobody has been executed for fornication, and no one seems likely to be. In the last act, the duke himself in effect becomes the law, the *lex loquens* or speaking law, as the Roman civil code and the speeches of James I would have it, an independent source of legal authority which transcends the city's ordinance, coming down like universal "power divine" to reveal the defects in a fallible local human system.[29] The pattern was already familiar in the London of 1604; it was to become more familiar with James's continuing intervention in the city's affairs. In *Measure for Measure* local authority is overridden by royal prerogative, by the principles of Roman civil law, which fostered the idea of the monarch as the embodiment of a general, mysterious, ultimate legal authority.

Throughout the play, the duke's style of intervention is associated, not with the common law, but with ecclesiastical jurisdiction in a markedly conservative form. He is garbed as a friar for most of the action, serving as a confessor and spiritual adviser to those in need of his ministrations. He appears and vanishes with mercurial suddenness, operating in hidden ways outside local boundaries and limits. In several instances, his methods correlate with procedure under the Roman law. As was the practice in the canon law courts (in marked contrast to the common law), he gathers testimony by interrogating witnesses in private and in advance of the trial. Given the secret way in which the relevant testimony was obtained, at ecclesiastical trials the truth often emerged with sudden and undeniable éclat once all the evidence was revealed.[30] Much the same effect is achieved in the duke's public exposure of Angelo. The trial scene, with its crowd of unruly onlookers, its attendant "clerics," and its emphasis on shaming and public reputation, has some of the quality of a trial in the contemporary bawdy courts, with their odd mix of the awesome and the carnivalesque.

In the end, when the duke throws off his ecclesiastical garb to act in his own person to confer validity on the play's irregular sexual unions, he is assuming a prerogative like that which James I and the Anglican church had asserted in 1604 as they tightened up the canon law governing valid marriage by insisting upon the proper license. Within the Vienna of the play, there are "outlaw" areas like Angelo's private garden "circummur'd with Bricke" and outlying areas like Mariana's lonely grange which appear analogous to the London suburbs, removed from the regular jurisdiction of the city. The duke's activities penetrate these places apart, redress the anomalous situations which have been tolerated there, and bring them under his authority, much as James I and the church were moving in to bring the London liberties under royal and ecclesiastical control. When the duke commands that Angelo and Mariana be immediately married, he is claiming ultimate authority over the system of ecclesiastical licensing. Ordinarily, by the 1604 canon, Angelo and Mariana would require a license from the bishop in order to be married "instantly," without the publication of banns. In this case, the license emanates not from a bishop but from the ultimate ecclesiastical power above the bishop, the *lex loquens* of the ruler.

There are also resemblances between the duke's style of justice and the English Court of Chancery. Traditionally, the chancellors of England had been clerics and the duke's disguise recalls that connection. Chancery was the final court of appeal in ecclesiastical cases involving matters of property (which often hinged upon the validity of marriage); it frequently reversed the severity of the lower common law courts, just as the duke alleviates the severity of the statute. According to one contemporary description, the chancellor "doth so *cancell* and *shut up* the *rigour* of the generall *Law*, that it shall not breake forth to the hurt of some one singular Case and person."[31] By abrogating a local statute in favor of "mercy" and equity, the duke acts, in effect, as his own Lord Chancellor, overriding local justices in the name of the Roman code and the royal dispensing power. The jurisdictional morass has been cleared away; pockets of secret license have been opened up to surveillance; and the duke has publicly established for himself and for the civil and canon law the ultimate right to adjudicate "Mortallitie and Mercie in *Vienna*."

In twentieth-century editions and productions of *Measure for Measure*, the trial scene usually takes place inside the city. The First Folio itself offers no such certainty as to place. As the scene begins, the duke is approaching the city gates: "Twice haue the Trumpetes sounded. / The generous, and grauest Citizens / Haue hent the gates, and very neere vpon / The Duke is entring" (TLN 2340–43). The folio stage directions which follow specify only that the "Duke, Varrius, Lords, Angelo, Esculus, Lucio" and "Citizens" enter "at seuerall doores" (TLN 2346–47). In some of the earliest editions of the play specifying the locus of the public trial which follows, the scene of the trial is described as "a publick Place near the City." [32] That added stage direction is interesting because it suggests that early editors of the play thought of Shakespeare's "Vienna" in terms of a topography very like London's: the City proper is a self-contained, walled unit surrounded by other urban areas, like the London liberties, which are not strictly part of it. What the scene enacts is the traditional public ritual by which civic authorities greet a visiting monarch. They meet the ruler with fanfare just outside the walls—the entry "at seuerall doores" suggesting that the different groups have come from different directions—to formally tender up their authority and accompany him through the gates. [33]

In this case, however, the entry is delayed as a result of the duke's proclamation inviting petitioners to approach him publicly for the redress of grievances. The pleas of Isabella and Mariana turn the usual scene of ceremonial transfer of authority into a forum for inquiring into the conduct of the deputy. The duke establishes his superior claim to govern the city from a location just outside the wall, outside its proper jurisdiction; then, much as James I had entered London in triumph in the year 1604, he enters the gates and proceeds in state to his "Pallace," formally taking possession of the place he has demonstrated a transcendent right to control. That which is merely local has been made to appear small, paltry and corruptible, by comparison with an authority which partakes of the divine and the universal, which cuts through jurisdictional tangles to establish a single, centralized, yet merciful standard of law.

It is easy to see how James I would have relished the play's depiction of victory for the Roman law with which he felt such sympathy and which, in 1604, he still hoped to use as the basis of a united Britain. There are many ways in which the play seems weighted toward the "Jacobean line." The city's own authorities are an unimpressive lot: even Escalus is too shortsighted to suspect the vice of Angelo. Unless

Claudio is played as an unusually repellant character, he tends to generate audience sympathy, at least by comparison with Angelo, just as his plight generates sympathy from onlookers within the play. Insofar as an audience takes the part of Claudio against Angelo and the rigor of the statute, they are being invited to side with the duke against the city—recognize the wisdom of the ruler's timely use of equity to redress a reforming zeal which has gone too far.

There were contemporaries who would have agreed with Angelo that death was not an excessive penalty for fornication, but they were the same zealots who were most vehement against the theater. They would not (it seems safe to say) have been part of the audience for *Measure for Measure*. To the extent that London theatrical audiences resented the reformers' endless campaigns against the public "enormity" of stage plays, they may have found it easy to applaud the duke's exposure of a civic leader who was overly precise. The place of the duke's highly theatrical trial just outside the jurisdiction of the city was, in London, the place of the stage itself. There is a natural topographical alliance between the theatricality of the duke and the institution which brought him to life on stage on the outskirts of London.

But for at least some members of a London audience in 1604, the play's victory over statute may have looked more like defeat. Whether or not the duke's influence is perceived as salutary depends to a marked degree on the audience's evaluation of the duke himself. For good or for ill, his *modus operandi* in the play is made to appear arbitrary, manipulative, imposed from without. In modern performances, he is often idealized as the wise exemplar of overarching authority called for by the play's "Jacobean line," a figure whose arbitrary gestures are justified as desperate counters to the rampant crimes of his surrogate. Almost as frequently in modern productions, however, the duke comes closer to Lucio's description of the "fantastical Duke of darke corners" or Angelo's equally disparaging language: "In most vneuen and distracted manner, his actions show much like to madnesse, pray heauen his wisedome bee not tainted" (TLN 2274–76). In modern productions, the duke can be a *deus ex machina* who descends by means of a whirligig, a shadowy trickster who delights in imposing unnecessary gyrations of misery upon his subjects merely to show his power. Like Jupiter in *Cymbeline*, he exists on a perilous boundary between the sublime and the grotesque.

In London, 1604, there may have been nearly as much potential for variability in the portrayal of the duke as there is in modern performance. Because of the heated conflicts over jurisdictional issues in the city, even relatively small alterations in the nervous balance between the duke and his antagonists could markedly have altered the political complexion of the play. Let us take one "localized" example of the problematics that contemporary performance could—perhaps fleetingly—have exploited. If a London audience saw a parallel between the duke of Vienna and James I as the promulgator of the new ecclesiastical laws regarding marriage, they could easily have been puzzled by his uncanonical behavior earlier in the play. The "bed trick" by which Mariana is substituted for Isabella to satisfy Angelo's lust was *not* lawful according to the church's new definition of marriage. The precipitous wedding ordered by the duke between Mariana and Angelo was also uncanonical unless, by some chance, they happened to be married in the parish church of one of them, or unless the duke's verbal "license" is taken to cancel out the usual rules. These are small details, perhaps: topicality thrives on what is almost too insignificant to notice. But they suggest that the duke, insofar as he is identified with James I, can be trusted to respect his beloved canon law no more than Angelo does the statute. That perception unleashes a potential for contemporary deconstruction of *Measure for Measure*'s Jacobean line. Like King James, the duke acts above the law, freely overriding even his own preferred code when it suits his purpose to do so. Contemporary viewers could surmount the seeming contradiction in the duke's position by making a "leap of faith" from the law to Christian mercy, by which all legal codes are confounded. As we will note further later on, *Measure for Measure*, like *King Lear*, is associated with St. Stephen's Day, at least through its performance at court, and therefore with the holiday inversion of law and ordinary hierarchy. But to regard the duke as transcending all law would undermine the play's appeal to the ruler as an alternative and superior source of law. In *Measure for Measure*, the rule of law is overthrown by something that may be divine transcendence, but can also look like royal whim, unruly "license," a mere recapitulation of the abuse it purports to rectify.

In London, 1604, one of the things on trial in *Measure for Measure* was the city's jealously guarded autonomy. Under such conditions, a strongly divided reaction to the duke and his triumph could easily have been generated by one and the same performance. Not all theatergoers were Londoners, of course; many were foreigners or visitors from the provinces for whom the conflict over law in its particular London form would have been less than familiar, although the general problem was familiar enough. For such viewers some of the intensity of the play's topicality "within the wall" might have been lost. Then too, even for many Londoners, the "honeymoon" between the new king and his people was not quite over. The reign was young enough that many subjects who would later become disaffected were still willing to grant the monarch the benefit of the doubt. The name of king exerted a powerful emotional pull, particularly when coupled, as in *Measure for Measure*'s last act, with evocations of sacred divinity. Yet if, in a given audience, on a given day, the passion for city liberties ran high enough, even a sympathetic portrayal of the duke would probably not have made palatable his conquest over a "Vienna" which looked so uncannily like London.

At the end of the play, there is one slight suggestion that the duke's victory may not be complete. His conquest over the city has also been a conquest of the chaste virgin Isabella, or so, at least, he assumes. Twice he publicly asks her to allow him to possess her as his wife, but both times she remains silent in one of Shakespeare's most intriguing "open silences."[34] What can her silence mean? Traditionally in performance, it has meant that no words are necessary: Isabella gladly gives him her hand. In very recent productions, it has sometimes meant refusal: instead of accepting the duke, Isabella turns her back and walks off. It is difficult for us to know whether or not such a stunning rejection of patriarchy and political authority by a "mere" woman could have been staged in Renaissance England. We know little enough about the conditions of Renaissance performance that we should not automatically discount the possibility. But a more muted version of the same response could easily enough have been acted. We, with our quaint late twentieth-century prejudice in favor of consensual marriage, find the notion of bridal reluctance or coercion profoundly shocking. In the Renaissance, it was all too familiar. Isabella could easily have held back, given evidence that she was being conquered against her wishes, before finally yielding to the duke. The effect would be to cast a shadow, however brief, upon his triumph.

For some modern readers and viewers of *Measure for Measure*, Isabella bears a muted resemblance to the dead Queen Elizabeth.[35] Elizabeth, like Isabella, had been an insistent, sometimes strident virgin who had valued her own inviolability above many other pressing matters. She had had her own set of imperial images—to some extent James I was merely adopting her symbology of power. After her death, however, the image of the queen signified political difference from James; she stood for nationalism and "local" identity. To the extent that the identification between the two virgins carries credence (and carried credence for contemporaries), the duke's conquest over Isabella can be seen as yet another dramatic marginalization of the mythos of Elizabeth, like those we have briefly observed already in several other plays we call Shakespeare. Through Isabella, the dead queen and her cult of virginity and national "intactness" are invaded and dominated by an alternative, Stuart ideology of male dominance and imperial conquest.

Despite the fact that she too had sometimes offended against London liberties, Elizabeth was becoming a powerful political symbol in Jacobean London. In the city, as in Parliament, and in contemporary plays and pamphlets, the figure of the queen was associated with resistance to royal absolutism and the maintenance of customary franchises and liberties. Some years later, the city erected a statue of the queen with hair flowing freely to symbolize her (and its own) celebrated "virgin" freedom and self-containedness. Isabella, Elizabeth, London: in terms of gender encoding, all three were associated with vulnerable boundaries stoutly maintained against violation. In Shakespeare's *Rape of Lucrece*, similarly, the "tyranny" of a "King" and the Tarquins' encroachment upon civic "laws and customs" are associated with sexual conquest.[36] Like the resolute virgin Isabella in *Measure for Measure*, the City of London had been called upon through James's coronation pageant and other royal initiatives to open its gates, become the submissive "bride" of the monarch, throw off its cherished inviolacy to become part of a larger "Union." To the extent that the symbolic parallel holds, Isabella's equivocal silence in the face of imperial conquest can resonate strongly with a parallel silence on the part of the city in the face of its incipient forced "marriage" to King James I.

WITHOUT THE WALL

But then, "Vienna" is not only London. It can also be taken as Vienna, or some more generalized depiction of a European city under absolutist or imperial rule. The conflict between local liberties and emerging central authority was not London's problem alone. It was the problem of towns and cities all across Europe, particularly in areas dominated by the Holy Roman Empire, which was successfully replacing local customary ordinances with the Roman code.[37] The Roman emperor Severus had been a prototype of the imperial reformer, going in disguise to spy out illicit dealings in ancient Rome. In nearly all of the Renaissance sources and analogues to Shakespeare's *Measure for Measure*, the climactic conflict lies between a corrupt local official who uses his powers of office to take sexual advantage of a woman who has trusted him to deal justly and the emperor (or some other powerful ruler) who steps in to redress the abuse in the name of a more general code of law. In George Whetstone's *Promos and Cassandra*, the offending official is a judge of the city of "*Iulio* (sometimes vnder the dominion of *Coruinus* Kinge of *Hungarie*, and *Boemia*)." Corvinus was a historical figure who was also an imperial elector, conqueror of Vienna, and aspirant to the imperial crown. He intervenes in Whetstone's play to save the judge from his own corruption. Whetstone's retelling in *An Heptameron of Civill Discourses* specifies further that Corvinus's goal in appointing magistrates like the judge of Iulio was to assure that his "free Cities" were well governed according to his own standards of law. In Cinthio's *Hecatommithi* and *Epitia*, the emperor Maximian intervenes similarly to right the injustice perpetrated by the governor of Innsbruck.[38]

There are also French variants of the story, some of them perhaps based upon an actual incident of 1548 which reverses the fictional pattern. In that year Bordeaux and its *banlieux* revolted against the French king's imposition of a salt tax "contrary to its ancient privileges." The constable of France, Anne de Montmorency, crushed the revolt and executed over a hundred "persons of note," falsely promising the wife of one of the rebels that he would spare her husband if she gave him her sexual favors. After she had yielded her body, Montmorency put her husband to death anyway, but instead of being punished for his perfidy, the constable was created duke and peer of France.[39]

What characterizes the imperial versions of the story in particular is that, like *Measure for Measure*, they culminate in an intervention which is salutary because it undoes local injustice. There are other literary variants too distant to be considered analogues, but related through their portrayal of the victory of unlocalized law. In Calderón's play *El Alcalde de Zalamea*, for example, Philip II of Spain appears in his own person as a *deus ex machina* to settle a dispute between an aristocratic colonel of one of his regiments and the lowborn mayor of a small town whose daughter has been ravished by a regimental officer. In this case, uncharacteristically, the town official takes the side of empire, declaring that the king's justice has to be one and indivisible. Philip (who was, of course, yet another Hapsburg, cousin of the Holy Roman emperor and ruler of a New World empire in his own right) settles the dispute in favor of the mayor, the advocate of "unlocalized" law, and against the privileges of the aristocrat.[40] What all the fictional versions of the encounter have in common is a conflict to some degree created but also resolved through a process of bureaucratic centralization and its imperative for legal reform. The tale seems to have sprung into existence in many different places at once—wherever a strong monarchy or imperial state was being transformed by what historians call "the Reception of Roman Law."[41]

In *Measure for Measure*, the first mention of Vienna does not come until Escalus's response to the duke's long expository speech at the beginning of the play. "*Esc*. If any in *Vienna* be of worth / To vndergoe such ample grace, and honour, / It is Lord *Angelo*" (TLN 25–27). For contemporary London audiences, that sudden naming of the city may have caused a jolt—all of the duke's previous disquisition on government, with its talk of the "*Cities Institutions*," "the Termes / For Common Iustice," and the formation of the commission of deputies, could easily have been imagined as referring to London, or at least to a less alien theatrical locale than Vienna. In the folio text, for readers of 1623 and after, the name *Vienna* is also withheld before Escalus's seemingly offhanded reference. Unlike *Twelfth Night*, for example, the folio does not use the initial stage directions to communicate the play's locale. They read simply "Enter Duke, Escalus, Lords." In *Measure for Measure* the withholding of place creates an aura of familiarity "within the wall," which is then suddenly shattered when it turns out that "here" is "*Vienna*."

The passage of *Measure for Measure* which associates the play most closely with contemporary Vienna has proved highly problematic for editors. It is clearly topical, but can be understood in diametrically opposite ways, depending on the degree to which an audience conceptualizes cultural distance and enters imaginatively into an alien locale. It occurs in one of the play's opening scenes. Lucio and two other gentlemen are discussing current events:

> Luc. If the *Duke*, with the other Dukes, come not to composition
> with the King of *Hungary*, why then all the Dukes fall vpon
> the King.
> 1. Gent. Heauen grant vs its peace, but not the King of *Hungaries*.
> 2. Gent. Amen.
> Luc. Thou conclud'st like the Sanctimonious Pirat, that went to
> sea with the ten Commandements, but scrap'd one out of the
> Table.
> 2. Gent. Thou shalt not Steale?
> Luc. I, that he raz'd.
> 1. Gent. Why! 'twas a commandement, to command the Captaine and
> all the rest from their functions: they put forth to· steale:
> There's not a Souldier of vs all, that in the thanks-giuing be-
> fore meate, do rallish the petition well, that praies for peace.
> (TLN 97–112)

On grounds that "the King of *Hungaries*" peace was not formally
ratified until 1606, some editors of the play have argued that this interchange must be a later (and irrelevant) topical interpolation into the
1604 text.[42] But that editorial maneuver is yet another evasion of the
unease of topicality. There is no particular internal reason why the passage should be set aside as "not Shakespeare" or not "the Originall."
In fact, the gentlemen's prayer to be saved from "the King of *Hungaries*" peace does not at all require a date of 1606. He intimates that
while peace is in prospect, it is not yet a *fait accompli*. That was the situation in 1604. The king of Hungary was then the emperor Rudolf II. The
duke and the "other Dukes" were all Hapsburg archdukes, all younger
brothers of Rudolf, all rulers of European states under the Holy Roman Empire. Discontented with the unstable Rudolf's administration
of the areas under his direct control, the "Duke and the other Dukes"
banded together to deprive him of effective power, eventually expel-
ling him (since he obstinately refused to "come to composition") from
the thrones of Hungary and Bohemia.[43]

Nor is it necessarily true, as those who suspect the passage have argued, that its business is irrelevant to the subject of the play. A reference to central-European affairs may appear to us too remote from
London to be comprehensible to the English, but in all likelihood,
it was not. Londoners followed events in Hungary and elsewhere under Hapsburg rule with particular avidity and dread because of their
strong feelings of kinship with beleaguered Protestants under Hapsburg domination. Transylvania in particular had a large and eminent
community of Calvinists—the largest under the empire. Sir Philip

Sidney had visited Hungary to help promote the Protestant military cause, and so had many other Englishmen. There was a lively cultural exchange between English and Hungarian Protestants: many books by English Puritan divines were to be found in Hungarian Protestant libraries.[44] In 1604 the king of Hungary was at war both with the Turkish invaders and with the Protestants under his authority. His idea of "peace" with the Protestants meant their complete eradication. Those Hungarians heretical enough to practice the Protestant religion could be punished with death, and many were driven into exile. In England, there were attempts to levy troops and money to aid the Hungarian "brethren."[45] Left-wing Protestant circles received the slightest news from the Continent with almost incredible speed and watched the Hapsburg suppression extremely closely. Once again, in the fleeting reference to the "King of *Hungaries*" peace, we encounter the motif of the loss of local liberties as a result of the inroads of empire, but this time the "liberties" in question are as much religious as secular.

In topical interpretation of the conversation about the duke and the other dukes, everything depends upon place. If Lucio and the two gentlemen are imagined to be speaking as proper Austrians and soldiers under the empire, then their interchange relates more than anything else to a fear of lost employment. So long as there is war in Hungary, they will be assured of military posts: Hungary will keep them from hunger. But the joke about the prayer for peace at mealtimes to some extent brings the interchange back to England by referring to a common form of English grace.[46] If the witty exchange is imagined as though it were taking place in London among Protestants, then its meaning flip-flops completely. For the English, the "King of *Hungaries*" peace meant "pacification" in the sense of religious persecution by fire and sword. Hungarian Protestants could live more freely under the heathen Turks than under zealous enforcers of the Catholic Counter-Reformation like Emperor Rudolf.

Small wonder, perhaps, that the topical passage is easier to elide as "not Shakespeare" than to accept in its chameleon indeterminacy. If the conversation is localized to Vienna, then "peace" means peace. But to the degree that "Vienna" evokes London and the milieu of English Protestantism, "peace" means war, annihilation. Depending on an audience's ability or willingness to extrapolate themselves from their own immediate cultural situation, the witty exchange can be taken topically either as favoring or as opposing the local customary "liberties" by which Hungarian Protestants claimed the right to freedom of worship. The "London" interpretation is more awkward in context than the "Viennese," since it sorts ill with the ensuing jokes about piracy. But the "Viennese" interpretation, from an English Protestant point of view, requires the audience to place themselves imaginatively in a milieu in which their own native values and priorities are turned completely around. To view the duke's activities sympathetically under such conditions of cultural alienation would require an extraordinary leap of disengagement.

If the duke of Vienna could be identified as a Hapsburg, which Hapsburg was he likely to be taken for? The range of possible answers was very different for viewers in 1604 from that for readers in 1623, if only because of the vast changes in the face of Europe in the years in between. According to the First Folio's cast list, the duke of Vienna is named Vincentio. The name does not occur within the play itself and most editors assume that it was supplied at some point after *Measure for Measure* was composed and probably by someone other than Shakespeare. I am inclined to agree that the name sounds like an afterthought, but that does not make it insignificant. It is one of several tantalizing incongruities between the cast list and the play. The addition of the name makes excellent sense in terms of the folio's general tendency to efface "local" meaning, if only because no contemporary Hapsburg duke was named Vincentio.[47] From a twentieth-century point of view, there is no need to hunt down a specific Hapsburg at all. Shakespeare's duke, who holds sway over the seat of imperial government, the hub of the Holy Roman Empire in terms of administrative and legal reform, can easily be taken as a generalized type of the Hapsburg ruler. Yet the project for localization demands that we at least probe into the matter: we must never underestimate either the intrigue or the rewards of contemporary political lock-picking.

There were no fewer than four Hapsburg dukes, all brothers, all sons of Maximilian II, who were active in 1604, and Shakespeare's duke has some affinities with all of them—particularly with Emperor Rudolf. Not coincidentally, Rudolf's most recent biographer in English has also found astonishing similarities in terms of personality and style of government between the emperor and England's James I.[48] The actual "Duke of Vienna" in 1604 was Archduke Matthias, who was about to take over Hungary, Bohemia, and the imperial crown from his elder brother. In terms of telling, detailed parallels and general familiarity to the English, however, there was an even better candidate for identification with Shakespeare's duke: the youngest of the Hapsburg brothers, Archduke Albert, the ruler of the Austrian Netherlands, a figure of much fascination and gossip in the period before 1604.

Archduke Albert had been a key administrator in the Catholic ecclesiastical hierarchy—cardinal of Toledo, chief primate of Spain, and head of the Spanish Inquisition. In 1598, Philip II of Spain had given Albert the Austrian (or Spanish) Netherlands with the understanding that he marry Philip's favorite daughter, the Infanta Isabella, and rule the Netherlands jointly with her. There are episodes of the courtship between Archduke Albert and Isabella which, to anyone inclined to the sport of topical identification, might have seemed remarkably similar to details of *Measure for Measure*. In order to marry, Albert had to defrock himself and give up his "red hat" for "new short rich garments." We may wonder whether Shakespeare's duke, when disguised as a friar, is a Blackfriar, just as Albert had been associated with the Dominican-run Inquisition. In any event, the duke displays a similar agility when it comes to the adoption and casting-off of a religious vocation. The Infanta Isabella, like Isabella in the play, displayed great piety and a strong devotion to the religious life. Even after her marriage to the archduke, she would go on frequent retreats to hermitages where she would subject herself to the most stringent rituals of asceticism. An order she particularly favored was the Poor Clares, which is Isabella's chosen order in the play. Until her wedding to Archduke Albert, she remained in seclusion in a convent, so that his "conquest" of her—a virgin "saved" by marriage from a religious vocation—had some of the quality of the duke's wooing of Isabella in the play. When he died (some years later) Albert had himself buried in the habit of a friar; Isabella was buried in the habit of a Poor Clare.[49]

In England, Albert and Isabella were the subjects of regular gossip, known in common parlance simply as "the Archdukes." The odd, colorful marriage of the ex-cardinal and the would-be nun aroused considerable interest. But familiarity did not necessarily breed affection. James I of England was on cordial terms with all of the Hapsburg archdukes, particularly Albert, but he, as king of Scotland, had never been at war with them. His new English subjects feared the House of Austria with a deep, irrational fear—the same fear they felt for the Spaniards, the Archdukes' close allies, who had repeatedly attempted invasion in the years since 1588. England was formally at war with both Spain and the Austrian Netherlands until 1604. Particularly during the final years of Elizabeth, there had been terrible waves of panic about the coming of the Spaniards and the Archdukes. Spain had sent armadas in 1596 and 1597, but both fleets had been wrecked by storms. There were renewed alarms in 1599. According to one Londoner, "Upon Monday toward evening came newes (yet false) that the Spaniardes were landed in the yle of Wight, which bred such a feare and consternation in this towne as I would litle have looked for, with such a crie of women, chaining of streets and shutting of the gates as though the ennemie had been at Blackewall."⁵⁰ A few weeks earlier there had been terror on the coast "because of a fleet discovered near the shore there, and supposed to be the enemy, though they were but Flemish merchants." In 1601, the Spanish attempted to land in Ireland and enlist local Catholics against the queen. Leaders of the Irish rebellion were known to be in contact with Spain and the Archdukes: in 1596, they had invited Albert to become their sovereign. The discovery of the Bye and Cobham plots in early 1603 convinced many in England that when it came to Hapsburg imperialism, their worst imaginings were justified.⁵¹

It is not only that the duke and Isabella in *Measure for Measure* display suggestive similarities to their Austro-Spanish historical counterparts, however. In the final years of Elizabeth's reign, the Archdukes came up repeatedly in Catholic circles (and elsewhere) as prime candidates for the English throne. The Infanta Isabella was mentioned with particular frequency; she and Elizabeth were often overtly compared (though not always to Isabella's advantage!). Robert Parsons, the English Jesuit, helped "set" the rumors "on foot" in a book advocating the succession: he also prepared a letter to the same effect for presentation to the English Parliament, once it was Catholic again. During the same period, Albert was striving to be elected emperor. If his plans had come to fruition, one of the prospective rulers of England would indeed have been "Duke" of Vienna, married to an Isabell, and England, yet another imperial state. In 1603, the Jesuits spread rumors that the archduke and Isabella had in fact been proclaimed sovereigns of England.⁵²

Measure for Measure was staged in London at a time when such rumors were still fresh and terrifying. In order to do an adequate "local" reading, we need to think ourselves back into a state of mind from which the play—so familiar, even tame, to us—could take on the coloration of a paranoid vision. In 1604, if interpreted "without the wall" in terms of the goals of international Catholicism, *Measure for Measure* could easily be perceived as an enactment of Catholic fantasy, of English Protestant nightmare: a Hapsburg duke marries an Isabella and takes over a Vienna markedly like London—or in the most extreme version of the nightmare, a London whose local identity has been obliterated, a London subsumed under Catholic Vienna, the controlling hub of empire.

Archduke Albert, meanwhile, was making overtures of peace toward England. After years of constant warfare, both his country and Spain were exhausted and financially depleted. But the archduke's talk of concord was widely distrusted. It was rumored (and not without some foundation) that his secret motive in suing for peace was the usual Hapsburg goal of "pacification" and restoring England to Catholicism. In one version of the Hapsburg scenario, peace with England was "the true road to the installation there of a prince of the House of Austria, or at least some Catholic prince with the heiress of that kingdom, which would not be a small foundation for maintaining there the good friendship and correspondence between [us] which can never be firm and durable between princes of contrary religion." In 1602, there was word of a plot between the archduke and English Catholics to take the coastal towns in England through "sudden spoil"; according to another source, "They say in Douay college that all priests made in English seminaries beyond seas are sworn by a Jesuit, before their coming into England, to be true to the Archduke and Infanta." The news during those years was full of the "desperate" men dispatched by the archduke as secret intelligencers, the Friars Minor he used as deputies and delegates, and the almost preternatural detail in which such agents had spied out conditions in England.[53] In such an atmosphere of cloak and dagger rumormongering, the strongly Catholic environment of Shakespeare's "Vienna" could not be a matter of indifference: the duke's secret machinations, his crafty methods of "intelligence" giving him a seemingly uncanny grasp of secret events, his use of friars as messengers—all of these tactics, if one shared the political nervousness of the time, could seem eerie echoes of the strategies of the Archdukes.

In the event, English fears about the Archdukes proved unjustified. Unlike some of his brothers, Albert was willing to consider religious toleration within his dominions. He suppressed the ancient "liberties" of the States General, and stood, like James I, upon Roman law and equity in preference to local ordinance, but he allowed the towns to keep some of their traditional privileges. Yet he scarcely looked like a moderate in his conduct of the long siege of Protestant Ostend. In one of the public ceremonies of which the Archdukes were fond, Isabella had been presented with "an image of Flandria [Flanders], richly set out, and in its foot a thorn, signifying Ostend, which she promised to pull out."[54] While Londoners feverishly sent money to aid Ostend and English troops joined the effort to lift the siege—at least three thousand from London in 1601 and 1602 alone—the Archdukes relentlessly battered the Protestant enclave, finally bringing Ostend to capitulation in 1604. After the victory Albert and Isabella entered Ostend in solemn procession to reestablish "true religion" there but found, to their chagrin, that nothing was left but ruins and burning rubble—a "new Troy."[55] From across the Channel, the devastation of free Protestant Ostend seemed yet another sinister example of Hapsburg "pacification"—the same fate the English themselves were likely to suffer if the direst rumors came true and the Hapsburgs came over to rule.

By 1604, of course, James I had safely ascended the throne, to all outward signs a staunch Protestant. But the Archdukes hoped he would soon declare himself a Catholic. From Holyrood Palace before he had even left for England he had written his "cousin" Albert that nothing was closer to his heart than renewing England's ancient friendship with the House of Austria. One of his first acts as king of England was to proclaim an end to hostilities against Spain and the Netherlands. He initially showed signs of leniency toward the English Catholics and, in a celebrated speech before Parliament, acknowledged the "Romane Church to be our Mother Church, although defiled with some infirmities and corruptions." Isabella wrote hopefully to the duke of Lerma, "Every day there are greater hopes that he will be a Catholic."[56] Her hope was English Protestants' fear.

From the perspective of English paranoia in 1603–4—if paranoia is indeed the correct term for perceptions which had some basis in reality—the similarities between Shakespeare's duke and James I in *Measure for Measure* take on a profoundly disquieting dimension. They intimate a doubling between Stuart and Hapsburg in which the distinction between the two modes of empire becomes blurred, perhaps extinguished. Imperial meaning, like empire itself, obliterates boundaries and separations between disparate areas of signification. In *Measure for Measure*, the play's topicality "without the wall" is also "without walls" in that it tends, like the imperial mythos itself, to invade and transform the merely local.

If James I is comparable to a "Duke" of the House of Austria, his dream of empire like theirs, his efforts to import Roman forms and practices (whether he realized it or not) part of the grand plan of Counter-Reformation imperialism, then the legal reform celebrated in *Measure for Measure* becomes a mode of Hapsburg "pacification." In the Austrian Netherlands, Albert and Isabella had pursued massive works of Baroque piety, building monasteries and convents, supporting the Jesuits, collecting and displaying relics, conducting lavish public ceremonials like the Veneration of the Virgin of Brabant to buttress the Catholic faith. To many in England, some of James's "innovations" seemed to be leading the kingdom in precisely the same superstitious direction. Within the context of such contemporary anxieties, Shakespeare's duke of Vienna becomes a mediating presence between Stuart and Hapsburg that allows imperial meaning to flow in and contaminate the play's "local" London topicality. By relocating English ecclesiastical practices within a space dominated by the Counter-Reformation and empire, the duke reinforces the homology between English and Roman Catholic usage. The effect is to confirm the basic identity which made such "relics of popery" suspect to many Protestants.

For instance, at the Hampton Court Conference and elsewhere, opponents of the English church courts likened their methods to the infamous Spanish Inquisition (and the two systems did in fact follow similar Roman procedure). The duke of Vienna, with his friar's garb, his fidelity to elements of ecclesiastical court procedure, his likeness both to James I of England and to a former Grand Inquisitor of Spain, embodies in his person the connection which Protestants so frequently made—he melds English usage back into its Roman Catholic simulacrum. Or to take another example, Protestant reformers and English parliamentarians objected to the growing tolerance for marriage licenses within the English church on grounds that they were revivals of the old, corrupt system of papal indulgences. In Latin documents of the Church of England, the term *license* was sometimes translated *indulgentia*—a reminder of the historical origins of ecclesiastical licensing. The duke's "licensing" of the play's various marriages in the markedly Catholic environment of Vienna reinforces the link between Anglican and Catholic "indulgence" in a way that would have been profoundly alienating for large segments of a London Protestant audience.[57] The topical *Measure for Measure* equivocates between different imperial modes. Is James's empire a purely British phenomenon, or a mere outpost of an empire centered elsewhere? Critics of the project for Great Britain likened its engulfment of national identities to the Hapsburg takeover of the Netherlands under Albert and Isabella.[58] In conceptual or practical political terms, could there be more than one empire? All it would take to activate the alternate "paranoid" interpretation of *Measure for Measure* and its victory for unlocalized law would be sufficient fear of an as yet uncertain future for England under a monarch not yet well known.

In terms of diplomatic issues "without the wall," the most important event in London, 1604, was surely James I's peace with Spain and the Archdukes, signed after several months of negotiations as the Treaty of London, officially dated August 19, 1604. During the negotiations, the city was filled with the pomp of the comings and goings of the foreign diplomats and their delegations, but also with open sentiment against the impending peace. Pamphlets and tracts circulating in manuscript argued that if it were concluded, England's Dutch Protestant allies in the free states north of the Austrian Netherlands would be isolated and easily overrun, deprived of their "states and liberties" by the Archdukes and Spanish "tyranny." The House of Commons voiced similar concern over the "rights and privileges" of the Dutch. But a deeper fear was for themselves: unless James moved to crush Spain altogether, there would be no end to the possibility that England could be overrun by the "most dangerous country in Christendom": for Spain "has always desired the . . . conquest of England and will use religion to stir up sedition" as she had in the past.[59] During the negotiations, London was atremble with "suspicions of small moment." According to one account, the Spanish ambassador was mobbed by hostile citizens. "Strange reports" circulated through the city about the gigantic bribes being spread among potentially friendly courtiers by the Archdukes and the Spaniards.[60] But the massive public suspicion did not prevent the conclusion of the peace.

Formal ratification of the Treaty of London was turned into a colorful public pageant. The Commissioners for Peace were escorted by fifty English gentlemen to Whitehall, where James I and Prince

Henry's oaths to preserve the peace were publicly read out. A celebratory banquet occupied the whole afternoon. As crowds of curious
onlookers watched, the king and queen exchanged elaborate toasts
and gifts with the chief negotiators: James gave the Spanish constable a
"fine" ring "for the marriage of peace," and priceless gold and enamel
pieces out of the royal treasure. In the middle of the banquet, the peace
was "solemnly proclaimed" with "sound of Trumpet." At the same
moment, the peace was also formally proclaimed "at Court Gate and
through the City" by royal heralds, the sheriff of London in scarlet
robes, honor guards of horsemen, and trumpeters. According to the
official proclamation, the English were "from henceforth to accompt
all Subjects of the said Kinge of Spaine and Archdukes of Austria
Dukes of Burgundy to bee our friends and allyes and so to use them as
they will answer the contrary at their perills." Later on at Whitehall,
there was dancing and bearbaiting with hordes of spectators looking on.[61]

Public response was disappointing. There was little of the euphoria
that James and the negotiators expected to mark the cessation of such
long and bitter hostilities. In London, only the Spanish ambassador
reported that the English received the proclamation "with great joy."
Perhaps he was treated to a specially staged demonstration; from other
quarters, the news was less positive. The French ambassador reported
that, contrary to the usual custom, there were no bonfires in London
or cannon salutes at the Tower in honor of the peace. Both he and officials of the court of James I noted that "the people did not seem
pleased." Additional evidence of the sullen recalcitrance of James's subjects is provided by a proclamation of the next year (1605), ordering the
English to desist from continuing hostilities toward the Hapsburg
powers and follow his majesty's own example: "imbrace and cherish"
a "perfect amitie and friendship" toward their "good brethren" of
Spain and Austria. But such appeals had little effect; even years later,
the peace was still remembered in anti-Stuart circles as "dishonorable"
to England, advantageous for the Hapsburgs.[62] In its lackluster response to the treaty with Spain and the Archdukes, the city was again
playing the silent "virgin" bride—mutely accepting a union it was
powerless to forestall.

It is possible, of course, to generate a "King James Version" of *Measure for Measure* in which the play becomes a propaganda piece for the
Treaty of London. To the extent that the duke of Vienna is identified

as a Hapsburg ruler, yet perceived as wise and compassionate—a model of virtuous government according to the principles of James I himself—the play can be taken as an eloquent attempt to defuse contemporary hostilities. Such an "official" *Measure for Measure* would have carried particular force in the court performance on St. Stephen's Day, December 26, 1604—another performance, like that of *King Lear* two years later, in which the topicality of the playtext is framed and reconceptualized by its resonance with the liturgical and festival message of the holiday. The St. Stephen's Day *Measure for Measure* would give a particularized political focus to the festival Collect's message of forgiveness for those who have wronged us: "Graunt us, o Lorde, to learne to love our enemies, by thexample of thy Martir sainct Stephen."[63] As St. Stephen forgave his persecutors, as Isabella pardoned Angelo, so the English should achieve concord with their traditional enemies and embark on a new era of amity and cooperation. St. Stephen was, of course, stoned anyway. The liturgical message in this political context carries ominous after-images of national martyrdom. But the hope would be that the treaty would hold on both sides, and that both would learn to "love their enemies."

Within such an interpretive milieu, the play's dangerous equivalences between England and "Vienna" would flip over once again toward the positive, becoming an argument for the abandonment of blind prejudice against the "alien," for the recognition of a vast human territory possessed in common. The official portrait commissioned to commemorate the Treaty of London shows all of the negotiators— English, Austrian, Spanish—sitting about a table as equals (figure 17), all of them sober bureaucrats almost indistinguishable from one another in terms of dress and manner. The dispassionate symmetry of the portrait appears calculated to dampen the distortions created by wartime hysteria. ("Which is the Merchant here and which the Jew?") The English, on the right, are more animated, more individualized, than the negotiators for the Hapsburgs, on the left, who share a uniform demeanor and Hispanic gravity. But the portrait's balance, despite the subtle differences, dissolves adversarial posturing into similarity and common purpose. Its "peacemaking" rhetoric is very much like that of the St. Stephen's Day *Measure for Measure*: the recognition of likeness becomes a prelude to amity.

Within the context of the Treaty of London, whether it was in prospect or just concluded, the play's topical interchange between Lucio

and the two gentlemen can take on yet a third contemporary signification which slides over the reference to internal division among the
Hapsburg "Dukes" or construes the "Dukes" as the Spaniards and the
Archdukes, and applies the prospect of impending peace to the situation of London itself. The gentlemen's protest against a peace with the
empire can be taken as parallel to the protest of martially inclined Londoners in 1603 and 1604 who were being deprived through the cessation of hostilities of their livelihood as soldiers and pirates against
Spain and the Archdukes. James I took great pains to halt English piracy against the nation's new allies, but had a great deal of trouble suppressing it. Pirates against Spain (Sir Walter Ralegh, for example) were
often celebrated as popular heroes in London.[64] Lucio, however, would
be hard to cast in such a role. He starts out well, but by the end of the
play, as he digs himself ever deeper into the pit of his own reckless
scandalmongering, he would be hard even for a contemporary audience to view with particular sympathy. The "Treaty of London" interpretation of the exchange among young blades in "Vienna" reduces
opposition to the peace from a matter of national pride and Protestant
principle to blatant self-interest. The effect, within a "King James Version" of the play, is to undermine the vehement contemporary protests
against the peace as mere fantastical scandalmongering "according to
the trick" like the unprincipled jangling of Lucio.

Thus understood, however, even a topical *Measure for Measure*
which celebrates the Treaty of London still registers contemporary
disquietude over the peace through the complaints of Lucio and the
two gentlemen. Given the climate of contemporary opinion, that
seemingly minor reference could function like a small crack in a
dike—create an access point for a flood of audience sentiment against
the peace. In performance at court, within the euphoria of the successfully concluded negotiations and in an environment to some extent
insulated from the public disgruntlement outside, the slippage might
be negligible. In the London theaters, even for viewers sympathetic to
James and his notions of world pacification, the erosion would be
more damaging. The "paranoid" alternative *Measure for Measure* might
not have existed in most people's perception as a continuous interpretation, but in an environment of profound hostility toward the
peace and the Hapsburgs, it would be difficult to black out altogether.
It might have appeared as an uncanny shadowing or doubling in Sigmund Freud's sense of the *Unheimlich*—that which is familiar rendered

17.   The Somerset House Conference (1604), artist unknown. Photo
courtesy of the National Portrait Gallery, London.

suddenly *other*. It might have appeared, in varying degrees depending
on the strength of a given viewer's political passions, as flickers of a
sudden change in locus like a momentary shift in light by which the
everyday suddenly appears sinister, reordered as some vague shape of
destruction. Local reading of *Measure for Measure* provides a new way
of coming at the idea of the play as a "problem play," with the problem of its uneven tone, its "double written" portrayal of the duke
and Isabella, inextricable from a deep division in the contemporary
audience.

There are other potential localizations of the play. Within the milieu
of the 1604 Treaty of London, it can be read, for example, as a piece of
out-and-out propaganda for the lifting of restrictions against English
Catholics. There were other contemporary plays taking such a stance—
The Noble Spanish Soldier, for example. The Archdukes and the Spaniards expected the peace to lead to an end to English persecution of the

Catholics. To the extent that the play depicts Catholic personages and institutions sympathetically, it can be taken as a plea for not only international but also national accommodation with the popish "enemy." The duke's act of saving Isabella from the convent, which is usually interpreted as a victory for Protestant chastity in marriage over sterile Catholic celibacy, might not have appeared particularly Protestant to contemporaries, given its topical echoes of the marriage of the ultra-Catholic Archdukes. That is not to say that all seventeenth-century Catholics would necessarily have approved of the play. In the 1632 Shakespeare folio possessed by the English College at Valladolid, *Measure for Measure* was the only play torn out, perhaps because in the interim peace had shattered, English Catholics had been subjected to renewed persecutions, and Anglo-Spanish hostilities had resumed.[65] But our emphasis here is on the London *Measure for Measure* of 1604, performed before an audience which was overwhelmingly Protestant and uneasy about Jacobean policy. From the perspective of the city, the benevolent Stuart interpretation was almost by definition "without the wall," an imposition of ideology from the outside which threatened city autonomy and identity. The topical *Measure for Measure* is a play that will not sit still; it both enacts contemporary division and provides a structure within which the fissure has to be perceived, mysteriously, as sameness. We can turn it and turn it as we might a Möbius strip, but never be able to identify the "right" side from the reverse because one leads seamlessly into the other.

Within an environment of hostility and fear, the "royal" version of *Measure for Measure* could have little appeal for Londoners, particularly for those of a strongly Protestant persuasion. What Shakespeare accomplished through the play's restlessly oscillating topicality was the initiation of a theatrical event which could be taken as Stuart propaganda, or as the expression of a contemporary nightmare, or most likely as both together. That portion of the audience blocked off by their preconceived beliefs from the play's line of Stuart moral instruction would not therefore be blocked off from the play; they would have the harrowing, titillating experience of seeing their worst political fantasies spring briefly but powerfully into life.

The play's strange doubling can also be seen as performing another function—one close to the interests of the theatrical company itself. As in the case of *Cymbeline* but to a much more significant degree, the play's potential for Hapsburg interpretation also helps to create an independent locus for the theater. Shakespeare's company, like the others, was dependent in numerous ways on the Jacobean line. Not only did the monarch provide direct patronage, he took over all the theatrical companies as royal monopolies and provided the very royal license—in the same year of 1604—by which the King's Men were exempted through the royal "dispensing power" from local ordinances outlawing theaters, by which they were freed to perform in spite of community opposition.[66] Members of the company had performed in James's coronation pageant—also in 1604. The shelter of royal benevolence was protective, certainly, but not necessarily always comfortable. The acting companies, as much as any other institution which was coming under the universalizing power of empire, were in danger of losing their own proper boundaries, their fragile emerging self-definition as a structure apart. The paranoid version of *Measure for Measure* creates a rift in the "natural" ideological and topographical alliance between the theatricality of the duke, who stages his show trial just outside the city walls, and the similarly situated institution of the London theater, dependent on the indulgence and "equity" of the monarch for its continuing survival. Through the rift, the play is assured of breathing space within its own secure boundaries even as it appears to echo the Jacobean line.

The First Folio provides a list of actors for *Measure for Measure*—one of the few in the volume—but in this case, the list is as puzzling as it is enlightening as to the persons of the play. It doubles characters who can easily be single in performance, names characters who were probably nameless in performance. I would like to make a case for its oddities as traces of the "paranoid" *Measure for Measure*. With the single exception of Pompey, the characters for whom there are major disparities between the language of the playtext and the "names of all the Actors" later on are those associated with institutional Catholicism or empire, or both. The duke is nameless in the playtext but named as Vincentio in the list of personae. The nun who advises Isabella is nameless in the playtext; in the names of the actors and folio stage directions she springs into greater visibility with the Spanish name Francisca. The friar is named Peter in the play's dialogue; through the stage directions and list of actors, he is transformed into "2. Friers"—"Friar Peter" and "Frier Thomas." There is a similar doubling and tripling of the shadowy figures surrounding the duke, except that this time the words of the playtext itself are more informative than the accompanying folio materials. When he is about to make his reentry into Vienna, the duke names several adherents, most of them with Roman names; they are but ciphers in the playtext and do not appear on the list of personae: Flavia, Valencius, Rowland, Crassus, and Varrius. Varrius is the only one of the duke's shadowy "friends" whose mute presence is actually acknowledged on stage; the others may have accompanied the duke in his triumphal reentry of the city, but they remain undefined, ambiguously apart from the action.[67] Given contemporary fears about the ubiquitous unseen presence of imperial agents throughout the kingdom, the duke's sudden naming of allies with suspiciously Roman names might well have vibrated for viewers and early readers of the play with anxieties about the agents of empire who passed unrecognized among them.

All of these disparities in the folio text of the play may be signs of earlier revision. Perhaps some acting versions of *Measure for Measure* were more strongly "imperial" than others. Whatever the origin of the incongruities, they map out a space of indefinition associated with the extent of empire, suggesting unease over the Hapsburg resonances of the play on the part of someone associated with it at some point between performance and publication. Through the inconsistencies between the extra information supplied for folio readers and the actual language of the folio text, the 1623 *Measure for Measure* registers continuing disquietude about the invisibility and silent spread of empire— as capable of sudden, unfathomable metastasis as the imperial characters themselves.

REVISIONS:
CORIOLANUS AND THE EXPANSION
OF CITY LIBERTIES

In *Coriolanus*, a city dominates the stage once more, but this time the city is Rome, a much more familiar locus for English Renaissance audiences than Vienna. On the basis of our experience with *Cymbeline* and *Measure for Measure*, we might expect the Rome of *Coriolanus* to be associated with the "unlocalized" code of Roman law. But the city in this play is not the Rome of empire—it is the Rome of the early republican period, a Rome which is, like early Jacobean London, expanding out to incorporate the suburban areas around it, and is, like Jacobean London, dominated by fierce civic pride and clamor for the preservation of local autonomy. In Parliament and in London, political leaders disgruntled with James's tendencies toward absolutism looked to republican Rome for alternatives to government by royal preroga- tive. For his part, James muttered aloud about the contemporary English "Tribunes" who stirred up sentiment against him. *Coriolanus* is overlaid with a language of civic "liberties and franchises" which does not occur in Shakespeare's sources, but which carries strong topi- cal reverberations with the jurisdictional battles in Shakespeare's Lon- don. In this play—perhaps four years after *Measure for Measure*—local law and privilege win out against the more global and arbitrary claims of absolutism.

The figure of Caius Martius Coriolanus cannot readily be equated with James I or with any other specific contemporary offender against the "freedoms" of London. But he is associated with abuses of local authority like those which the City of London was contesting in the early Stuart period, whether the transgressors against civic ordinance were agents of the king or aristocrats sheltered by the royal dispensing power. In *Coriolanus*, through the person of the arrogant, isolated warrior, royal and aristocratic privilege is symbolically banished from a city whose political divisions make it readily comparable to London. Coriolanus is a figure who would have been far more at home within a climate of empire than in Rome of the Republic. He, like the Tarquins in *Lucrece*, is a violator of civic liberties. And he, like them, is cast off. As a result of his inability to function within the turbulent republican system "within the wall," he is banished "without," turned into a scapegoat whose expulsion both makes possible and bears witness to the expansion of the city and its "liberties."

Coriolanus is yet another of the folio plays which does not exist in an earlier printed version. Like some of the others we have discussed, it is so laden with highly charged topical materials that we may be tempted to speculate it was withheld from earlier publication for that reason alone. The usual date assigned to it is 1608, and the usual basis for the dating is the strong correlation between the grain riots which open the play and the grain rioting that year and the year before in England. In some ways, the civil disorders of the play are closer to the English situation in 1607–8 than to that of the early Roman Republic. According to the standard classical sources, the dearth in Rome had been caused by the peasants' failure, amid the throes of political up- heaval, to plant their crops as usual. In *Coriolanus*, by contrast, the gods made the dearth, or at least a significant part of it. As in the English famine in 1607 and 1608, disastrous weather is to blame, along with hoarding of produce by some institutions and individuals. In the Midlands, where the worst rioting took place, "Levellers" tore down hedges and filled up ditches that enclosed land which had once been held in common. They saw themselves quite clearly as defending their ancient "liberties" against a new breed of aristocratic encroachment. It was a rural version of the familiar London conflict between the city's customary rights and "walled off" enclaves of special privilege— royal, courtly, ecclesiastical—which were surrounded by the city but immune from its jurisdiction.[68]

In London, too, dearth and hoarding were acute problems in the famine of 1608. There was some rioting; the problem of supply was compounded by a longstanding jurisdictional dispute between the London Corporation and officials of the court—particularly the Warders of the Tower of London, where foodstuffs arriving by water were unloaded—over who had the right to collect customs on the cargo and distribute it. The shortages inevitably made the conflict more pressing. In the play, the arrogant Coriolanus incites the hatred of the Roman rioters by insisting that the grain supply be kept out of their hands: they have not done the state sufficient service to "deserue Corne gratis" (TLN 1822). So strongly is he identified with the withholding of food that the citizens assume they have only to do away with him to achieve abundance: "Let vs kill him, and wee'l haue Corne at our own price" (TLN 13–14). Coriolanus's rigid stance recapitulates the attitude of court officials in London who claimed the special privilege of receiving and distributing foodstuffs in violation of the customs of the city. Some Tower officials even took it upon themselves to exact their own private percentage of every cargo unloaded, much to the prejudice of the shipmen, who lost their profit and began taking their produce elsewhere, and of the public, who ended up paying higher prices.[69] In the Rome of *Coriolanus*, as in contemporary London, hunger is rampant, but hunger for civic respect pinches worse: the touchy citizens regard flagrant violation of their local "laws" and customs as a crime almost more heinous than any other.

What the citizens want most is precisely what Coriolanus refuses to give them. If there is any one precipitating cause behind his rejection as consul, it is his inability to act within what the aristocrats scoffingly refer to as the citizens' "rotten Priuilege and Custom" (TLN 882). As

Mark Kishlansky has observed, the portrayal of civic election in the "Rome" of *Coriolanus* has no prototype in the play's classical sources; instead, it accurately replicates the process of English parliamentary selection or of wardmote selection to the London Common Council.[70] In order to be elected consul, Coriolanus can be chosen by acclamation, but must also observe ancient civic ritual, which he would prefer to "o'erleap." He must don the robe of humility, ask individual citizens for their votes according to the "Custome of Requests," and show his wounds to the assembled populace. With poor grace, he manages to perform the "Custome of Requests," but he cannot bring himself to show his wounds. That too is a departure from Shakespeare's classical sources—in Plutarch, Coriolanus shows his wounds.[71] The seemingly minor alteration focuses attention on the aristocrat's contempt for the "rotten," dusty customs of the city. He has been amply advised that "the People must haue their Voyces, / Neyther will they bate one iot of Ceremonie" (TLN 1360–61), but it is precisely the idea of "the People" as possessing a voice and identity apart from his own that he cannot stomach. To show them his wounds would be to grant them a kind of authority over his secret vulnerability, demean him to their level, "vnbuild the Citie" and "lay all flat," bring the "Roofe to the Foundation, / And burie all" (TLN 1908–17). The fastidiously specific procedures which the citizens insist upon in the name of their ancient privileges are, for Coriolanus, both inconsequential and outrageous, an opening into chaos.

Throughout the play, Coriolanus's arrogant assumption that he can freely override the "liberties and franchises" of the city is interpreted by Roman citizens and tribunes in terms of the language of Stuart absolutism. Coriolanus has "resisted laws" and would "winde" himself "into a power tyrannical," "affecting one sole Throne without assistance." The tribunes charge that he "would depopulate the city, & be euery man himself" (TLN 1995). That feared engulfment of identity is very much like the obliteration of autonomy and local meaning associated in London with the menacing claims of empire. At one point during the civic tug of war, a brief riot erupts as the "peoples Magistrates" attempt to arrest Coriolanus but are beaten off by the aristocrats. That conflict closely mimics the undignified skirmishes of the streets of Jacobean London in which local JPs were prevented from making an arrest by royal marshals claiming higher jurisdiction. Finally Coriolanus is expelled as a tyrant and "Enemy to the People" through the same city gates he had earlier entered in triumph. In *Measure for Measure* a public trial earns the duke the right to marry and reclaim his city; in *Coriolanus*, a public trial issues in "divorce" and estrangement, the hero's perpetual banishment "without the wall." Even as the city rejects him, Coriolanus almost comically banishes the city (TLN 2411)—as though its monuments and topography can be uprooted as easily as he.

The charges against Coriolanus are, of course, not altogether justified. The vacillating citizens on their own appear willing to affirm him as consul, but they are inflamed against him by their tribunes, who need to vanquish the contemptuous aristocrat in order to protect their own authority. Coriolanus's monumental narcissism may or may not have specifically imperial ambition behind it (in terms of Roman history, such ambition might have been anachronistic in the early republican period). But his martial specialty, reflected in his honorific surname Coriolanus, is highly threatening to the concept of civic liberties. He excels in the solitary penetration of walled cities—Corioles, Antium. War in the play is a "Ravisher" of cities and he is its phallic agent, daring to penetrate alien walls alone, threatening to invade even his "mother city" Rome in an act which would "treade" on his "Mothers wombe / That brought thee to this world" (TLN 3478–80). As in *Lucrece* and *Measure for Measure*, there is a strong link between political autocracy and sexual conquest. For Coriolanus, the citizens and their quaint claims to authority "within the wall" are incomprehensible, inchoate, achieving definition only insofar as they are dominated with the sword from without.

In interesting ways, *Coriolanus* recasts the emerging Renaissance preoccupation with personal and political authorship. Coriolanus strives to be "author of himself" in much the same way that Renaissance writers—even the Stuart monarch—were beginning to claim authorship as a way of overriding the endless, protean multiplicity of "local" meaning. Coriolanus perceives the people as pieces, scabs, fragments; he is a unity, self-identical, self-contained like a sword. He is frequently associated with the gods; at the height of his fleeting popularity after the victory over Corioles, the nobles bend to him as to "*Ioues* statue" (TLN 1196)—unalterable, impervious, like marble. If he is to earn the consulship, the citizens demand that he participate in a civic pageant of which he is not sole "author." Like England's James I, he is but a reluctant performer—"It is a part that I shall blush in acting"—and finally refuses to participate in a ritual of which he will not be the controlling focus. His preferred form of civic pageantry is the military triumph to the sound of trumpets, centering gloriously upon himself "crown'd with an Oaken Garland, with Captaines and Souldiers, and a Herauld" (TLN 1061–63). He can only relate to the citizens from a Jove-like eminence apart, and cannot imagine a form of civic government which is not an aristocratic hegemony. "When two Authorities are vp, / Neither Supreame; How soone Confusion / May enter 'twixt the gap of Both, and take / The one by th'other" (TLN 1803–6). His formulation is a strong justification for absolutism. Brutus complains, "You speak a'th' people, as if you were a God, / To punish; Not a man, of their Infirmity" (TLN 1773–74). At one point the hero appears to take on a composite identity, like a Stuart monarch: "as if that whatsoeuer God, who leades him, / Were slyly crept into his humane powers" (TLN 1138–39). A god, Jove-like, self-created, partaking of the "sacred body" of kingship—the language surrounding Coriolanus is the language of Stuart power, particularly as refracted through the complaints of contemporaries who found it threateningly excessive.

To view the play's political conflict from the perspective of civic liberties is to gain a somewhat more sympathetic view of the Roman citizens and their leaders than is often brought out in performance. On stage, as in recent critical analysis, the tense balance between the plebeians and the aristocrat can tilt either way, depending on how sympathetically either flawed entity is presented. We need, as usual, to assume that there could have been an almost equal flexibility in Renaissance performance, depending on place and circumstance. One of the play's characters muses that "Our Vertue[s], / Lie in th'interpretation of the time" (TLN 3140–41): there could scarcely be a better epigraph for the nature of topicality itself and its capacity to take on different colorations as a result of even slight adjustments of character and dramatic action. As recent performances have shown, a powerful lead actor can easily move the major locus of the play's conflict away from the political and toward the personal and psychological. To the extent that the tragedy in performance focuses on the plight of Coriolanus alone, his dilemma becomes an entrapment between two ideas of the city: between the volatile Rome of the citizens and the demanding Rome of Volumnia, cruel nurturant. In London, 1608, however, there were special factors that would have moved the play back toward the locus of political conflict which I have suggested here. In that year, in addition to the problems we have already seen recapitulated in the play, there was a landmark victory for the city and its liberties.

The most important circumstance linking *Coriolanus* topically to the year 1608 (or a little before or after) has scarcely surfaced in discussions of the play. In 1608, after much parleying back and forth, James I granted London a new charter which rescinded some of the abuses aired in the play and gave the city increased authority over several of the enclaves within it which had traditionally been exempt from its jurisdiction. The dark scenario of empire was not unfolding in London according to the direst expectations of its citizens in 1603 and 1604. Instead, even as the clashes between rival officials continued, James I was increasingly inclined to make accommodation with the city's franchises and liberties and with the "Tribunes of the People." He acted partly out of increasing recognition of London's sensitivity to the issue, but much more out of a financial embarrassment which the city could do much to repair. The monarch was "hungry" too: many of the parliamentary debates in the period before *Coriolanus* focused on matters of royal supply. Two years later in the Parliament of 1610, Menenius's Parable of the Belly and the Members came up in debate in connection with the matter of royal supply. According to contemporary report, James's "price" for the new London charter was funds to build a new royal banqueting house—again, as in *Coriolanus*, the issue of abundant foodstuffs is balanced against civic respect.[72]

The new London charter gave the city greatly increased jurisdiction over Blackfriars, Whitefriars, West Smithfield, and the precincts of Duke's Place. Perhaps more important, it gave London justices of the peace the right to act in criminal matters without hindrance by other keepers of the peace or royal ministers. No longer, if the charter was observed, would there be the inglorious spectacle in the London streets of local officials trying to make an arrest but finding themselves detained by royal marshals instead. The charter also reaffirmed London's customary control over shipping and unloading of boats on the Thames; in theory at least, the citizens and the London Corporation now had the control of foodstuffs within their own hands. Last but not least, the charter explicitly stated that the liberties it guaranteed to London superseded royal proclamations to the contrary. It was an important victory for the city, an official guarantee of an end to some of the worst inroads by absolutist government against London's precious liberties and franchises.[73]

Samuel Taylor Coleridge once remarked, with reference to *Coriolanus*, on the "wonderful philosophic impartiality in Shakespeare's politics."[74] It is true that the play identifies serious flaws on both sides of the Roman civic conflict. Coriolanus's massive arrogance is balanced off against the vacillation of the Roman citizens, who display little of the steadiness and "civility" they will need if they are to execute the political functions granted them in theory through the election of their own tribunes as well as the military functions they have taken on themselves through their banishment of the warrior. But the play does not end impartially. It is a tragedy for the aristocrat, a victory for the citizens, despite the Volscian forces massed threateningly outside the walls. Coriolanus, who has contemned the citizens as scraps, meaningless pieces, is himself reduced to little more, cut down by multiple stab wounds within the boundaries of an enemy city. Having refused his part in civic pageantry while alive, he is doomed to fulfill it in death: when his body is carried through the streets of Antium, he finally shows his wounds to a group of gazing citizens. As Janet Adelman's keen analysis has pointed out, the isolate Coriolanus does not permit audience sympathy: his very nature "insists that we keep our distance." The play "separates and limits" rather than permitting resolution and reconciliation.[75] In that sense, *Coriolanus* effects a more complete "divorce" between the city and the aristocracy than that worked in contemporary London, where the bargain struck between monarch and city over the new 1608 charter preserved a measure of reciprocity. In the play, the conflict is implacable, cast in extreme form. The Enemy of the People has been destroyed; Rome has been made militarily vulnerable as a result; but her precious "liberties and franchises" remain intact and the cornerstone of her future greatness has been laid. For republican Rome, as for its enemy Aufidius, the death of Coriolanus becomes a source of new invigoration: "Therefore shall he dye, / And Ile renew me in his fall" (TLN 3703–4).

In critical analysis or performance of *Coriolanus*, it is easy enough to take sides for or against the aristocrat. From the perspective of localization, however, what the play *does* is more important: it enacts a civic victory like the expansion of London authority; it does so by casting out a symbolic representative of the artificial constraints imposed on the city from above. Coriolanus is a direct threat to city liberties, but also an externalization of the self-contempt and collective self-disparagement which would keep the city down, perhaps even diminish its capacity for local pride and identity by encouraging the inroads of imperial ideology and making the citizens "of no more Voyce / Then Dogges" (TLN 1618–19). The 1608 *Coriolanus* invites Londoners to don a robe of humility of their own and wear it more productively than Coriolanus—see their own weaknesses as a group reflected in their Roman counterparts so that they can cast off their unsettled, fragmented factionalism and prepare themselves for increased political autonomy. In a sense, the citizens are invited to assume as part of their new "Authoritie" a new sense of "authorship" over their collective political actions. What will thereby be created is, of course, an urban entity which moves toward an imperialist potential of its own— toward the vision of Dryden's *Annus Mirabilis* a half century later, in which the city itself becomes empress, glorious, conquering Imperia. But that is another story. What concerns us here is the earlier stage which is delineated in *Coriolanus*: the city casts off a privilege that overrides its own, an "unlocalized" law by which civic identity is eroded. *Coriolanus* turns *Measure for Measure* on its head.

The play can also be seen as creating a space for itself—for the genre of Jacobean tragedy—out of the expulsion of the aristocrat from the city. Coriolanus has refused his part in civic pageantry "within the wall." As a result of his contempt for the "liberties" and "charters" of Rome and its "violent, testy magistrates," he is banished without—to the place of the London stage, just outside the city's jurisdiction. Thereafter, the language he uses in describing his predicament becomes increasingly theatrical. As he tells his wife and mother from outside the gates of Rome, "Like a dull Actor now, I haue forgot my part, / And I am out, euen to a full Disgrace" (TLN 3390–91). He is condemned to "act" in his own tragedy in the "place of the stage" outside the city, since he will not conform to the demands of "custom" within it. We may be reminded of the fact that in ancient Athens the word *hubris* could refer either to overbearing pride or to an offense against the city deemed punishable by death.[76] The arrogant power and prerogative voided from the city convert to dramatic representation outside it: the play offers a recipe for the creation of Jacobean tragedy. Perhaps it is not mere happenstance that in the First Folio, *Coriolanus* is listed first among the tragedies. It marks out a "local" space for the others, displaying a mechanism by which the menace of aristocracy in London is transformed into a safer mode of enactment outside it. Many Londoners feared the theater for its associations with arbitrary rule, its flouting of local ordinances and liberties. In *Coriolanus*, the enactment of tragedy—the self-imposed fall of a noble general—does not so much flout the laws and customs of the city as display their increasing power.

Epilogue

In 1793 Edmund Malone had the Stratford bust of Shakespeare white-washed, and so it remained until 1861.[1] He found its garish painted colors offensive in a funerary monument, particularly one dedicated to the Bard, and suspected that they had been added in the course of an earlier restoration. His gesture is a fitting enough representation of the denial of Shakespearean topicality. Whitewashing moves the author of the sacred texts in the direction of enduring marble—serene, aloof detachment from the turbulent flow of time and particulars, a seeming permanence like that of the monuments of antiquity. Malone did not know that some of the ancient statuary which seemed so admirable in its pale, impassive whiteness had once been brightly painted—rather like the bust of Shakespeare.

It is easy enough to ridicule Malone's drastic attempt to eradicate the traits which made the Stratford bust of Shakespeare unacceptably "local"—more the visage of a plump provincial burgher than a figure for Art Itself. But what needs to be examined at this point is the congruence between Malone's enterprise and our own. The project for localization sets itself resolutely against the general and the universal, but has its own ways of creating generalities, leaping over difference in order to construct an alternative order of "essences" out of the materials of history. In poststructuralist criticism, there usually comes a moment in which the critic stops to acknowledge a silent complicity in the universe of certainties which it is his or her overt effort to unsettle. That universe, or pieces of it, continue to exist "under erasure" as the defining ground against which the critic's strategies are directed but by which they are also constituted. Poststructuralist iconoclasm preserves the icon, if only as a continuing ground for its own energies of defacement and dispersal.

In the project for localization, the basic problem is the same but figure and ground are as often as not reversed. What is obvious on the surface of critical discussion is frequently a series of seemingly lucid syntheses, narrative and argumentative structures built up out of historical and textual data. To outward appearances it is an admirably positivist exercise—except for anyone who would, as we would, deny the epistemological bases of positivism. Localization depends on an odd breed of temporary, provisional positivism: we have to have enough confidence in our historical data to be able to perceive homologies and differences between the texts we are working with and other social formations; we have to get our texts to coalesce into identifiable patterns long enough to allow us to sort out their idiosyncratic ways of creating meaning. The surface of our critical discourse is for that reason sometimes deceptively orderly. What lies "under erasure" but can never be evaded entirely is the endless flux of history itself, the unbridgeable terrains of unknowing that mock our attempts at interpretation building even as we make them. Paul Ricoeur has talked of the "*risk* of interpretation."[2] That risk is more obvious in "local" reading than in many other critical approaches because the project is so massively and obviously dependent on meanings which are fleeting, elusive even in the recovery.

The most striking area in which the present study has whitewashed its own raucous colors is in the matter of the Shakespearean texts themselves. In every case, we proceed as though we *have* texts which are sufficiently identified with the time of early performance to allow us to construct strong and telling local readings. Yet, for Shakespeare at least, our texts are all at considerable distance from the milieu of dramatic production—both in terms of time and in terms of their static fixity as printed documents. Like a whitewashed monument, they are only pale replicas of the color, motion, and variability of performance. Interpretation under such conditions of temporal distance and textual uncertainty is a dancing upon air, and quite self-consciously so. We have to use the early texts we have, since they are all we have; we have to recognize that they can never yield us the reassuring, rock-ribbed certainties that are sometimes sought through historical investigation.

Another whitewash—or at least inevitable flattening of contrast—comes from the fact that we depend so closely on texts to begin with. Localization would be far more telling if it could be performed instead of written (and occasionally, it has been)—performed before a twentieth-century audience somehow already magically cognizant of some of the major preoccupations circulating within the play's early historical milieu. An approximation of the effect has been achieved through the seeking-out in modern performance of twentieth-century motifs which can capture some of the immediacy and shock value of their Renaissance equivalents. But there will almost inevitably be a falsification about such attempts (unless, perhaps, they are produced during periods of unusual intensity like wartime), simply because late twentieth-century culture is so much more compartmentalized than Renaissance culture was. For us the "political," the realm of public events, appears a realm apart, a realm we can look on with a measure of detachment because it seems to be separable from ourselves. In the Renaissance, as I have argued, such a segmentation of worlds did not exist. What we would call the political was inextricable from other aspects of life, a realm people could not imagine themselves living apart from any more than they could stop breathing the air.

As a mode of written criticism, localization requires an enormous amount of detailed historical narration in order to give us anything approaching the immersion in Renaissance events and information which contemporaries would have had almost automatically. But the very process of historical reconstruction inevitably throws us back into the musty world of scholarship—back into another realm apart, the ivory tower of learning we were trying to escape to begin with. The very discursivity required by our efforts to familiarize ourselves with a distant culture creates an overlay of order and predictability about local reading—first this happened, then this, then this; something can mean this, or this, or this. That overlay radically alters the spotty, intermittent, multilayered ways in which topical meaning was likely to be registered by contemporaries. Like King James I, we find ourselves striving to "make sense" in traditional discursive terms even when we seek to depart from traditional modes of interpretation. I have identified techniques by which certain playtexts invite a linear style of interpretation which is akin to our own expository methods— in part, like *Cymbeline*, by insisting on their own "authored" textuality, in part, like *Measure for Measure*, through the repetition of culturally commonplace patterns. But we need to be careful not to mistake a linear interpretive style for the whole of local reading, or to confuse our own narrativizing and argumentative ordering of topical materials with topical interpretation as it might have unfolded during a Renaissance performance.

The two-pronged nature of my method throughout the present

study makes that confusion particularly likely. On the one hand, I argue for the variability and indeterminacy of Shakespearean topicality in order to account for its scruffy, low-life reputation among traditional critics, who have gone out of their way to avoid it. On the other hand, I make a case for what is seemingly ephemeral and throwaway as a contact point with broader themes and structures unrecoverable by more conventional methods of interpretation. Topical reading allows us to enter into alien areas of signification, which quickly spread beyond the fleeting contemporary reference to create a new field for interpretation. The field is not new in the sense that it has never before existed, but it is new in the sense that it has regularly been closed off in favor of more general, less "parochial" systems for organizing meaning. The project for localization is always a balancing act between the collection of details which build toward a single structure and the identification of mechanisms for deconstruction and dispersal. The two sides of the method are always pulling against each other, competing for dominance within a discursive space which can only entertain one at a time. What needs to be recognized at any given point is that the other "half" of the method is always lurking in the shadows, waiting to emerge into dominance itself.

The present study emphasizes collection over dispersal. I have chosen that emphasis in part because it goes against the grain of much recent critical work: dispersal is easy for us; collection is more difficult. We generally find the scattering of previously encoded meaning more congenial and exhilarating than the painstaking process of gathering up meaning afresh, only to see it fragmented and scattered in its turn. But my emphasis on collection as opposed to dispersal is also designed to induce a greater capacity for critical empathy with a time—the late Renaissance—in which the activity of gathering and building meaning, of drawing seemingly disparate materials into unified patterns, was emerging for many would-be authors as a more fascinating pursuit than dispersal. Postmodernist readings of Renaissance texts regularly interpret incipient efforts to build up stable meaning as attempts, instead, to dismantle it. Both kinds of activity existed in the Renaissance and much can be gained by distinguishing one from the other. In either case, however, what we are likely to be dealing with in topical interpretation is not fully articulated meanings but patches and glimmers of meaning that cause a play to gravitate toward some areas of signification and cultural functioning rather than others.

To do local reading is inevitably to generalize and to universalize—but only up to a point. It is to choose, from among the flood of possible meanings, those which seem most likely to have been accessible to the widest contemporary audience. It is to assume, along with the recognition of vast cultural difference, that we have enough common ground with Renaissance audiences to be able to recover meanings at all. Such recovery is always suspect. Given the exigencies of critical discourse in our time, we will choose what is fresh and startling over what has been aired before. We will also choose what is politically and aesthetically congenial to us—if only because of its capacity to induce a liberating alienation from past interpretive closure. We are always limited by what we can imagine and construct, by the range of cultural materials we have been able to dig up. Even as we stretch ourselves toward the apprehension of difference, we can speculate about what has escaped us, the things which are too culturally other or too deeply buried for us to gain access to at all. Our "recovery" of the past is always interpretation and self-interpretation, but it is not less significant for that.

There is a more specific bias built into the project for localization—that is, quite obviously, a bias toward the local as opposed to the more general. I have argued that in the Renaissance, a preference for "local" place and local meaning tended to correlate with resistance to various forms of political and cultural totalization. If that correlation holds, then local reading will almost inevitably gravitate toward antitotalizing interpretations. I have tried to suggest that the degree to which such bias appears "licensed" is quite variable from one playtext to another. But given the parameters of our specific critical enterprise, the bias toward the local will always be there for us to find and triumphantly identify—it is built into the mode of inquiry. I have sought to counterbalance it by offering, from time to time, local readings which are also profoundly totalizing—as in the 1608 Whitehall *King Lear*. More often, I have happily submitted to the bent of the enterprise and shied away from broad statements in favor of fragments and specificities—particularly when it comes to the definition of the jumbled, fascinating puzzle we call Shakespeare.

A reflective epilogue like this one might appear the proper place for redressing such an atomizing method, for drawing large conclusions and tying together disparate threads of the argument. Yet I find myself resisting such rituals of closure. I would rather leave the set of functions we call "Shakespeare" open and end the present investigation with the emphasis remaining on the variability of the Shakespeares we have constructed rather than on the points of contact among them. Certain motifs have surfaced more than once during the discussion—motifs like theatrical scapegoating, the marginalization of the woman ruler, the attractions and perils of empire, of political hegemony, of linear systems of signification, the rise of "authorship" and of resistance to it. But these motifs have come to prominence through the topical reading of only a handful of plays, and those plays seem as often to jostle and negate each other as to accumulate toward larger synthesis. The Shakespeare we have identified is more segmented than unified, discontinuous not only through time but even within a given cross-section of it. To recognize that, we need only consider that plays as mutually self-canceling in terms of "local" meaning as *Cymbeline* and *Coriolanus* very likely date from the same year.

No endeavor which depends on historical data can deny the existence of a man—actor, poet, we think, playwright—called Shakespeare. Insofar as we have attempted to define the shadowy historical person behind the giant name, we have identified a playwright who used topicality not to limit, select, and shape his audiences in ideological terms but to disperse ideology prismatically so that his plays—at least the ones we have been able to examine—would take on different colorations in different settings and times. To a marked degree, the playtexts themselves resist self-identity, shake out, each of them, into a kaleidoscope of related but discrete entities. Insofar as we want to define "Shakespeare" what we find is a similar bewildering, spectacular array—an evasion of the linear even in the act of generating it, a set of diverse engines for producing multiplicity even amid the gathering of likenesses. To describe "Shakespeare" thus is, of course, to give ourselves the Shakespeare we want. Yet even here, I detect an odd motion back to the idea of Shakespeare as in some sense Universal. Generating a plenitude of particulars is not the same as appealing to a realm of ultimate truths, yet there may be important ways in which the two activities are functionally similar. The peculiar agility with a plenitude of local meanings which we have labeled "Shakespeare" begins edging back toward the Universal as soon as we step back from local reading and begin to assemble a given play's various texts and potential interpretations together as parts of a single entity. For a while longer now, we need to keep our various "Shakespeares" apart. The

Shakespeare we want is not a man, a set of describable data, but an "ongoing cultural activity" or set of related, often competing, activities which need to remain open in order to retain their vitality.[3] When local reading begins to move toward closure and codification rather than the generation of new meanings and functions, it will be time to abandon it and move on to something else.

Notes

1. The complaints are cited from M. H. Spielmann's discussion in *The Title-Page of the First Folio of Shakespeare's Plays* (London: Oxford Univ. Press, 1924), 26–32; and W. W. Greg, *The Shakespeare First Folio: Its Bibliographical and Textual History* (Oxford: Clarendon Press, 1955), 451. Blake's reaction is discussed in Spielmann, 51. My discussion of the title page is strongly indebted to Greg, 449–55.

2. William Prynne, *Histrio-Mastix* (London, 1633), unpaginated preface "To the Christian Reader," marginal note. Jaggard himself had numerous Puritan connections, but also produced playbills and books with more polished title pages. For examples of his more elaborate work, see Edwin Eliott Willoughby, *A Printer of Shakespeare: The Life and Times of William Jaggard* (1934; reprinted New York: Haskell House, 1970).

3. For the analysis of title pages here in the text and in the notes accompanying the illustrations, I am indebted to Margery Corbett and Ronald Lightbown, *The Comely Frontispiece: The Emblematic Title-Page in England 1550–1660* (London: Routledge & Kegan Paul, 1979). For Samuel Daniel's title page, see also the explication in Laurence Michel's edition, *The Civil Wars* (New Haven: Yale Univ. Press, 1958), 339–41n.

My discussion will also display a strong debt to Michel Foucault, "What Is an Author?" trans. Josué V. Harari, in *Textual Strategies: Perspectives in Post-Structuralist Criticism*, ed. Harari (Ithaca: Cornell Univ. Press, 1979), 141–60.

4. Cited from the Norton facsimile edition of *The First Folio of Shakespeare*, ed. Charlton Hinman (New York: W. W. Norton, 1968), A2r; citations from this edition will hereafter appear in the text. I have kept folio spellings but have silently expanded contractions and changed stage directions from italics to roman when quoted in isolation. References to the texts of the plays as opposed to the front matter are indicated by "through line number" (TLN) in my text.

5. See Roy Strong, *The English Renaissance Miniature* (Ashton-under-Lyne, Lancashire, and Tokyo: Thames & Hudson, 1983), 10; his *Tudor and Jacobean Portraits* (London: Her Majesty's Stationery Office, 1969), 1:283; and Arthur M. Hind, *Engraving in England in the Sixteenth and Seventeenth Centuries: A Descriptive Catalogue with Introductions* (Cambridge: Cambridge Univ. Press, 1952–64), 2:354–59. As other Droeshout portrait engravings collected by Hind demonstrate, Droeshout regularly produced work which had a much more finished appearance.

6. See also the Purchas frontispiece (figure 5) in which the portrait of the author is in complicity with the title page's message of *memento mori*. The vol-

ume itself celebrates New World discovery; the title page, which was published shortly before the author's death, undercuts the marvels of voyaging with the image of the New Jerusalem and numerous messages about death, the final resting place of all voyaging. The author holds out for our examination a copy of the Bible open to Psalm 39, a text that emphasizes the vanity of restless human "sojourning." Some memorial volumes had a simple picture of the deceased across from an unadorned title page. See, for example, the Newberry Library copy of the posthumous edition of William Whately's *Prototypes* (London: for G. Edwards, 1640).

7. Spielmann, 2–4 and 52.

8. The portraits from *Herωologia Anglica* are reproduced in Hind, beginning on p. 145. For Pembroke, see in particular Margot Heinemann, *Puritanism and Theatre: Thomas Middleton and Opposition Drama under the Early Stuarts* (Cambridge: Cambridge Univ. Press, 1980), 162–67.

9. See Greg's discussion, 17–26.

10. See Greg, 449–50. In my discussion, I have followed Greg's hypothetical numbering of unnumbered pages.

11. See J. L. Nevinson, "Shakespeare's Dress in His Portraits," *Shakespeare Quarterly* 18 (1967): 101–6; Ann Jennalie Cook, *The Privileged Playgoers of Shakespeare's London, 1576–1642* (Princeton: Princeton Univ. Press, 1981), 40–43, 121–23; and for the volume's elevation of the dramatist and player, G. E. Bentley, *The Professions of Dramatist and Player in Shakespeare's Time, 1590–1642*, one-volume paperback edition (1971 and 1984; reprinted Princeton: Princeton Univ. Press, 1986), *Dramatist*, 38–61, and *Player*, 18 and 46–47. As Laura Caroline Stevenson has pointed out, however, neither "Mr." nor "gentle" was used exclusively of gentlemen, although both did imply respect. See her *Praise and Paradox: Merchants and Craftsmen in Elizabethan Popular Literature* (Cambridge: Cambridge Univ. Press, 1984), 84–86 and chap. 9, "The Gentle Craftsman in Arcadia," 180–213.

12. These and subsequent citations from the quartos are from *Shakespeare's Plays in Quarto*, ed. Michael J. B. Allen and Kenneth Muir (Berkeley: Univ. of California Press, 1981).

13. Bentley, *Dramatist*, 52–61; I am also indebted to Leonard Tennenhouse, *Power on Display: The Politics of Shakespeare's Genres* (New York: Methuen, 1986), 4–13.

14. These examples as well as many from the ensuing discussion are taken from the invaluable survey in the Introduction to David Bevington, *Tudor Drama and Politics: A Critical Approach to Topical Meaning* (Cambridge, Mass.: Harvard Univ. Press, 1968), 1–26, and from p. 106. There are many other specific examples in Marie Axton, *The Queen's Two Bodies: Drama and the Elizabethan Succession* (London: Royal Historical Society, 1977).

15. See Bevington, 10–13; Annabel Patterson, *Censorship and Interpretation: The Conditions of Writing and Reading in Early Modern England* (Madison: Univ. of Wisconsin Press, 1984), 44–48; Stephen Greenblatt's introduction to *The Power of Forms in the English Renaissance*, ed. Greenblatt (Norman, Okla.: Pilgrim Books, 1982), 3; and Lacey Baldwin Smith, *Treason in Tudor England: Politics and Paranoia* (Princeton: Princeton Univ. Press, 1986), 261–69 and 315n. Smith sees the Renaissance passion for political decoding as linked to a paranoid personality structure created by modes of early education. He offers persuasive evidence on the passion itself, but I would question whether a trait which is culturally accepted and even normative should be labeled in a way that implies deviance.

16. Bevington, 7; Virginia Crocheron Gildersleeve, *Government Regulation of the Elizabethan Drama* (1908; reprinted New York: Burt Franklin, 1961), 19, 108.

17. In *Censorship and Interpretation*, Annabel Patterson has argued that there were implicit agreements between writers and the authorities over how topical meanings could be insinuated without the presumption of sedition. Although I am indebted to her discussion, I see the interpretive situation in the Renaissance as far less orderly than she does. See also Philip J. Finkelpearl, "'The Comedians' Liberty': Censorship of the Jacobean Stage Reconsidered," *English Literary Renaissance* 16 (1986): 123–38.

For the point about dreams and psychoanalysis, I am indebted to Robert J. Leider, M.D., personal communication, Nov. 16, 1975.

18. Foucault, "What Is an Author?" 148; Patterson, *Censorship and Interpretation*, 26, 48; and the discussions of the Essex affair listed in note 15 above.

19. John M. Wallace, "Examples Are Best Precepts: Readers and Meanings in Seventeenth-Century Poetry," *Critical Inquiry* 1 (1974): 273–90. The complaint is from Jonson, surely one of the seventeenth-century authors least willing to abandon his work to the irresponsibility of audiences. His rage over loss of authority over his texts may be atypical, but it is a register of new authorial expectations that other seventeenth-century writers also had.

20. Nevertheless, as I have argued in *The Politics of Mirth: Jonson, Herrick, Milton, Marvell, and the Defense of Old Holiday Pastimes* (Chicago: Univ. of Chicago Press, 1986), topical readings were regularly built into masques and poems. The fact that authors were reluctant to explicate or even acknowledge their own highly topical "arguments" has made such things easy for us to overlook or dismiss as inconsequential.

21. Wallace, "Examples Are Best Precepts," 277–85.

22. As later sections of the argument will make clear, I am using the term *humanist* in order to engage with recent attacks upon it, particularly those launched by British cultural materialists. See Jonathan Dollimore, *Radical Tragedy: Religion, Ideology and Power in the Drama of Shakespeare and His Contemporaries* (Chicago: Univ. of Chicago Press, 1984), 153–81; Dollimore and Alan Sinfield, eds., *Political Shakespeare: New Essays in Cultural Materialism* (Ithaca: Cornell Univ. Press, 1985); and John Drakakis, ed., *Alternative Shakespeares* (London: Methuen, 1985).

23. For this point I am indebted to Richard Helgerson, personal communication, Oct. 18, 1986.

24. This summary of recent shifts is indebted to Robert Weimann, "Textual Identity and Relationship: A Metacritical Excursion into History," in *Identity of the Literary Text*, ed. Mario J. Valdés and Owen Miller (Toronto: Univ. of Toronto Press, 1985), 274–93. See, as examples, Dollimore, *Radical Tragedy*, and the recent collections cited in note 22 above.

25. The phrase is borrowed from Dollimore, *Radical Tragedy*, 250–71. The "we" of my discussion does not, however, include only those critics who identify themselves as cultural materialists or new historicists: as David Bevington's enthusiastic reception of Dollimore's book (quoted on the flyleaf) testifies, the critical mainstream is becoming increasingly receptive toward attacks on "essentialist humanism."

26. The point has been sufficiently belabored recently that examples are perhaps superfluous, but see, as one key text, Cleanth Brooks, *The Well Wrought Urn: Studies in the Structure of Poetry* (1947; reprinted London: Dennis Dobson, 1949), 199.

27. Alfred Harbage, "*Love's Labors Lost* and the Early Shakespeare," *Philological Quarterly* 41 (1962): 18–36; the quotation is from p. 23; see also Mary Ellen Lamb, "The Nature of Topicality in 'Love's Labours Lost,'" *Shakespeare Survey* 38 (1985): 49–59.

28. Richard Levin, *New Readings vs. Old Plays: Recent Trends in the Reinterpretation of English Renaissance Drama* (1979; reprinted Chicago: Univ. of Chicago Press, 1982), 167–71, and Appendix, 209–29. For examples of the method, see Lilian Winstanley, *Hamlet and the Scottish Succession* (Cambridge: Cambridge Univ. Press, 1921); and her *Macbeth, King Lear and Contemporary History* (Cambridge: Cambridge Univ. Press, 1922).

29. E. K. Chambers, "The Disintegration of Shakespeare," Annual Shakespeare Lecture, 1924, in *Proceedings of the British Academy 1924–1925* (London: Oxford Univ. Press, [1925]), 89–108.

30. J. Thomas Looney, *"Shakespeare" Identified in Edward de Vere the Seventeenth Earl of Oxford* (1920; reprinted New York: Duell, Sloan & Pearce, 1949), v; see also Looney's letter to *Newsletter: The Shakespeare Fellowship—American Branch* 1, no. 2 (1939): 5.

31. Letter by Louis P. Bénézet, *Newsletter: The Shakespeare Fellowship—American Branch* 1, no. 1 (1939): 2; see also another letter by Thomas Looney in vol. 5, no. 2 (1944), which states explicitly that his *"Shakespeare" Identified* was an effort to keep humanity alive during the First World War.

32. *Newsletter* 1, no. 6 (1940): 9–10; 2, no. 3 (1941): 34–35; 3, no. 1 (1941): 9; Dorothy and Charlton Ogburn, *This Star of England: "William Shakespeare" Man of the Renaissance* (New York: Coward-McCann, 1952), 329–34; Charlton Ogburn, *The Mysterious William Shakespeare: The Myth and the Reality* (New York: Dodd, Mead, 1984); William Plumer Fowler's pamphlet, *Shake-speare's "Phoenix and Turtle"* (Portsmouth, N.H.: Peter E. Randall, 1986); and Fowler, *Shakespeare Revealed in Oxford's Letters* (Portsmouth, N.H.: Peter E. Randall, 1986).

33. See in particular Terence Hawkes's brilliant essay "*Telmah*," in *Shakespeare and the Question of Theory*, ed. Patricia Parker and Geoffrey Hartman (New York: Methuen, 1985), 310–32; Hawkes, *That Shakespeherian Rag: Essays on a Critical Process* (New York: Methuen, 1986); Alan Sinfield's "Introduction: Reproductions, Interventions," the essays in that section by Sinfield, Graham Holderness, and Margot Heinemann, and Raymond Williams's "Afterword" in *Political Shakespeare*, ed. Dollimore and Sinfield, 130–239; Derek Longhurst, "'Not for All Time but for an Age': An Approach to Shakespeare Studies," in *Re-Reading English*, ed. Peter Widdowson (London: Methuen, 1982), 150–63; and Malcolm Evans, *Signifying Nothing: Truth's True Contents in Shakespeare's Text* (Athens: Univ. of Georgia Press, 1986).

34. See Don Wayne, "Power, Politics, and the Shakespearean Text: Recent Criticism in England and the United States," and Walter Cohen, "Political Criticism of Shakespeare," in *Shakespeare Reproduced: The Text in History and Ideology*, ed. Jean E. Howard and Marion F. O'Connor (London: Methuen, 1987); I am grateful to Jean Howard for supplying me with these parts of the volume in manuscript so that I could make use of them here. See also Jean E. Howard, "The New Historicism in Renaissance Studies," *English Literary Renaissance* 16 (1986): 13–43; and Fredric Jameson, *The Political Unconscious: Narrative as a Socially Symbolic Act* (1981; reprinted Ithaca: Cornell Univ. Press, 1985), 54n.

Jameson argues against the idea that American "splinter-group" politics can operate in the same way that, say, French antitotalizing movements do: following his analysis, my attempt to import a model would be a version of the political evasiveness of which American new historicists are frequently accused, yet another example of our displacement of present-day political issues onto texts from the past. On the other hand, it can be argued that those critics who make an unequivocal statement about the placement of their work in terms of contemporary politics sometimes fail to separate their intent from an actual impact which it may be too early to determine. My own view of the politics of localization is closer to that expressed in Michael Ryan, *Marxism and Deconstruction: A Critical Articulation* (Baltimore: Johns Hopkins Univ. Press, 1982), 114–16.

35. See, for example, Clifford Geertz, "Deep Play: Notes on the Balinese Cockfight," *Daedalus* 101 (1972): 1–37 (a special issue of *Daedalus* entitled "Myth, Symbol, and Culture"); Geertz, *Negara: The Theatre State in Nineteenth-Century Bali* (Princeton: Princeton Univ. Press, 1980), 98–129; *The Interpretation of Cultures* (New York: Basic Books, 1973); and *Local Knowledge: Further Essays in Interpretive Anthropology* (New York: Basic Books, 1983).

36. See, for example, Natalie Zemon Davis, *Society and Culture in Early Modern France* (Stanford: Stanford Univ. Press, 1975); Emmanuel Le Roy Ladurie, *Le Carnaval de Romans: De la Chandeleur au mercredi des Cendres, 1579–1580* (Paris: Gallimard, 1979); and Robert Darnton, *The Great Cat Massacre and Other Episodes in French Cultural History* (1984; reprinted New York: Vintage Books, 1985), 257–63. See also the critique of Geertz in James Clifford and George E. Marcus, *Writing Culture: The Poetics and Politics of Ethnography* (Berkeley: Univ. of California Press, 1986).

37. On the novel, see J. Hillis Miller, "Narrative and History," *ELH* 41 (1974): 455–73; Patricia Parker, "The (Self-)Identity of the Literary Text: Property, Propriety, Proper Place, and Proper Name in *Wuthering Heights*," in *Identity of the Literary Text*, ed. Valdés and Miller, 92–116, and the studies cited in Parker's note 7, p. 214. I am indebted to all the essays in this volume, to Alan Liu, who generously presented me with a copy at just the moment I needed it most, and to Jay Clayton's introduction to a forthcoming study tentatively entitled "Narrative and Power: Deconstruction to the New Historicism," presented at the Draft Group, Univ. of Wisconsin–Madison Department of English, 1986. On Shakespearean deconstruction, see, for example, James R. Siemon, *Shakespearean Iconoclasm* (Berkeley: Univ. of California Press, 1985), 29–30.

38. In making these suggestions, I am indebted to Edward W. Said, "The Text, the World, the Critic," in *Textual Strategies*, ed. Harari, 161–88; Jerome McGann, *The Beauty of Inflections: Literary Investigations in Historical Method and Theory* (Oxford: Clarendon Press, 1985), 4–18; and Stephen Greenblatt's Introduction to *The Power of Forms in the English Renaissance*, 5–6.

39. The discussion which follows is strongly dependent on Richard Schechner, *The End of Humanism* (New York: Performing Arts Journal Publications, 1982). Behind Schechner, of course, stand figures like Antonin Artaud, *The Theater and Its Double*, trans. Mary Caroline Richards (New York: Grove Press, 1958). For a rich sense of links between the postmodern theater and the Renaissance, see Jonathan Goldberg, *Voice Terminal Echo: Postmodernism and English Renaissance Texts* (New York: Methuen, 1986).

40. See in particular Robert Weimann, "Mimesis in *Hamlet*," in *Shakespeare and the Question of Theory*, ed. Parker and Hartman, 275–91.

41. Cited from Michael Rudman's Director's Notes to his National Theatre *Measure for Measure* (set on a Caribbean island) in Thomas Clayton, "Theatrical Shakespearegresses at the Guthrie and Elsewhere: Notes on 'Legitimate Production,'" *New Literary History: A Journal of Theory and Interpretation* 17 (1985–86): 511–38. I am also indebted to Stephen Orgel, who got me thinking about the meaning of stage relocalizations in his helpful written comments on my proposed project, June 6, 1986.

42. Cited from *Shakespeare's Sonnets*, ed. Stephen Booth (New Haven: Yale Univ. Press, 1977), 49, 57, 101.

43. I would like to discuss this point in much more detail, but this is not the place to do so. I have a longer study of law, literature, and the politics of intentionality in the planning stages.

44. See Diana Benet's essay on Carew, forthcoming in *The Muse's Commonwealth*, ed. Claude J. Summers and Ted-Larry Pebworth; and recent reinterpretations of Jonson in Katharine Eisaman Maus, *Ben Jonson and the Roman Frame of Mind* (Princeton: Princeton Univ. Press, 1984); John Gordon Sweeney III, *Jonson and the Psychology of Public Theater: To Coin the Spirit, Spend the Soul* (Princeton: Princeton Univ. Press, 1985); Don Wayne, "Drama and Society in the Age of Jonson," *Renaissance Drama* 13 (1982): 103–29; and the brilliant and funny discussion of Jonson in Peter Stallybrass and Allon White, *The Politics and Poetics of Transgression* (Ithaca: Cornell Univ. Press, 1986), 66–79.

45. See Chambers, "The Disintegration of Shakespeare," note 29 above; and Greg, *The Shakespeare First Folio*, 83–88.

46. I am indebted to Margreta de Grazia, "Prelexical Possibilities in Shakespeare's Language," presented at the Annual Shakespeare Association of America conference, Nashville, 1985, and to her paper "Bibliographic Holds on Shakespeare," presented at the Modern Language Association, December 1985, which traces editorial shifts in the handling of the texts between the First Folio and the end of the eighteenth century. See also E. A. J. Honigmann, *The Stability of Shakespeare's Text* (London: Edward Arnold, 1965); Stephen Orgel, "What Is a Text?" *Research Opportunities in Renaissance Drama* 24 (1981): 3–6; and Jonathan Goldberg, "Textual Properties," *Shakespeare Quarterly* 37 (1986): 213–17. All of the most recent textual revisionism is indebted, of course, to Steven Urkowitz, *Shakespeare's Revision of King Lear* (Princeton: Princeton Univ. Press, 1980); and Gary Taylor and Michael Warren, eds., *The Division of the Kingdoms: Shakespeare's Two Versions of King Lear* (Oxford: Clarendon Press, 1983).

As I have already implied and will further suggest later on, the arrangement and presentation of plays in the First Folio may also have had specific "local" meanings at the time of publication.

47. Stanley Wells, *Re-Editing Shakespeare for the Modern Reader* (Oxford: Clarendon Press, 1984), 33–34. In citing Wells, I do not mean to suggest that he is unusually culpable. Much of what I here identify as evasion of ideology is not conscious (or necessarily even unconscious) suppression of ideology on the part of each editor, but sometimes the mere continuation of editorial tradition which has long since winnowed ideology out.

48. See Greg, 236–37. The reasons for its omission were presumably political. In light of the Essex affair and Elizabeth's identification of herself with Richard II, the deposition scene could be taken as a staging of the queen's overthrow. It may also have been omitted from some performances. See the sources in note 15 above.

49. Goldberg, "Textual Properties." My emphasis on textual matters is also indebted to Jerome J. McGann, *A Critique of Modern Textual Criticism* (Chicago: Univ. of Chicago Press, 1983); and *The Beauty of Inflections*, although, as Goldberg notes, some of McGann's assumptions about the recoverability of "correct" texts need to be seriously modified when we are dealing with Renaissance drama, particularly Shakespeare.

50. Of the many recent discussions of the playing scene in *Hamlet*, I am particularly indebted to Robert Weimann, "Mimesis in *Hamlet*," in *Shakespeare and the Question of Theory*, ed. Parker and Hartman, 275–91; on the carnivalesque in the play more generally, see also Michael D. Bristol, *Carnival and Theater: Plebeian Culture and the Structure of Authority in Renaissance England* (New York: Methuen, 1985), 185–92.

51. Philip C. McGuire, *Speechless Dialect: Shakespeare's Open Silences* (Berkeley: Univ. of California Press, 1985), xiii–18; on the Mechanicals and suppressed violence, see also Bristol, *Carnival and Theater*, 172–78; and Theodore Leinwand, "'I believe we must leave the killing out': Deference and Accommodation in *A Midsummer Night's Dream*," *Renaissance Papers 1986* (Durham, N.C.: Southeastern Renaissance Conference, 1986), 11–30.

CHAPTER 2

1. For examples of Disintegrationism, see John Dover Wilson's edition of *The First Part of King Henry VI* (1952; reprinted Cambridge: Cambridge Univ. Press, 1968), vii–lv; his "Malone and the Upstart Crow," *Shakespeare Survey* 4 (1951): 56–68; and the useful overview in *Evidence for Authorship: Essays on Problems of Attribution*, ed. David V. Erdman and Ephim G. Fogel (Ithaca: Cornell Univ. Press, 1966), 438–50. The problems of authorship, dating, and sequence have been discussed by almost every editor of the play. See in particular Peter Alexander, ed., *The Heritage Shakespeare: The Histories* (New York: Heritage Press, 1958), 574–87; Alexander's *Shakespeare's Henry VI and Richard III* (Cambridge: Cambridge Univ. Press, 1929); and Madeleine Doran, *Henry VI, Parts II and III: Their Relation to the "Contention" and the "True Tragedy,"* University of Iowa Studies, Humanistic Studies vol. IV, no. 4 (Iowa City: Univ. of Iowa, 1928). The consensus now is that the early quarto editions are not sources for Shakespeare's *Henry VI* plays, but either pirated editions of Parts 2 and 3 based on stage performance or (as seems even more likely) actual performance versions. See Steven Urkowitz's parallel argument for the *Richard III* quarto as acting text in "Reconsidering the Relationship of Quarto and Folio Texts of *Richard III*," *English Literary Renaissance* 16 (1986): 442–66. The best explanation I have encountered of how the *Henry VI* plays could have been composed in chronological order with Part 1 coming first, yet receive contemporary notice when they did, is Hanspeter Born, "The Date of *2, 3 Henry VI*," *Shakespeare Quarterly* 25 (1974): 323–34.

2. *The Works of Thomas Nashe*, ed. Ronald B. McKerrow, 1 (London: A. H. Bullen, 1904), 212. It is now generally agreed that Nashe's comment is a reference to Shakespeare's play.

Since my discussion will be complex enough already, I am not dealing with variant reactions to the play—those of devout Catholics, for example, who might have been sympathetic toward French ritualism, or the reactions of women in the audience as differentiated from men. To a large degree, they probably shared the response recorded by Nashe—those were years during which the appeal to national unity overrode many other factors. Nevertheless, I should make clear in advance that my discussion will be geared toward what was perceived by Nashe as the universal response.

3. See the introduction to John Dover Wilson's edition, cited in note 1 above; S. C. Sen Gupta, *Shakespeare's Historical Plays* (London: Oxford Univ. Press, 1964), 69 (Gupta is citing A. W. Ward's characterization of *1 Henry VI*); Thomas Marc Parrott, *Shakespearean Comedy* (1949; reprinted New York: Russell & Russell, 1962), 207; W. Schrickx, "Nashe, Greene and Shakespeare in 1592," *Revue des langues vivantes* 22 (1956): 55–64; and Leo Kirschbaum's spirited polemic against the Disintegrators, "The Authorship of *I Henry VI*," *PMLA* 67 (1952): 809–22.

4. See Gupta, *Historical Plays*, 63; Parrott, *Shakespearean Comedy*, 209–10; Hardin Craig, *An Interpretation of Shakespeare* (1948; reprinted New York: Citadel Press, 1949), 47–56; and E. M. W. Tillyard's discussion of critics' attitudes toward Joan of Arc in *Shakespeare's History Plays* (New York: Barnes & Noble, 1944), 162–68.

In a related maneuver, George Bernard Shaw argued that Shakespeare wanted to make Joan a "beautiful and romantic figure" but was forced by his company to cater to contemporary taste, producing as a result a play that was "poor and base in its moral tone," *Saint Joan: A Chronicle Play in Six Scenes and an Epilogue* (New York: Brentano's, 1924), xxxvi.4.6.

5. From Sir Robert Cecil's 1603 letter to Sir John Harington, printed in *Nugae Antiquae: Being a Miscellaneous Collection of Original Papers . . . by Sir John Harington and by Others*, ed. Thomas Park (London: J. Wright, 1804), 1:345.

6. See Ernst Kantorowicz, *The King's Two Bodies: A Study in Mediaeval Political Theology* (Princeton: Princeton Univ. Press, 1957), 7–14; and Marie Axton, *The Queen's Two Bodies: Drama and the Elizabethan Succession* (London: Royal Historical Society, 1977), 38.

7. See Winfried Schleiner's important article, "*Divina Virago*: Queen Elizabeth as an Amazon," *Studies in Philology* 75 (1978): 163–80. For other references to the queen's androgynous image and related strategies, see Jonathan Goldberg, *Endlesse Worke: Spenser and the Structures of Discourse* (Baltimore: Johns Hopkins Univ. Press, 1981), 150–53; Louis Adrian Montrose, "'Shaping Fantasies': Figurations of Gender and Power in Elizabethan Culture," *Representations* 1 (1983): 61–94; and Leonard Tennenhouse, *Power on Display: The Politics of Shakespeare's Genres* (New York: Methuen, 1986). For Elizabeth's explicit use of the doctrine of the king's two bodies, see her speech before the Lords cited in Axton, *Queen's Two Bodies*, 38.

The fullest account of Tilbury by a biographer of Elizabeth is in Alison Plowden, *Elizabeth Regina: The Age of Triumph 1588–1603* (New York: Times Books, 1980), 10–12. Contemporary accounts of Tilbury vary considerably and there is no way of being certain which is the most accurate version. Like Elizabeth's coronation, the episode remains shadowy despite its prominence: it was too anomalous to fit readily into contemporary descriptive categories.

The queen's speech was apparently not printed until 1651, but that version is regarded by historians as reasonably reliable. As she spoke, her chaplain took down her words and they were read later to the troops who were too far away to hear her. The manuscript circulated widely. See Paul Johnson, *Elizabeth I: A Biography* (New York: Holt, Rinehart & Winston, 1974), 320 (I have cited the speech from Johnson's text); and J. E. Neale's discussion of the text of the speech in "The Sayings of Queen Elizabeth," *History* n.s. 10 (1925–26): 212–33. We will never know precisely what the queen said at Tilbury, but there is corroboration of key elements of her speech as we have it from unexpected places. See notes 30 and 31 below.

8. Schleiner, *"Divina Virago,"* 173; Johnson, *Elizabeth I,* 79.

9. As Plowden points out (*Elizabeth Regina,* 10–11) Leicester suggested Elizabeth's visit to his camp at Tilbury, east of London, at least in part as a way of diverting her from going down to the coast to meet the enemy in person. Her martial appearance at the camp was a symbolic display, not a genuine military encounter. However, there remained the possibility of such an encounter later on, since the Spaniards were expected to return.

10. Quoted in J. E. Neale, *Elizabeth I and Her Parliaments, 1559–1581* (London: Jonathan Cape, 1953), 107–8. I am also indebted to Allison Heisch's study, "Queen Elizabeth I: Parliamentary Rhetoric and the Exercise of Power," *Signs* 1 (1975): 31–55, which gives excerpts from many of Elizabeth's speeches in the queen's manuscript versions.

11. Neale, *1559–1581,* 149–50. At least some of her contemporaries noted the skill with which she used the strategy. See Neale, *Elizabeth I and Her Parliaments, 1584–1601* (London: Jonathan Cape, 1957), 248–49.

12. John Knox, *The First Blast of the Trumpet against the monstrous regiment of Women (1558),* ed. Edward Arber (London: English Scholar's Library, 1878), 23. Knox's marginal note attributes the analogy to one of the homilies of Chrysostom, but it was so familiar that Elizabeth was not necessarily alluding directly either to Knox or to Chrysostom.

As is well known, Knox somewhat amended his views out of deference to the Protestant queen, but the move came belatedly and grudgingly.

13. See Paul L. Hughes and James F. Larkin, eds., *Tudor Royal Proclamations,* Vols. 2 and 3 (New Haven: Yale Univ. Press, 1969). For illustrations of the masculinization of epithets, see, for example, 2:100, 103, 144, 210, 258, 273; 3:119, 121, 125, 185, 193, 198, 236, 242, 245, 256; for proclamations issued during a plague, 2:236, 317, 321, 345, 420, 430, and for the later, more masculine plague-time proclamations, 3:121; for feeding the hungry, 3:193–94. Another place where she kept the feminine forms was in contexts which also mentioned her father, but even that vestige dropped out in time. See 2:364, 435, and 3:97.

For examples of the use of *princess* to imply demeaned status, see Neale, *1584–1601,* 127; George P. Rice, Jr., ed., *The Public Speaking of Queen Elizabeth* (1951; reprinted New York: AMS Press, 1966), 89–91; and G. B. Harrison, ed., *The Letters of Queen Elizabeth* (1935; reprinted New York: Funk & Wagnalls, 1968), 180 and 219.

14. Cited from Edmund Plowden in Kantorowicz, *The King's Two Bodies,* 23, 407.

15. Neale, *1584–1601,* 385, 388–92, 432.

16. See Johnson, *Elizabeth I,* 111; and Sir Robert Naunton, *Fragmenta Regalia,* ed. Edward Arber (1870; reprinted New York: AMS Press, 1966), 15.

17. Johnson, *Elizabeth I,* 323–24; Neale, *1584–1601,* 392; see also Louis Montrose, "'Eliza, Queene of shepheardes' and the Pastoral of Power," *English Literary Renaissance* 10 (1980): 153–82.

18. On the ruler as hermaphrodite see Edgar Wind, *Pagan Mysteries in the Renaissance,* 2d ed. (London: Faber & Faber, 1968), 214. The Holy Roman

Empire, and indirectly the emperor, had been depicted symbolically as an Amazon on a famous map of Europe reproduced in Schleiner, 166, from Sebastian Münster's *Cosmography* (Basel, 1588).

For Elizabeth's male analogues, see Roy Strong, *The Cult of Elizabeth* (Wallop, Hampshire: Thames & Hudson, 1977), 122–24; and his *Portraits of Queen Elizabeth I* (Oxford: Clarendon Press, 1963), 68, 156–57; David Bevington, *Tudor Drama and Politics: A Critical Approach to Topical Meaning* (Cambridge, Mass.: Harvard Univ. Press, 1968), 6; and Frances A. Yates, *Astraea: The Imperial Theme in the Sixteenth Century* (London: Routledge & K. Paul, 1975), 42–51.

19. Johnson, *Elizabeth I*, 195–96, 201; Lacey Baldwin Smith, *Treason in Tudor England: Politics and Paranoia* (Princeton: Princeton Univ. Press, 1986), 13.

20. See, for example, her letter to Anjou in *Letters of Queen Elizabeth*, 145; and on the courtship in general, the detailed account in Martin Hume, *The Courtships of Queen Elizabeth*, rev. ed. (London: E. Nash, 1904).

21. *Nugae Antiquae*, 1 : 177–78.

22. William Camden, *Annales*, trans. R. N[orton], 3d ed. (London: for Benjamin Fisher, 1635), 469. (Like other contemporary writers, Camden also more than once alludes to the "masculine" virtues by which Elizabeth exceeded her sex.) In "Eliza, Queene of shepheardes," Louis Montrose has noted the queen's "paradoxical analogy" without attempting to explicate it. Her parliamentary speeches often seem deliberately to befuddle her gender identification in regard to the marriage issue. See Neale, *1559–1581*, 127.

23. See Carole Levin, "Queens and Claimants: Political Insecurity in Sixteenth-Century England," in *Gender, Ideology, and Action: Historical Perspectives on Women's Public Lives*, ed. Janet Sharistanian (New York: Greenwood Press, 1986), 41–66. See also Hume, *The Courtships of Queen Elizabeth*, 334–61. Examples of the queen presented as the nation's mother are easy to come by. See Neale, *1584–1601*, 74; Montrose, "Shaping Fantasies"; and Heisch, "Parliamentary Rhetoric," 54.

24. See Juliet Dusinberre, *Shakespeare and the Nature of Woman* (New York: Barnes & Noble, 1975), 95.

25. *Proclamations*, 1 : 308. Of course, the issue of her princehood may have had important personal dimensions for her. To say that all those involved in her birth and upbringing had hoped for a boy would be to understate the matter.

26. Such separation is always, of course, a matter of degree. For discussion of non-Western analogues, see Sherry B. Ortner and Harriet Whitehead, eds., *Sexual Meanings: The Cultural Construction of Gender and Sexuality* (Cambridge: Cambridge Univ. Press, 1981), especially the essays by Fitz John Porter Poole, 116–65, and Ortner, 359–409; Shirley Ardener, ed., *Defining Females: The Nature of Women in Society* (New York: John Wiley, 1978), Introduction, 41 and 47; and Kirsten Hastrup's essay, 49–65. I am indebted to Judith Kegan Gardiner for suggesting both these references. A familiar if partial Western analogue is, of course, the Virgin Mary. See Geoffrey Ashe, *The Virgin* (London: Routledge & K. Paul, 1976). I am also indebted to William Blake Tyrrell's provocative analysis, *Amazons: A Study in Athenian Mythmaking* (Baltimore: Johns Hopkins Univ. Press, 1984).

27. There is, by now, a fairly massive literature on the subject. See Natalie Zemon Davis, "Women on Top: Symbolic Sexual Inversion and Political

Disorder in Early Modern Europe," in *The Reversible World*, ed. Barbara A. Babcock (Ithaca: Cornell Univ. Press, 1978), 147–90, reprinted with minor revisions from Davis's book *Society and Culture in Early Modern France* (Stanford: Stanford Univ. Press, 1975); David Underdown, *Revel, Riot, and Rebellion: Popular Politics and Culture in England 1603–1660* (Oxford: Clarendon Press, 1985), 102–11; and Peter Stallybrass, "'Drunk with the Cup of Liberty': Robin Hood, the Carnivalesque, and the Rhetoric of Violence in Early Modern England," *Semiotica* 54 (1985): 113–45.

28. Cited from Phillip Stubbes in Linda Woodbridge, *Women and the English Renaissance: Literature and the Nature of Womankind, 1590–1620* (Urbana: Univ. of Illinois Press, 1984), 139. As Woodbridge's discussion indicates (139–51), moralists linked the idea of women in masculine attire with the idea of male effeminacy.

29. See Schleiner's survey of Amazon portraits in *"Divina Virago,"* note 7 above; and Roy Strong, *Portraits of Queen Elizabeth I*, note 18 above. There is a painting of Elizabeth at Tilbury, believed to be contemporary, in St. Faith's Church, Gaywood, King's Lynn, Norfolk, reproduced as the color frontispiece to A. M. Hadfield, *Time to Finish the Game: The English and the Armada* (London: Phoenix House, 1964), which shows Elizabeth surveying the troops. She appears to be carrying a sword, but not wearing a breastplate. Her head is surrounded with a ring rather like a halo.

In addition to the foreign and post-Elizabethan depictions mentioned by Schleiner, Constance Jordan has argued for the Siena 'Sieve' portrait of Elizabeth as a study in royal androgyny in her "The Siena Portrait of Queen Elizabeth I and Contemporary Conceptions of Women's Rule," which she was kind enough to let me read in manuscript.

30. James Aske, *Elizabetha Triumphans* (London, 1588), cited from John Nichols's reprint in *The Progresses and Public Processions of Queen Elizabeth* (London: John Nichols, 1823), 2:545–82.

31. *The Copie of a Letter sent out of England to Don Bernardin Mendosa, Ambassadour in France for the King of Spaine, declaring the State of England . . . found in the Chamber of Richard Leigh, a Seminarie Priest, who was lately executed for High Treason, committed in the time that the Spanish Armada was in the Seas* (London, 1588), reprinted in *The Harleian Miscellany*, ed. William Oldys and Thomas Park, vol. 1 (London: for John White and John Murray, 1808), 142–60. Given the letter's purpose, which was to account for the failure of English Catholics to rise to the aid of the Spaniards, we should not perhaps expect the author to record anything but the strength of English patriotism. This account of Tilbury does not mention Amazonian attire—only that the queen marched "curiously" to survey the troops with her sword carried before her. It does, however, give a paraphrase of the key part of her speech, 152.

32. Knox, *First Blast of the Trumpet*, 12–13. I am not, of course, arguing that Knox's views were universally accepted, only that they expressed fears which many other people shared, at least partially and part of the time. As an antidote to Knox, see [John Aylmer,] *An Harborowe for Faithfvll and Trewe Svbiectes* (Strassburg, 1559), which includes a favorable comparison between Elizabeth and Joan of Arc. See also the discussion of other Amazon figures in popular materials from the 1570s and 1580s in Laura Caroline Stevenson, *Praise and Paradox: Merchants and Craftsmen in Elizabethan Popular Literature* (Cambridge: Cambridge Univ. Press, 1984). In *Famous Victories of Henry V* (1586), for example, it is suggested that a cobbler's Amazonian wife would be

a better soldier in France than he, 167–68. This is very different from the marginalization of female power which we will briefly notice later on in Shakespeare's version of *Henry V.*

33. Aske is cited from John Nichols's reprint, *The Progresses and Public Processions of Queen Elizabeth,* 2:545. See also Woodbridge's survey of similar ideas in contemporary moralists, *Women and the English Renaissance,* 139–41; and the brief survey of other poems in Leicester Bradner, "Poems on the Defeat of the Spanish Armada," *Journal of English and Germanic Philology* 43 (1944): 447–48. Aske's comparison of himself as a writer to the "mother" of his work is, of course, sixteenth-century commonplace, but suggestive of more than mere commonplace in combination with his earlier statement.

On the parallel with Long Meg and the density of cultural preoccupation with the Amazon in the immediate post-Armada period, I am also indebted to Gabriele Bernhard Jackson's "Topical Ideology: Witches, Amazons, and Shakespeare's Joan of Arc," forthcoming in *English Literary Renaissance* during 1988, which she has kindly sent me in manuscript. Working independently, she and I have arrived at remarkably similar conclusions about Joan and Elizabeth I.

34. These are brought out with particular clarity in David Bevington's notes, *The Complete Works of Shakespeare,* ed. David Bevington, 3d ed. (Glenview, Ill.: Scott, Foresman, 1980), 560.

35. For elements of the controversy, see Woodbridge, *Women and the English Renaissance,* 139; and Stephen Greenblatt, "Fiction and Friction," in *Reconstructing Individualism: Autonomy, Individuality, and Self in Western Thought,* ed. David Wellbery and Thomas C. Heller (Stanford: Stanford Univ. Press, 1986), 30–52. The two accounts may appear contradictory, but Greenblatt is discussing physiology and Woodbridge, gender construction. It could be argued that sixteenth-century gender distinctions carried some of the cultural force they did because men and women were taken to be so physiologically homologous. In our own time, the opposite situation exists: men and women are perceived as quite distinct physiologically, and gender categories are much less clearly and rigidly defined.

36. There is one minor exception: Holinshed refers to a movement after Joan's death to rehabilitate her memory and associate her with "Debora." *Holinshed's Chronicles of England, Scotland, and Ireland,* vol. 3 (London: for J. Johnson et al., 1808), 172.

37. Doran, *Henry VI, Parts II and III* (note 1 above), 57–59. Doran makes a strong case for the early quartos as good acting versions of Parts 2 and 3. At the time she made the argument, it was heresy; now more and more textual scholars are coming around to the same position.

If *1 Henry VI* follows the pattern of these other plays, the figure of Joan would have carried most of her virulence in performance. It would have been structurally impossible to leave her out of the play altogether. Another possibility is that the references which link Joan most closely with Elizabeth were inserted later on. This strikes me as unlikely, but it cannot be ruled out altogether. The reading offered here is predicated on the assumption that Joan of Arc—in some form recognizably related to the version we have—was part of *1 Henry VI* in 1591–92 performance. That is when the figure would have had the most powerful "local" significance.

38. Cited from Thomas Nashe, *A Countercuffe to Martin Junior* (1589), in Smith, *Treason in Tudor England,* 114.

39. *Shakespeare: The Complete Works*, ed. G. B. Harrison (1948; reprinted New York: Harcourt, Brace & World, 1968), 116n.

40. See the sources cited above in notes 1, 3, and 4, especially John Dover Wilson's edition of *1 Henry VI*, which has elaborate textual notes surveying editorial opinion about the authorship of each scene. The quotation is from p. 165.

41. Cited from Levin, "Queens and Claimants," 58–59; and F. G. Emmison, *Elizabethan Life: Disorder* (Chelmsford, Essex: County Council, 1970), 42–43. On the ease with which such rumors were propagated, see Smith, *Treason in Tudor England*, 136–37.

42. Emmison, *Elizabethan Life: Disorder*, 42. Emmison's evidence relates to Essex, but the suspension of earlier vigilance against treasonous remarks was a widespread phenomenon.

43. John Stubbs, *The Discoverie of a Gaping Gulf whereinto England is Like to be Swallowed* (n.p., 1579), sig. A4, B3, C2, and D3. Stubbs points out at some length that Elizabeth's marriage would plunge England into more civil wars like those of the reign of Henry VI. I am also indebted to Lloyd E. Berry, *John Stubbs' Gaping Gulf with Letters and Other Relevant Documents* (Charlottesville: Univ. Press of Virginia, 1968).

44. Mendoza is quoted in Berry's preface to Stubbs, *Discoverie of a Gaping Gulf*, xxxiii. Camden is cited from his *Annales: The True and Royall History of the famous Empresse Elizabeth*, trans. Abraham Darcie (London, 1625), Book 3, pp. 16 and 67. Protestant fears were no doubt fueled by the fact that the very statute by which Elizabeth had Stubbs punished was one dating from the Catholic times of Philip and Mary.

45. See Berry's discussion in *Stubbs' Gaping Gulf*, ed. Berry, li–liv. Another example is *Willobie His Avisa* (1594), which is, whatever else it may be, a satire on the various suitors of Elizabeth. See the edition by G. B. Harrison, ed., *Willobie His Avisa* (London: John Lane, 1926); and B. N. De Luna, *The Queen Declined: An Interpretation of Willobie His Avisa* (Oxford: Clarendon Press, 1970), which gets lost in detail but does point out the numerous parallels between the attributes of Avisa and Eliza. On the basis of the nexus of topical ideas discussed here, I would be willing to add another equally speculative possibility: the Willobie whom Avisa (Eliza) scorns might have reminded contemporaries of Lord Willoughby, whom Elizabeth had neglected to aid in France. The High Commission appears to have agreed that the work had dangerous political implications: it was ordered burned in the late 1590s.

46. Cited from the reprint of the proclamation in Stubbs, ed. Berry, 150–51 (Appendix I). Stubbs's tract and the earl of Northampton's answer to it also mention the Wars of the Roses in connection with the royal marriage, Northampton claiming that the contention would indeed be "set on foot again, if such usurpations of royal dignity continue." See Berry's edition, 65 (Appendix II).

47. In the analogy, Anjou, of course, was the snake. Stubbs, *Discoverie of a Gaping Gulf*, A2r. It is tempting to speculate that Stubbs's emphasis on womanly weakness as something the queen must at all costs avoid, his subtle turning of the queen's own "male" rhetoric against the proposed French match, may have been one of the things she found most intolerable about his tract.

48. The episode is, of course, borrowed from the chronicles; most of the other instances of inversion are not.

49. *State Papers Relating to the Defeat of the Spanish Armada*, ed. John Knox Laughton (London: Navy Records Society, 1894), 2:69. See also Hadfield, *Time to Finish the Game*, note 29 above, pp. 89–90 (on the queen's irresolution before the event) and 152–74; Michael Lewis, *The Spanish Armada* (New York: Macmillan, 1960), 175–83; Garrett Mattingly, *The Defeat of the Spanish Armada* (London: Jonathan Cape, 1959), 285–97; and R. B. Wernham, *After the Armada: Elizabethan England and the Struggle for Western Europe 1588–1595* (Oxford: Clarendon Press, 1984), to which the following discussion is indebted.

I am also indebted to the following topical studies which link the play to military events of the 1590s or more general anxieties of the period: Geoffrey Bullough, "The Uses of History," in *Shakespeare's World*, ed. James Sutherland and Joel Hurstfield (London: Edward Arnold, 1964), 96–115; Bullough, ed., *Narrative and Dramatic Sources of Shakespeare*, vol. 3 (New York: Columbia Univ. Press, 1975), 24–25; T. W. Baldwin, *On the Literary Genetics of Shakespeare's Plays 1592–1594* (Urbana: Univ. of Illinois Press, 1959), 333–34; John Dover Wilson's introduction to *Henry VI Part 1*, note 1 above; A. C. Hamilton, *The Early Shakespeare* (San Marino, Calif.: Huntington Library, 1967), 14–15; Emrys Jones, *The Origins of Shakespeare* (1977; reprinted Oxford: Clarendon Press, 1978), 119–26 (Jones's is by far the most sensitive topical reading to date); Hereward T. Price, *Construction in Shakespeare*, University of Michigan Contributions in Modern Philology, no. 17 (Ann Arbor: Univ. of Michigan Press, 1951), 25–33 (one of the best general readings of the play); Ernest William Talbert, *Elizabethan Drama and Shakespeare's Early Plays: An Essay in Historical Criticism* (Chapel Hill: Univ. of North Carolina Press, 1963), 163–64; and more generally, C. G. Thayer, *Shakespearean Politics: Government and Misgovernment in the Great Histories* (Athens: Ohio Univ. Press, 1983), which argues that the problem of succession toward the end of Elizabeth's reign was one impetus behind Shakespeare's history plays.

50. As Emrys Jones has pointed out, 120–21, Shrewsbury had been the longtime jailor of Mary Queen of Scots: he was in many ways strongly associated with the anti-Catholic cause. The assertion about Shrewsbury and Talbot at Tilbury comes from the letter to Mendoza, note 31 above, and is perhaps not trustworthy, but the general point about Shrewsbury's perceived public role remains valid. Shrewsbury himself was apparently not present at Tilbury, or was there only briefly, since Leicester sent him a letter describing the queen's visit.

51. See in particular Thomas Coningsby, *Journal of the Siege of Rouen, 1591*, ed. John Gough Nichols, *The Camden Miscellany, Volume the First* (n.p.: Camden Society, 1847); and John Dover Wilson's discussion in his introduction to *1 Henry VI*, note 1 above. Several of the discussions of topicality cited in note 49 also mention the similarities. See also Schrickx, "Nashe, Greene and Shakespeare in 1592," note 3 above, which points out parallels between contemporary pamphlet discussions of the French wars and Shakespeare's play, but uses them to argue against Shakespeare's authorship.

Much ink has been spilt over whether or not the play makes use of the Rouen materials as an actual source. It is a crucial matter for dating the writing of Part 1, but not crucial in terms of audience perception of the plays in performance. Whether or not Shakespeare intended the details to recall specific episodes in France, they certainly would have been interpreted generally in terms of the French situation.

52. See the detailed discussion in Wernham, *After the Armada*, note 49 above, 148–76. Direct quotations are from pp. 167 and 172.

53. Wernham, *After the Armada*, 171, 174–75; for Stubbs's participation see also *Stubbs' Gaping Gulf*, ed. Berry, xlii and xlvi.

54. There is a very helpful discussion of these plays in Bevington, *Tudor Drama and Politics*, 187–211. He, however, portrays Shakespeare's *Henry* plays as moderate by the standards of other patriotic plays of the period. My reading of Joan will question that characterization.

55. See David Underdown's discussion in *Revel, Riot, and Rebellion*, 38–40. On the dynamics of witchcraft beliefs more generally, see Mary Douglas, *Purity and Danger: An Analysis of Concepts of Pollution and Taboo* (London: Routledge & K. Paul, 1966), Introduction and 98–107; Keith Thomas, *Religion and the Decline of Magic: Studies in Popular Beliefs in Sixteenth- and Seventeenth-Century England* (1971; reprinted Harmondsworth, Middlesex: Penguin Books, 1973), 515–680; Michael MacDonald, *Mystical Bedlam: Madness, Anxiety, and Healing in Seventeenth-Century England* (Cambridge: Cambridge Univ. Press, 1981); and Alan MacFarlane, *Witchcraft in Tudor and Stuart England: A Regional and Comparative Study* (New York: Harper Torchbooks, 1970).

56. Witchcraft against Elizabeth is mentioned in James R. Siemon's excellent study *Shakespearean Iconoclasm* (Berkeley: Univ. of California Press, 1985), 55. See also Strong, *Portraits of Queen Elizabeth I*, note 18 above, 32, 40–41. For the queen's association with demonism, see Sir John Harington, *Nugae Antiquae*, note 5 above, 1:165; Paul Johnson, *Elizabeth I*, note 8 above, 223–24; and Garrett Mattingly, *The Defeat of the Spanish Armada*, note 49 above, 166–67. As Mattingly notes, there had been a series of well-known and alarming prophecies about a disaster which was to occur in the year 1588.

57. Cited from John Nichols, *The Progresses and Public Processions of Queen Elizabeth*, 2:216; there is more information about the case on p. *249n (an extra page added to the text). See also Paul Johnson, *Elizabeth I*, 345.

My discussion of rituals against ritual in this section is indebted throughout to Steven Mullaney, "Strange Things, Gross Terms, Curious Customs: The Rehearsal of Cultures in the Late Renaissance," *Representations* 3 (Summer 1983): 40–67.

58. Nichols, 2:216–17 (letter from Topcliffe to the earl of Shrewsbury).

59. See, for example, other portions of Topcliffe's letter (Nichols, 2:218), which describe the French overtures to Elizabeth as part of the same set of fears. Stubbs's *Gaping Gulf* appeared the next year.

60. Frances Yates, *Astraea*, note 18 above, 79. For ultra-Protestant objections to the cult, see Roy Strong, *The Cult of Elizabeth*, 125–26.

61. Nichols, *Progresses of Elizabeth*, 2:217.

62. Ibid., *249n.

63. The best discussion to date for our purposes here is Ernest B. Gilman, *Iconoclasm and Poetry in the English Reformation: Down Went Dagon* (Chicago: Univ. of Chicago Press, 1986), 48. On the psychological impact of iconoclastic burning more generally, see Gilman's chap. 2, "At the Crossroads: The Poetics of Reformation Iconoclasm," pp. 31–59. As Gilman points out, the idea of ritual burning exerts a curious spell in Fox's *Book of Martyrs*: in that book, the purgative element of the ritual is tied up with ideas about Protestant martyrdom. Gilman suggests that for iconoclasts, the sight of any image aroused thoughts about its breaking. The possibility is interesting in terms of its implications for the image of Elizabeth I.

64. Garrett Mattingly, *The Defeat of the Spanish Armada*, 190–91; Nichols, *Progresses of Elizabeth*, 2:537; *The Harleian Miscellany*, ed. Oldys and Park, note 31 above, 1:133.

65. Roy Strong, *Portraits of Queen Elizabeth I*, 5–6, 9; and his *English Renaissance Miniature* (Ashton-under-Lyne, Lancashire: Thames & Hudson, 1983), 118. As Strong notes, licentious and defamatory portraits of Elizabeth were circulated abroad as propaganda against England.

On Smithfield and the burning of heretics there, see Henry Morley, *Memoirs of Bartholomew Fair* (London: Chapman & Hall, 1859), 78–79, 144.

66. See in particular Sigurd Burckhardt, "'I am but Shadow of Myself': Ceremony and Design in *1 Henry VI*," *Modern Language Quarterly* 28 (1967): 139–58; and Hereward T. Price, *Construction in Shakespeare*, note 49 above, 25–36.

67. Nichols, *Progresses of Elizabeth*, 2:143. Elizabeth is referred to in the pageant text as the "Phoenix" who quenched the flame of division, 143; later portions compare her to Deborah, Judith, Esther, and Martia, "sometime Queene of England," 145.

68. All of these examples are taken from Patricia-Ann Lee, "Reflections of Power: Margaret of Anjou and the Dark Side of Queenship," *Renaissance Quarterly* 39 (1986): 183–217. See also Celeste Turner Wright, "The Elizabethan Female Worthies," *Studies in Philology* 43 (1946): 628–43. I am also indebted to Phyllis Rackin, "Anti-Historians: Women's Roles in Shakespeare's Histories," *Theatre Journal* 37 (1985): 329–44; Robert A. Ravich, "A Psychoanalytic Study of Shakespeare's Early Plays," *Psychoanalytic Quarterly* 33 (1964): 388–410; David Bevington, "The Domineering Female in *1 Henry VI*," *Shakespeare Studies* 2 (1966): 51–58; and Irene G. Dash's discussion of the spectacular role of Margaret and factors which have hindered its discovery by prominent actresses, *Wooing, Wedding, and Power: Women in Shakespeare's Plays* (New York: Columbia Univ. Press, 1981), 159–93.

There have been many discussions of the disintegration of succession in the trilogy. See, in addition to the critics cited in notes 4 and 49 above, Edward I. Berry, *Patterns of Decay: Shakespeare's Early Histories* (Charlottesville: Univ. Press of Virginia, 1975); Charles R. Forker, "Shakespeare's Chronicle Plays as Historical-Pastoral," *Shakespeare Studies* 1 (1965): 85–104; David Riggs, *Shakespeare's Heroical Histories: Henry VI and Its Literary Tradition* (Cambridge, Mass.: Harvard Univ. Press, 1971); and Mark Rose, *Shakespearean Design* (Cambridge, Mass.: Harvard Univ. Press, 1972), 126–33.

69. See Leslie Fiedler's discussion in *The Stranger in Shakespeare* (New York: Stein & Day, 1972), 43–81. He notes that in *1 Henry VI*, Joan of Arc, the countess of Auvergne, and Margaret could all have been played by a single actor, since they never appear on stage together (p. 47). As Fiedler's views suggest, our own reactions to both Joan and Margaret are likely to be far more positive than those of contemporary audiences. But see also my caveat in note 2 above.

70. W. Carew Hazlitt, *Faiths and Folklore: A Dictionary of National Beliefs, etc* (London: Reeves & Turner, 1905), 2:268–69. On St. George customs more generally, see E. K. Chambers, *The English Folk-Play* (Oxford: Clarendon Press, 1933), 156–74.

71. See James George Frazer, *The New Golden Bough*, ed. Theodor H. Gaster (1959; reprinted Garden City, N.Y.: Anchor Books, 1961), 298–99, 354–70; Yves-Marie Bercé, *Fête et révolte: Des mentalités populaires du XVIᵉ au*

XVIIIe siècle (Paris: Hachette, 1976), 46–85; and David Underdown, *Revel, Riot, and Rebellion*, note 27 above, 70.

72. See the sources in note 55 above. For both English and non-Western examples of the use of witchcraft beliefs to effect social and structural changes, see Mary Douglas, ed., *Witchcraft Confessions and Accusations* (London: Tavistock, 1970), especially xviii, which gives an example of witchcraft accusations being used to effect a village's fission into two separate villages—a non-Western analogue, perhaps, of the English expansionism of the 1590s. For a comparable argument about English witchcraft, see Keith Thomas's *Religion and the Decline of Magic*, note 55 above; and his essay "The Relevance of Social Anthropology to the Historical Study of English Witchcraft," in Douglas, ed., 47–79.

73. Knox, *First Blast of the Trumpet*, 53. In all of the instances of Protestant burning in England, there seems to be strong ambivalence about whether the image is to be eradicated altogether (the ultra-Protestant position) or only purified. I see the same ambivalence operating in *1 Henry VI*: can the icon of the queen be emptied of its "popish" superstition, or must the image of queenship be eradicated?

74. See in particular Stephen Greenblatt's essay on Marlowe in *Renaissance Self-Fashioning: From More to Shakespeare* (Chicago: Univ. of Chicago Press, 1980), 193–221; and David Bevington's examples of theatrical scapegoating in *Tudor Drama and Politics*, chap. 14, "War Fever."

My argument here depends on our taking the plays as having been written and staged in the folio order; I am willing to risk circularity of argument and argue that the structure of repetition itself supports the view that *1 Henry VI* came first.

75. I have cited the folio stage directions. The quarto calls for the enactment of the scene, but does not include the elaborate stage directions.

76. First Folio, TLN 2994; *Shakespeare's Plays in Quarto: A Facsimile Edition of Copies Primarily from the Henry E. Huntington Library*, ed. Michael J. B. Allen and Kenneth Muir (Berkeley: Univ. of California Press, 1981), 71. In neither version is there a clear connection between the killing of the rebel and the burning motif. On the ambivalence of ritual violence in the Jack Cade episodes, see Stephen Greenblatt, "Murdering Peasants: Status, Genre, and the Representation of Rebellion," *Representations* 1 (1983): 1–29; and Michael D. Bristol, *Carnival and Theater: Plebeian Culture and the Structure of Authority in Renaissance England* (New York: Methuen, 1985), 89–90.

77. For the quarto version, see *Shakespeare's Plays in Quarto*, ed. Allen and Muir, 85; see also the discussions of the variations between quarto and folio in Madeleine Doran, *Henry VI, Parts II and III*, note 1 above. For discussion of the York episode, see in particular David M. Bergeron, "The Play-within-the-Play in *3 Henry VI*," *Tennessee Studies in Literature*, vol. 22, ed. Allison R. Enser (Knoxville: Univ. of Tennessee Press, 1977), 37–45; and Anne Righter, *Shakespeare and the Idea of the Play* (London: Chatto & Windus, 1962), 119–26.

78. First Folio, TLN 138–43; *Shakespeare's Plays in Quarto*, ed. Allen and Muir, 334. On the instability that continues along with the cycle's motion toward consolidation, see the fine essay by Jonathan Dollimore and Alan Sinfield, "History and Ideology: The Instance of *Henry V*," in John Drakakis, ed., *Alternative Shakespeares* (London: Methuen, 1985), 206–27.

79. I refer to Dr. Richard James's story about the name change in *Henry IV* from Oldcastle to Falstaff. His explanation of the change as a result of the

offense taken by Oldcastle's descendants was made in reply to a "young gentlewoman" who had been reading the folio version of the histories and asked how Sir John Falstaff could die in the reign of Henry V, yet live again to be banished for cowardice under Henry VI. Such are the new questions that emerge when the plays are read instead of seen on stage, and read in the folio order. For one account of the incident (among many others) see S. Schoenbaum, *William Shakespeare: A Documentary Life* (New York: Oxford Univ. Press, 1975), 144. Modern editions usually tidy up the problem by turning Falstaff of the *Henry VI* plays into Fastolfe, Holinshed's version of the name.

80. The older view that Greene was accusing Shakespeare of plagiarism is, by now, accepted by very few scholars. The decisive argument against plagiarism was made by Peter Alexander in his Introduction to *The Heritage Shakespeare: The Histories*, note 1 above, 574–87.

81. Alison Plowden, *Two Queens in One Isle* (Brighton, Sussex: Harvester Press, 1984), 82, 89; *Calendar of State Papers*, Spain, 1:364. I am indebted to the generosity of Carole Levin for the Spanish reference. She is working on a book-length study of Elizabeth which will bring together many interesting new materials. See also Louis Adrian Montrose, "The Elizabethan Subject and the Spenserian Text," in *Literary Theory / Renaissance Texts*, ed. Patricia Parker and David Quint (Baltimore: Johns Hopkins Univ. Press, 1986), 303–40; Marie Axton, *The Queen's Two Bodies*, note 6 above; Bevington, *Tudor Drama and Politics*, note 18 above; and Mortimer Levine's discussion of other texts in *The Early Elizabethan Succession Question 1558–1568* (Stanford: Stanford Univ. Press, 1966).

82. Malcolm Evans, *Signifying Nothing: Truth's True Contents in Shakespeare's Text* (Athens: Univ. of Georgia Press, 1986), 117. Evans's deconstructive reading of *As You Like It* is a bracing antidote to the passion for establishing set meanings for comedy. See also Donald K. Hedrick, "Merry and Weary Conversation: Textual Uncertainty in *As You Like It*, II.iv," *ELH* 46 (1979): 21–34.

83. David Underdown, *Revel, Riot, and Rebellion*, note 27 above, 37–38.

84. Underdown, *Revel, Riot, and Rebellion*, 38–39; and his contribution "The Taming of the Scold: The Enforcement of Patriarchal Authority in Early Modern England," in Anthony Fletcher and John Stevenson, eds., *Order and Disorder in Early Modern England* (Cambridge: Cambridge Univ. Press, 1985), 116–36; Allison Heisch, "Queen Elizabeth I and the Persistence of Patriarchy," *Feminist Review* 4 (1980): 45–56; and Linda Woodbridge, *Women and the English Renaissance*, note 28 above, 139–41.

85. For Chancery law, see the discussion by the legal historian George W. Keeton, *Shakespeare's Legal and Political Background* (London: Pitman & Sons, 1967), 136–48.

86. For near-contemporary examples of players' mimicry of known individuals, see G. E. Bentley, *The Professions of Dramatist and Player in Shakespeare's Time, 1590–1642*, one-volume paperback edition (1971 and 1984; reprinted Princeton: Princeton Univ. Press, 1986), *Dramatist*, 188–91 and his note 43, pp. 189–90. One play that brought Elizabeth onto the popular stage was Jonson's *Every Man Out of His Humor*, which had to be changed because "bringing the Queen upon the stage in person" was not "relished." See *Ben Jonson*, ed. C. H. Herford and Percy and Evelyn Simpson, 11 vols. (Oxford: Clarendon Press, 1925–52), 1:374 and 3:602–3. *Histriomastix* (1598–99) appears to have attempted something similar with the final descent of Astraea.

What is interesting for our purposes is that these representations were actually staged in the public theater, even if only briefly.

87. On the Skimmington and related shaming rituals, see Underdown, *Revel, Riot, and Rebellion,* note 27 above, 102–11; Peter Burke, *Popular Culture in Early Modern Europe* (New York: New York Univ. Press, 1978), especially chap. 7, 178–204; and Bercé, *Fête et révolte,* note 71 above, 45–49. For a lively description of how the ritual could be adapted to fit specific social situations, see Robert Darnton, *The Great Cat Massacre and Other Episodes in French Cultural History* (1984; reprinted New York: Vintage Books, 1985), 75–104.

There are, of course, other forms of ritualism behind the plays. I am particularly indebted to C. L. Barber, *Shakespeare's Festive Comedy* (1959; reprinted New York: Meridian, 1963); see also my brief discussion in *The Politics of Mirth: Jonson, Herrick, Milton, Marvell, and the Defense of Old Holiday Pastimes* (Chicago: Univ. of Chicago Press, 1986), 163 and its note 37.

88. On the subject of cross-dressing in Shakespearean comedy, nearly every recent study of the plays has had something interesting to say. It is worth emphasizing in advance that my analysis of one "local" area of signification is not meant to cancel out the possibility of others. In particular, I am indebted to Juliet Dusinberre, *Shakespeare and the Nature of Woman,* note 24 above, 231–71; Carolyn Lenz et al., eds., *The Woman's Part: Feminist Criticism of Shakespeare* (Urbana: Univ. of Illinois Press, 1980), Clara Claiborne Park's essay "As We Like It: How a Girl Can Be Smart and Still Popular," 100–116; Robert Kimbrough, "Androgyny Seen through Shakespeare's Disguise," *Shakespeare Quarterly* 33 (1982): 17–33; Catherine Belsey, "Disrupting Sexual Difference: Meaning and Gender in the Comedies," in *Alternative Shakespeares,* ed. Drakakis, note 78 above, 166–90; and Phyllis Rackin, "Androgyny, Mimesis, and the Marriage of the Boy Heroine on the English Renaissance Stage," *PMLA* 102 (1987): 29–41. Rackin is interested in accounting for some of the same peculiarities about the Shakespearean androgyne as I am. Her assessment of decline is arguably more pessimistic than it would need to be because she focuses on marriage and chooses Ben Jonson as her sole Jacobean example. If she had chosen someone like Dekker, she might have come up with a different pattern.

Imogen in *Cymbeline* is a variant of the type which will be discussed in the next chapter. For a view of theatrical androgyny which emphasizes the element of deviance and homoerotic display, see Lisa Jardine's interesting discussion in *Still Harping on Daughters: Women and Drama in the Age of Shakespeare* (Sussex: Harvester Press, 1983), 9–36; I am also indebted to Jonathan Dollimore's forthcoming work on androgyny and transgression in Jacobean comedy, presented at "New Perspectives on Stuart Drama," Modern Language Association, Washington, D.C., December 28, 1984.

89. See (among many other studies) Wernham, *After the Armada,* 567–68; and C. G. A. Clay, *Economic Expansion and Social Change: England 1500–1700* (Cambridge: Cambridge Univ. Press, 1984), 1:18. For the recurrence of old rumors about the succession, see Carole Levin, "Queens and Claimants," note 23 above, 58–59.

90. The best single compendium of such images is Simon Shepherd, *Amazons and Warrior Women: Varieties of Feminism in Seventeenth-Century Drama* (New York: St. Martin's Press, 1981), which discusses various phases of recapitulation of the image of Elizabeth as "warrior woman." As Shepherd notes, *If you know not me* gives to Elizabeth lines from Shakespeare's *Richard II* and

Henry V: "she slips into the role of male monarch" (p. 29)—a very customary role for her, we might add. What had appeared deviant in the sixteenth century became acceptable after the queen's death: Elizabeth as an Amazon protecting Protestant Europe was a motif invoked by militant Protestants against the Stuart policy of conciliation in Europe. See also Mary Beth Rose's "Women in Men's Clothing: Apparel and Social Stability in *The Roaring Girl*," *English Literary Renaissance* 14 (1984): 367–91; and Juliet Dusinberre, *Shakespeare and the Nature of Woman*, 303–7. Marston's Queen Sophonisba, whom Dusinberre mentions, also uses familiar rhetorical strategies associated with Queen Elizabeth I.

91. It would be interesting, in particular, to consider the local impact of *Macbeth* after the Gunpowder Plot, which institutionalized Protestant ritual burning in the form of Guy Fawkes Day with its bonfire immolation of Fawkes. The play has no burnings, but can be read as having a similar scapegoating structure with regard to hindrances to the Jacobean succession. On the play's echoes of the Darnley murder (another instance of spectacular explosion and fire) and kindred Scottish events associated with James and the succession, see an old book which cries out for reworking, Lilian Winstanley, *Macbeth, King Lear and Contemporary History* (Cambridge: Cambridge Univ. Press, 1922). See also Peter Stallybrass's fine essay "*Macbeth* and Witchcraft," in John Russell Brown, ed., *Focus on Macbeth* (London: Routledge & K. Paul, 1982). Less methodologically sophisticated Stuart readings of the play have been made in Henry N. Paul, *The Royal Play of Macbeth: When, Why, and How It Was Written by Shakespeare* (New York: Macmillan, 1950); and Arthur Melville Clark, *Murder under Trust or the Topical Macbeth and Other Jacobean Matters* (Edinburgh: Scottish Academic Press, 1981). But see also the counter-readings noted below. In asserting that *Macbeth* was "revived" on the public stage in 1611, I am following a standard editorial line, but the fact is that we do not know definitely when or if *Macbeth* was staged before that date.

92. See, for example, Jonathan Goldberg's "Speculations: *Macbeth* and Source," in *Shakespeare Reproduced: The Text in History and Ideology*, ed. Jean Howard and Marion F. O'Connor (London: Methuen, 1987), chap. 11; Malcolm Evans, *Signifying Nothing*, note 82 above, 133–40; Steven Mullaney, "Lying Like Truth: Riddle, Representation and Treason in Renaissance England," *ELH* 47 (1980): 32–47; and Michael Hawkins's essay, "History, Politics and *Macbeth*," in Brown, ed., *Focus on Macbeth*, 155–88. Arthur Kinney is working on a book-length historical "unreading" of the Stuart *Macbeth*.

CHAPTER 3

1. See Margot Heinemann, *Puritanism and Theatre: Thomas Middleton and Opposition Drama under the Early Stuarts* (Cambridge: Cambridge Univ. Press, 1980), 166–69; and Annabel Patterson, *Censorship and Interpretation: The Conditions of Writing and Reading in Early Modern England* (Madison: Univ. of Wisconsin Press, 1984), 73–79.

2. My discussion here is based on an argument made in my "City Metal and Country Mettle: The Occasion of Ben Jonson's *Golden Age Restored*," in David M. Bergeron, ed., *Pageantry in the Shakespearean Theater* (Athens: Univ. of Georgia Press, 1985), 26–47.

3. See G. Wilson Knight, *The Crown of Life*, 2d ed. (London: Methuen,

1948), 129–202; and W. W. Greg's survey of critical opinion in *The Shakespeare First Folio: Its Bibliographical and Textual History* (Oxford: Clarendon Press, 1955), 413–14. As Greg points out, even E. K. Chambers, who opposed most Disintegrationism, regarded the Descent of Jupiter as a "spectacular theatrical interpolation"; there has, however, been massive disagreement as to precisely where the "interpolation" begins and ends.

4. *The Triumphs of King James the First* (London, 1610), 50–51.

5. C. H. McIlwain, ed., *The Political Works of James I* (Cambridge, Mass.: Harvard Univ. Press, 1918), 24; see also Jonathan Goldberg, *James I and the Politics of Literature* (Baltimore: Johns Hopkins Univ. Press, 1983), 142. On James's imitation of Elizabethan tactics with Parliament, see, for example, his attempt to constitute the Addled Parliament as a "parliament of love," Thomas L. Moir, *The Addled Parliament of 1614* (Oxford: Clarendon Press, 1958).

6. McIlwain, ed., *The Political Works of James I*, 280, 286, 290, 292, 306. See also the important analysis in Jonathan Goldberg, *James I and the Politics of Literature*, to which my own discussion is indebted. However, I differ from Goldberg in that I want to highlight James's claims of sincerity rather than their internal instability in terms of his ideas about absolutism. That instability was variable. I am less interested in it as a permanent feature of James's self-definition than in the specific junctures at which it became particularly visible. On contemporary comparisons between James and Elizabeth, see, for example, Robert Ashton, ed., *James I by His Contemporaries* (London: Hutchinson, 1969), 7–8. Some of Goldberg's ideas are applied to *Cymbeline* in David M. Bergeron, *Shakespeare's Romances and the Royal Family* (Lawrence: Univ. Press of Kansas, 1985). See also Annabel Patterson's discussion of the 1604 speech and its reception in *Censorship and Interpretation*, 66.

7. James is cited from James F. Larkin and Paul L. Hughes, eds., *Stuart Royal Proclamations*, Vol. 1, *Royal Proclamations of King James I 1603–1625* (Oxford: Clarendon Press, 1973), v–vi. For the bishops, see William Barlow, *The Svmme and Svbstance of the Conference . . . at Hampton Court, Ianuary 14, 1603* [for 1604] (London: for Mathew Law, 1604), 84.

8. See Stephen Orgel and Roy Strong, *Inigo Jones: The Theatre of the Stuart Court*, 2 vols. (Berkeley: Univ. of California Press, 1973); my *The Politics of Mirth: Jonson, Herrick, Milton, Marvell, and the Defense of Old Holiday Pastimes* (Chicago: Univ. of Chicago Press, 1986), which includes several detailed political readings of court masques; and on perspective, Roy Strong, *Art and Power: Renaissance Festivals 1450–1650* (1973; reprinted Berkeley: Univ. of California Press, 1984), 32.

9. *The Workes of the Most High and Mightie Prince, Iames*, ed. James [Montagu] (London, 1616), sig. B2v. My discussion of James's authorship is strongly indebted to Richard Helgerson and Michael O'Connell's unpublished essay "Print, Power, and the Performing Self," which the authors were kind enough to send me in manuscript. A much revised version has appeared under Richard Helgerson's name as "Milton Reads the King's Book: Print, Performance, and the Making of a Bourgeois Idol," *Criticism* 29 (1987): 1–25.

10. Michael Ryan, *Marxism and Deconstruction: A Critical Articulation* (Baltimore: Johns Hopkins Univ. Press, 1982), 3–8. As numerous historians have pointed out, however, James's saving grace was his incapacity for consistency in practice and his state's technological incapacity for thorough enforcement of the Jacobean "line."

11. Cited from the *Calendar of State Papers Venetian* in Ashton, ed., *James I by His Contemporaries*, 96.

12. Sir John Harington, *Nugae Antiquae: Being a Miscellaneous Collection of Original Papers . . . by Sir John Harington and by Others*, ed. Thomas Park (London: J. Wright, 1804), 1:367–68. Other instances are recorded in Ashton, ed., *James I by His Contemporaries*, 140–67.

13. See Mark Breitenberg's analysis in "' . . . the hole matter opened': Iconic Representation and Interpretation in 'The Quenes Majesties Passage,'" *Criticism* 28 (1986): 1–25, to which my discussion is deeply indebted. On the "easy" allegories characteristic of Tudor popular literature, see also Laura Caroline Stevenson, *Praise and Paradox: Merchants and Craftsmen in Elizabethan Popular Literature* (Cambridge: Cambridge Univ. Press, 1984), 120–23.

14. See *Ben Jonson*, ed. C. H. Herford and Percy and Evelyn Simpson, 11 vols. (Oxford: Clarendon Press, 1925–52), 7:90–91; Breitenberg's article cited above; and the analyses of James's pageant in Goldberg, *James I and the Politics of Literature*, 31–33 and 50–54; and Graham Parry, *The Golden Age Restor'd: The Culture of the Stuart Court, 1603–42* (New York: St. Martin's Press, 1981), 1–9.

In terms of the general project of recovering recondite meanings, I am also indebted to Edgar Wind, *Pagan Mysteries in the Renaissance* (1958; reprinted London: Faber & Faber, 1968), 15; E. H. Gombrich, "*ICONES SYMBOLICAE*: The Visual Image in Neo-Platonic Thought," *Journal of the Warburg and Courtauld Institutes* 11 (1948): 163–92; and Gary Schmidgall's study of elitist modes of signification, *Shakespeare and the Courtly Aesthetic* (Berkeley: Univ. of California Press, 1981).

15. *Ben Jonson*, ed. Herford and Simpson, 7:90–91. Neither Tudor nor Stuart pageant designers were so optimistic as to suppose that the pageant as staged would be as easily "opened" as a printed description—hence the habit during both reigns of publishing an account of the royal entertainment immediately after the event.

16. S. Schoenbaum, *William Shakespeare: A Documentary Life* (New York: Oxford Univ. Press, 1975), 220; G. E. Bentley, *The Professions of Dramatist and Player in Shakespeare's Time, 1590–1642*, one-volume paperback edition (1971 and 1984; reprinted Princeton: Princeton Univ. Press, 1986), *Player*, 63.

17. For particulars of the debate, see Wallace Notestein, *The House of Commons 1604–1610* (New Haven: Yale Univ. Press, 1971), 250–54; David Harris Willson, ed., *The Parliamentary Diary of Robert Bowyer 1606–1607* (Minneapolis: Univ. of Minnesota Press, 1931), 257n, 269, 282, and 287–88; and for James's views, McIlwain, ed., *The Political Works of James I*, 291. Comparison of James to the Thunderer had also come up in earlier Commons debates. In 1604, for example, his answer to a parliamentary petition was received by the solemn and amazed MPs like a "thunderbolt." See G. B. Harrison, *A Jacobean Journal: Being a Record of Those Things Most Talked of during the Years 1603–1606* (London: George Routledge and Sons, 1941), 131.

18. Orgel and Strong, *Inigo Jones: The Theatre of the Stuart Court*, 1:105–14; and D. J. Gordon, *The Renaissance Imagination*, ed. Stephen Orgel (1975; reprinted Berkeley: Univ. of California Press, 1980), 173–77.

19. For the purposes of this reading, I am taking the (by now) standard position that the Jupiter scene is as much "Shakespeare" as the rest of the play, and that it was regularly included in the play as performed. Problems with this position will be discussed later on.

20. As in earlier chapters, I cite the play from the First Folio (1623) and indicate "through line numbers" (TLN) to that edition in my text.

21. *Willobie His Avisa* uses a somewhat similar technique, offering an initial group of suitors to Avisa who can readily be identified in terms of the courtships of Elizabeth I, followed by much more opaque composites that refuse to yield similar identifications. See B. N. De Luna, *The Queen Declined: An Interpretation of Willobie His Avisa* (Oxford: Clarendon Press, 1970). There is, however, a key difference between the two texts: *Cymbeline's* riddles all finally yield unitary messages whereas, in my view at least, those in *Willobie His Avisa* do not and are not intended to, De Luna's efforts at decipherment notwithstanding. In *Avisa*, the ease of the initial decodings stimulates burning, endless speculation about the more cryptic and finally "illegible" figures that occur later on.

22. Warren D. Smith, *Shakespeare's Playhouse Practice: A Handbook* (Hanover, N.H.: Univ. Press of New England, 1975), 32n. The exactitude was easily achievable in the printing house, since the same block of type could have been used both times. Nevertheless, it is tempting to see the precise repetition as indicative of reverence—or mock reverence—for the text in question.

23. See Geoffrey of Monmouth, *Histories of the Kings of Britain*, trans. Sebastian Evans (London: Dent, 1904), 99–104; *Shakespeare's Holinshed*, ed. Richard Hosley (New York: Putnam's Sons, 1968), 4–8; and Kenneth Muir, *The Sources of Shakespeare's Plays* (London: Methuen, 1977), 258–66. Of course, the story of Posthumus has fictional analogues in novellas by Boccaccio and others. David Bergeron notes that there is a Posthumus among the Roman analogues to Shakespeare's play and that Augustan Rome stands behind the play as a "kind of paradigm." See his "*Cymbeline*: Shakespeare's Last Roman Play," *Shakespeare Quarterly* 31 (1980): 31–41, especially his note 19. If so, the Roman allusions he cites work against the play's overt idealization of Augustan Rome and contribute to the stalemating I will discuss later on.

24. The present study is particularly indebted to G. Wilson Knight, *The Crown of Life*, 129–202; and to the topical interpretations of Emrys Jones, "Stuart Cymbeline," *Essays in Criticism* 11 (1961): 84–99; Howard Felperin, *Shakespearean Romance* (Princeton: Princeton Univ. Press, 1972), 188–95; and Glynne Wickham, especially *Shakespeare's Dramatic Heritage: Collected Studies in Mediaeval, Tudor and Shakespearean Drama* (New York: Barnes & Noble, 1969); and his "Riddle and Emblem: A Study in the Dramatic Structure of *Cymbeline*," in *English Renaissance Studies Presented to Dame Helen Gardner*, ed. John Carey (Oxford: Clarendon Press, 1980), 94–113.

In *Shakespeare's Military World* (1956; reprinted Berkeley: Univ. of California Press, 1973), Paul A. Jorgenson sees the play as displaying ambivalence about its own denigration of Elizabethan nationalism in favor of the Jacobean "Forrest of Olives," 202–4. Frances Yates takes a narrower view in *Shakespeare's Last Plays: A New Approach* (London: Routledge and K. Paul, 1975), arguing (28–53) that Shakespeare's play speaks for the strongly Protestant group surrounding Prince Henry and Princess Elizabeth; her interpretation underestimates the importance of empire to James I himself. Recent treatments of the play in its Jacobean political context include D. E. Landry, "Dreams as History: The Strange Unity of *Cymbeline*," *Shakespeare Quarterly* 33 (1982): 68–79; the discussion building up to *Cymbeline* in Jonathan Goldberg, *James I and the Politics of Literature*, 231–41 and 287n; and David Bergeron, *Shakespeare's Romances and the Royal Family*, note 6 above. See also Hallett Smith's attempt to reduce all topical approaches to the play to absurdity in *Shakespeare's Romances: A Study of Some Ways of the Imagination* (San Marino, Calif.: Huntington Library Publications, 1972), which is a good example of the kind of critical overhostility that my book seeks to come to terms with.

25. See the analysis of the coronation pageant in Graham Parry, *The Golden Age Restor'd: The Culture of the Stuart Court, 1603–42*, 1–39; and in the early sections of Jonathan Goldberg's *James I and the Politics of Literature*, note 5 above. See also Wickham, "Riddle and Emblem," 100–102; and Wickham, *Dramatic Heritage*, 250–54. For James I's proclamations, see Larkin and Hughes, eds., *Stuart Royal Proclamations*, Vol. 1, *Royal Proclamations of King James I 1603–1625*, 18–19 and 94. For the coin, see Wallace Notestein, *The House of Commons 1604–1610*, note 17 above, 247.

The idea of uniting the kingdoms was not a new one, but had been brought up on several previous occasions. See G. W. T. Omond, *The Early History of the Scottish Union Question* (Edinburgh: Oliphant, Anderson & Ferrier, 1897), 9–51; and Gordon Donaldson, "Foundations of Anglo-Scottish Union," in *Elizabethan Government and Society: Essays Presented to Sir John Neale*, ed. S. T. Bindoff et al. (London: Athlone Press, 1961), 282–314. As Donaldson notes, during the sixteenth century in particular there had been a gradual linguistic and cultural amalgamation between the two peoples.

26. The comment was made by the French ambassador (quoted in Notestein, *The House of Commons 1604–1610*, 211–12). My discussion is indebted to the general studies of the Project for Union by D. H. Willson, "King James I and Anglo-Scottish Unity," in *Conflict in Stuart England*, ed. W. A. Aiken and B. D. Henning (London: Jonathan Cape, 1960), 43–55; Omond, *The Early History of the Scottish Union Question*, 68–83; and Notestein's detailed account of the parliamentary debates on union, especially 79–80 and 215–54.

27. Thomas Campion, *Lord Hay's Masque*, dedicatory poem to James I, quoted in Wickham, "Riddle and Emblem," 112; as Gordon shows (*The Renaissance Imagination*, 169), contemporaries recognized the political reference. See also the Sibyl's prophecy at the end of Campion's *The Lords' Masque*, in Orgel and Strong, *Inigo Jones: The Theatre of the Stuart Court*, 1:246; Graham Parry, *The Golden Age Restor'd*, 102–6; and for the theme of union in Ben Jonson's *Hymenaei*, Gordon, 157–84; and the addition to Gordon's argument in my "Masquing Occasions and Masque Structure," *Research Opportunities in Renaissance Drama* 24 (1981): 7–16. For the Union-as-marriage motif on coins, see Omond, *The Early History of the Scottish Union Question*, 68–69.

28. This is, of course, a brief summary of a set of complex issues. See Wallace Notestein, *The House of Commons 1604–1610*, 233–35; D. Harris Willson, *King James VI and I* (London: Jonathan Cape, 1956), 253–56; Willson's "King James I and Anglo-Scottish Unity," in Aiken's collection *Conflict in Stuart England*; McIlwain, *The Political Works of James I*, 292 and Appendix B, pp. lxxxvii–lxxxix; and especially R. C. Munden's corrective to Willson, "James I and 'the growth of mutual distrust': King, Commons, and Reform, 1603–1604," in Kevin Sharpe, ed., *Faction and Parliament: Essays in Early Stuart History* (Oxford: Clarendon Press, 1978), 43–72; and Brian P. Levack, "The Proposed Union of English Law and Scots Law in the Seventeenth Century," *Juridical Review* n.s. 20 (1975): 97–115. See also Levack, *The Formation of the British State: England, Scotland, and the Union, 1603–1707* (Oxford: Oxford Univ. Press, 1987). I regret that this book appeared too late for me to use in my own discussion.

More general aspects of the controversy over law are discussed in J. G. A.

Pocock, *The Ancient Constitution and the Feudal Law* (Cambridge: Cambridge Univ. Press, 1957), 20–69; and in the debate over law in Christopher Brooks and Kevin Sharpe, "History, English Law and the Renaissance," *Past and Present* 72 (1976): 133–42.

29. On Scottish resistance to James's ecclesiastical reforms, see Samuel R. Gardiner, *History of England from the Accession of James I to the Outbreak of the Civil War* (London: Longmans, Green, 1884), 1: 303–6; and Willson, "King James I and Anglo-Scottish Unity," 49. On the Roman law in Jonson's masque, see my reading in "Masquing Occasions and Masque Structure," 9–11.

30. Notestein, *The House of Commons 1604–1610*, 240. Notestein discounts the claim, made by the French ambassador, that Scots were being denied precedence (212) on grounds that it may have come from the Scots themselves and that James I would not have tolerated such behavior. But as the whole debate over union demonstrates, James did not have all that much control over English attitudes and comportment, particularly when he was not present. The hostile climate in England would tend rather to support the claim. See Willson, *King James VI and I*, 252–55; and Willson, "King James I and Anglo-Scottish Unity," 45–48.

31. There is a detailed discussion of the case and the controversy surrounding it in Samuel Gardiner, *History of England*, 1: 301–57. The major documents of the case, including the arguments of Sir Francis Bacon, counsel for Calvin in the Exchequer, the 1608 report of Sir Edward Coke, and the opinion of James's chancellor Sir Thomas Egerton, are reprinted in T. B. Howell, ed., *A Complete Collection of State Trials*, 2 (London: Hansard and Longman, 1816), cols. 559–696. Egerton's arguments were published at the request of James I in 1609. On some of the contradictions surrounding the case and their effects on the arguments which preceded the American Revolution, see Harvey Wheeler, "Calvin's Case (1608) and the McIlwain-Schuyler Debate," *American Historical Review* 61 (1956): 587–97.

32. For examples of the many public ways in which James I associated himself and the Scots with the lion, see Emrys Jones, "Stuart Cymbeline," note 24 above, 88–93; Wallace Notestein, *The House of Commons 1604–1610*, 80; and Wickham, "Riddle and Emblem," 95–106. The lion was also associated with Britain and was considered to have been the heraldic animal of King Brute himself.

Frances Yates's argument in *Shakespeare's Last Plays* (51–59) that *Cymbeline* was revived to celebrate the marriage of the palsgrave Frederick and Princess Elizabeth is linked to my own in that Frederick was also an alien, also associated with the heraldic imagery of the lion, his marriage yet another example of James's policy for peace and empire. But otherwise there are few similarities between him and Posthumus. Frederick was not a despised alien, but quite popular in England. His marriage with Elizabeth was eventually torn by strife (the Thirty Years' War) but not until well after the play had been written.

33. See, for example, Notestein, *The House of Commons 1604–1610*, 251.

34. See, in particular, Posthumus's contract with Iachimo (TLN 458–72), where his language of "Couenants" and "Articles" seems excessively legalistic for the bargain being concluded. G. Wilson Knight (*The Crown of Life*, 178) has taken general note of the play's preoccupation with law.

35. G. R. Hibbard, "Politics in the Romances," *Filoloski Pregled* 2–3 (1964): 103–16, as summarized in *The Garland Shakespeare Bibliographies: Cymbeline*, ed. Henry E. Jacobs (New York: Garland Publishing, 1982), 37.

36. See, in particular, Frances Yates's discussion in *Shakespeare's Last Plays*; and David M. Bergeron, *Shakespeare's Romances and the Royal Family*.

37. See Joan Hartwig, "Cloten, Autolycus, and Caliban: Bearers of Parodic Burdens," in *Shakespeare's Romances Reconsidered*, ed. Carol McGinnis Kay and Henry E. Jacobs (Lincoln: Univ. of Nebraska Press, 1978), 91–103; James Edward Siemon, "Noble Virtue in 'Cymbeline,'" *Shakespeare Survey* 29 (1976): 51–61; and for the characterization of Cloten, H. N. Hudson, *Lectures on Shakespeare*, 2, 2d ed. (New York: Scribner, 1857), 215–16.

38. Stephen Booth, "Speculations on Doubling in Shakespeare's Plays," 1979; reprinted in *King Lear, Macbeth, Indefinition, and Tragedy* (New Haven: Yale Univ. Press, 1983), 149–53. Other critics have made the same suggestion.

39. McIlwain, ed., *The Political Works of James I*, 271–73, 292; Larkin and Hughes, eds., *Stuart Royal Proclamations*, Vol. 1, 18–19, 94–98. As D. J. Gordon demonstrates (*Renaissance Imagination*, 162–79), this organic political imagery was not only to be found in the speeches of James; it was endemic to discussions of the Union, and, indeed, to discussions of the body politic, though far from universally accepted in terms of its Jacobean political implications, as we shall note below. For a study of some of the general political implications of the play's imagery of rape and bodily fragmentation, see Ann Thompson's fine study, "Philomel in 'Titus Andronicus' and 'Cymbeline,'" *Shakespeare Survey* 31 (1978): 23–32.

40. Bergeron, *Shakespeare's Romances and the Royal Family*, 41 (citing Antonia Fraser's biography of James).

41. Wickham, "Riddle and Emblem," 111–12.

42. See Glynne Wickham, "Shakespeare's Investiture Play: The Occasion and Subject of 'The Winter's Tale,'" *Times Literary Supplement*, Dec. 18, 1969: 1456; Wickham, "Romance and Emblem: A Study in the Dramatic Structure of *The Winter's Tale*," in *The Elizabethan Theatre, III*, ed. David Galloway (London: Macmillan, 1973), 82–99; Robert Speaight, *Shakespeare: The Man and His Achievement* (London: Dent & Sons, 1977), 337; and for Daniel's masque and the investiture symbolism, John Pitcher's essay, "'In those figures which they seeme': Samuel Daniel's *Tethys' Festival*," in David Lindley, ed., *The Court Masque* (Manchester: Manchester Univ. Press, 1984), 33–46.

43. The hilariously apt term *polyanagnorisis* is borrowed from Philip Edwards, *Threshold of a Nation: A Study in English and Irish Drama* (Cambridge: Cambridge Univ. Press, 1979), 91.

44. On Augustus, the redescent of Astraea, and the birth of Roman law, see Yates, *Shakespeare's Last Plays*, especially p. 42; McIlwain, ed., *The Political Works of James I*, 271–73 (James's 1603 speech before Parliament); and for the impact of the birth of Christ, especially Northrop Frye, *A Natural Perspective: The Development of Shakespearean Comedy and Romance* (New York: Columbia Univ. Press, 1965), 66–67.

For arguments for the citizenship of the Post Nati on the basis of the *jus gentium*, see Notestein, *The House of Commons 1604–1610*, 225–27; and Howell, *State Trials*, 2, cols. 563–696. See also Margaret Atwood Judson, *The Crisis of the Constitution* (1949; reprinted New York: Octagon, 1964), 134–35, 165–66. Matters were complicated by the fact that, as Wheeler points out, the anti-union forces also marshaled arguments from the civil law, no doubt to counter the tactics of the king's supporters. Caesar Augustus was, of course, the reputed founder of Roman civil law.

45. Wickham, "Riddle and Emblem," 102.

46. McIlwain, ed., *The Political Works of James I*, 305; for the immediate context, see Wallace Notestein, *The House of Commons 1604–1610*, 245.

47. E. K. Chambers, *William Shakespeare: A Study of Facts and Problems* (Oxford: Clarendon Press, 1930), 2:338–39. Forman's note leaves the performance date unclear. Chambers argues for 1611 but conjectures that the play would have been written the previous year.

48. Those who hold that the Descent is theatrical interpolation can argue that it dates from after the performance in 1610 or 1611. Given its particular reverberation with parliamentary affairs in 1606–8, I find that viewpoint implausible.

49. This point has been emphasized in many recent discussions. See in particular David Bergeron, *Shakespeare's Romances and the Royal Family*, 147–57; and Meredith Skura's essay "Interpreting Posthumus' Dream from Above and Below: Families, Psychoanalysis, and Literary Critics," in *Representing Shakespeare: New Psychoanalytic Essays*, ed. Murray M. Schwartz and Coppélia Kahn (Baltimore: Johns Hopkins Univ. Press, 1980), 203–16.

50. See Glynne Wickham, "From Tragedy to Tragi-Comedy: 'King Lear' as Prologue," *Shakespeare Survey* 26 (1973): 33–48. On the gulf between the genre of tragicomedy (or romance) and topicality, I am also indebted to Howard Felperin, *Shakespearean Romance*, note 24 above, 194–96; and Fredric Jameson, *The Political Unconscious: Narrative as a Socially Symbolic Act* (1981; reprinted Ithaca: Cornell Univ. Press, 1985), 148–50.

51. See, in particular, Nicholas Abraham and Maria Torok, *The Wolf Man's Magic Word: A Cryptonymy*, trans. Nicholas Rand, Theory and History of Literature, vol. 37 (Minneapolis: Univ. of Minnesota Press, 1986), and the foreword by Jacques Derrida, which reincrypts the authors' operation of decrypting. In dealing with the Wolf Man, the authors are not, for obvious reasons, taking on a patient who can be "cured" of the fissures which separate some areas of his experience from others. However, the kinds of vertical splits which Abraham and Torok describe are very much like the narcissistic splits discussed in therapeutic terms in the works of Heinz Kohut. See in particular his *The Analysis of the Self: A Systematic Approach to the Psychoanalytic Treatment of Narcissistic Personality Disorders* (1971; reprinted New York: International Universities Press, 1974); and *The Search for the Self: Selected Writings of Heinz Kohut: 1950–1978*, ed. Paul H. Ornstein, 2 vols. (1978; reprinted New York: International Universities Press, 1984). I hope to explore these fascinating matters further in a separate study; suffice it to say for the present that Kohut's work allows for the building of many connections between the fissuring of individual psyches and the larger social formations within which such divisions function.

52. On the doctrine of essences as a subject for debate, I am particularly indebted to R. C. Munden, "James I and 'the growth of mutual distrust,'" note 28 above, 64.

53. Felperin, *Shakespearean Romance*, 195; E. K. Chambers, *William Shakespeare: A Study of Facts and Problems*, 2:352. For a detailed account of Charles's policies toward the Scottish Kirk, see Gardiner, *History of England from the Accession of James I to the Outbreak of the Civil War*, 7:274–98; and among many other recent studies of the possible impact of Caroline ecclesiastical policy, Conrad Russell, ed., *The Origins of the English Civil War* (New York: Harper & Row, 1973), especially the Introduction (1–31), and the essays by Michael Hawkins, Nicholas Tyacke, Robin Clifton, and P. W. Thomas.

54. Here and throughout the discussion my text is the facsimile of the Pied Bull quarto in *Shakespeare's Plays in Quarto: A Facsimile Edition of Copies Primarily from the Henry E. Huntington Library*, ed. Michael J. B. Allen and Kenneth Muir (Berkeley: Univ. of California Press, 1981). Page numbers in the text will be to this edition. We surmise that 1606 was the year of performance because the quarto was entered in the Stationer's Register in 1607.

For topical readings of *The Winter's Tale* in terms of the Project for Union, see the studies by Glynne Wickham cited in notes 24 and 50 above; there are also suggestive hints in David M. Bergeron, *Shakespeare's Romances and the Royal Family*, 157.

55. I am indebted in particular to Annabel Patterson, *Censorship and Interpretation*, 58–73; Marie Axton, *The Queen's Two Bodies: Drama and the Elizabethan Succession* (London: Royal Historical Society, 1977), 131–47; Steven Urkowitz, *Shakespeare's Revision of King Lear* (Princeton: Princeton Univ. Press, 1980); and Gary Taylor and Michael Warren, eds., *The Division of the Kingdoms: Shakespeare's Two Versions of King Lear* (Oxford: Clarendon Press, 1983).

56. See Margaret Judson, *The Crisis of the Constitution*, 25–27, 145; for uses of the idea in contemporary pageantry, see my "City Metal and Country Mettle," note 2 above.

57. See, for general discussion, George W. Keeton, *Shakespeare's Legal and Political Background* (London: Pitman & Sons, 1967); O. Hood Phillips's survey, *Shakespeare and the Lawyers* (London: Methuen, 1972), 89–90; and McIlwain, ed., *The Political Works of James I*, Appendix B, lxxxviii–ix.

58. See Larkin and Hughes, eds., *Stuart Royal Proclamations*, Vol. 1, 92–93.

59. See John Kerrigan's essay "Revision, Adaptation, and the Fool in *King Lear*," and Gary Taylor's essay "*King Lear*: The Date and Authorship of the Folio Version," both in *Division of the Kingdoms*, ed. Taylor and Warren, 195–243 and 351–468. Possible reasons behind the alterations are discussed by Taylor, who argues for artistic motives in his essay "Monopolies, Show Trials, Disaster, and Invasion: *King Lear* and Censorship," in *Division of the Kingdoms*, 75–119; and by Annabel Patterson in *Censorship and Interpretation*, 61–71; she contests Taylor's dismissal of censorship or the fear of it as a motivating factor behind the alterations.

I am also indebted to my former colleague Richard Knowles, who has supplied me with enough evidence against Urkowitz and Taylor's bibliographical arguments to convince me that I do not have enough expertise to enter that particular fray. See Knowles's reviews of Urkowitz in *Modern Philology* 79 (1981–82): 197–200; and of Taylor and Warren in *Shakespeare Quarterly* 36 (1985): 115–20.

60. See, for example, his heated speech against monopolies recounted in *The Hastings Journal of the Parliament of 1621*, ed. Lady Evangeline de Villiers, Camden Miscellany, vol. 20 (London: Offices of the Royal Historical Society, 1953), 27–29. At the beginning of the reign, James had revoked existing monopolies, but it soon became clear that he was sweeping away the old ones to make room for his own. See Larkin and Hughes, eds., *Stuart Royal Proclamations*, Vol. 1, 11–14; but also the more favorable account in R. C. Munden, "James I and 'the growth of mutual distrust,'" 50–53.

61. I have made a detailed argument for this proposition in *The Politics of Mirth: Jonson, Herrick, Milton, Marvell, and the Defense of Old Holiday Pastimes,*

note 8 above; both there and in the present discussion, I am also strongly indebted to Philip J. Finkelpearl, "'The Comedians' Liberty': Censorship of the Jacobean Stage Reconsidered," *English Literary Renaissance* 16 (1986): 123–38; and to Stephen Orgel's statement of the problem in "Making Greatness Familiar," 1981; reprinted in David M. Bergeron, ed., *Pageantry in the Shakespearean Theater*, 19–25.

62. See Steven Urkowitz, *Shakespeare's Revision of King Lear*; and all the essays in *Division of the Kingdoms*, ed. Taylor and Warren. As my discussion will make clear, however, I do not regard either text we have as definitive in the sense that these careful scholars claim for it.

63. The quarto version of the phrase reads "Like Rats oft bite those cordes in twaine, / Which are to intrench, to inloose" (677). The wording is interesting because it can be interpreted as a highly equivocal reference to the matter of essences: something tied together is either to be further tied (intrenched) or loosened. The reading is admittedly shaky and, in this case, I am willing to go along with modern editors who argue that the quarto version is probably garbled. I would accept a reading closer to the folio version, "Like Rats oft bite the holy cords atwaine, / Which are t'intrince, t'vnloose" (TLN 1147–48).

64. See Urkowitz, *Shakespeare's Revision of King Lear*, 80–128; and Randall McLeod, "Gon. No more, the text is foolish," in *Division of the Kingdoms*, 153–94. But see also Marion Trousdale's critique of the critical assumptions behind the differentiations in "A Trip through the Divided Kingdoms," *Shakespeare Quarterly* 37 (1986): 218–23.

65. See the descriptions of the holiday in R. Chambers, *The Book of Days* (London: Chambers, n.d.), 2:763–65; and Margaret Hotine, "Two Plays for St. Stephen's Day," *Notes and Queries* 227 (1982): 119–21. The carol of King Wenceslaus dates only from the nineteenth century. See Percy Dearmer et al., *The Oxford Book of Carols* (London: Humphrey Milford, 1928), 271.

66. W. Carew Hazlitt, *Faiths and Folklore: A Dictionary of National Beliefs, Superstitions and Popular Customs* (London: Reeves and Turner, 1905), 2:564.

67. Like Margaret Hotine, to whose work I am indebted for the parallels, I have used the 1559 *Book of Common Prayer*, but I have also checked the cited passages against the 1604 *Book of Common Prayer*. Biblical passages are from Hotine's citations of the Bishop's Bible version. There is another discussion of the liturgical context of *King Lear* in R. Chris Hassel, Jr., *Renaissance Drama and the English Church Year* (Lincoln: Univ. of Nebraska Press, 1979), 28, which points out the play's use of the holiday motif of forgiveness of one's enemies. That idea will be brought up below.

68. See in particular Roger Warren, "The Folio Omission of the Mock Trial: Motives and Consequences," *Division of the Kingdoms*, 45–57. Warren's major argument for the omission is on theatrical grounds—the scene slowed the play down too much. Given the festival context of the quarto version, I would suggest that much more was at stake. In the court setting, the slower quarto version might have been more moving and effective than the swifter and more perfunctory folio version.

69. See Larkin and Hughes, eds., *Stuart Royal Proclamations*, Vol. 1, *Royal Proclamations of King James I 1603–1625*, 103–4, and the similar order for the spring holidays, 21–22. See also my more extended discussion in *The Politics of Mirth*, 1–85.

70. Arthur Wilson, *The History of Great Britain* (London: for Richard Lownds, 1653), 35.

71. Hotine, "Two Plays for St. Stephen's Day," 120. See also Joseph Wittreich, *"Image of that Horror": History, Prophecy, and Apocalypse in King Lear* (San Marino, Calif.: Huntington Library, 1984), 16–33, 57–58, and 114–22.

72. See the rather massive evidence collected by Annabel Patterson, Gary Taylor, and Marie Axton, all cited in note 55 above; Margaret Hotine has shown parallels between Lear's fits and a hallucinatory disorder suffered by James I in "Lear's Fit of the Mother," *Notes and Queries* 226 (1981): 138–41.

73. See Stephen Greenblatt, "Shakespeare and the Exorcists," in Patricia Parker and Geoffrey Hartman, eds., *Shakespeare and the Question of Theory* (New York: Methuen, 1985), 163–87; and, for another fine essay that discusses similar issues of evacuation and deidealization, Franco Moretti, "'A Huge Eclipse': Tragic Form and the Deconstruction of Sovereignty," in Stephen Greenblatt, ed., *The Power of Forms in the English Renaissance* (Norman, Okla.: Pilgrim Books, 1982), 7–40.

CHAPTER 4

1. See Mark Eccles, ed., *A New Variorum Edition of Shakespeare: Measure for Measure* (New York: Modern Language Association, 1980), 292–94. My discussion throughout is strongly indebted to Eccles, also to J. W. Lever, ed., *Measure for Measure* (London: Methuen, 1965), who discusses textual problems on pp. xi–xxxi; and to W. W. Greg, *The Shakespeare First Folio: Its Bibliographical and Textual History* (Oxford: Clarendon Press, 1955), 354–56.

2. See Lever's survey, p. xxxii; I am also indebted to Jonathan Dollimore, "Transgression and Surveillance in *Measure for Measure*," in *Political Shakespeare: New Essays in Cultural Materialism*, ed. Jonathan Dollimore and Alan Sinfield (Ithaca: Cornell Univ. Press, 1985), 72–87.

3. *The Letters of John Chamberlain*, ed. N. E. McClure, Memoirs of the American Philosophical Society 12 (Philadelphia: Lancashire Press, 1939), 1: 48 (letter of October 20, 1598); *Middlesex County Records (Old Series)*, Vol. 1, ed. John Cordy Jeaffreson (1886) (reprinted London: Greater London Council, 1972), 234–35, 263, 270, 287. (These cases date from about 1598 to 1604.)

4. That is not to say that contemporary Puritans would have agreed that Claudio's offense falls within the statute. Angelo's interpretation is extreme, even by contemporary Puritan standards. Here and elsewhere, I use the term *Puritan* as opposed to *Protestant* to delineate that group within contemporary Protestantism which was devoted to thorough liturgical reform and restructuring of the ecclesiastical hierarchy.

See the accounts of contemporary Puritan opinion in John Strype, *The Life and Acts of John Whitgift, D.D.* (Oxford: Clarendon Press, 1822), 2:17; G. B. Harrison, "Extreme Tenets of the Puritans," in *The Elizabethan Journals: Being a Record of Those Things Most Talked of during the Years 1591–1603* (1928–33; reprinted as one volume, New York: Macmillan, 1939), 208–9; and the survey of Reformation legal opinion in Gerald Strauss, *Law, Resistance, and the State: The Opposition to Roman Law in Reformation Germany* (Princeton: Princeton Univ. Press, 1986), 191–239. Reformation planning and ideology on the Continent regularly included the death penalty for adultery, if not for fornication. In practice, such ordinances tended to be fleeting. See Steven E. Ozment, *The Reformation in the Cities: The Appeal of Protestantism to Sixteenth-Century Germany and Switzerland* (New Haven: Yale Univ. Press, 1975), 104–57; and E. William Monter, "Crime and Punishment in Calvin's Geneva, 1562," *Archiv für Reformationsgeschichte* 64 (1973): 281–87.

5. For James's pageant, see Jonathan Goldberg, *James I and the Politics of Literature* (Baltimore: Johns Hopkins Univ. Press, 1983), 31–33 and 50–54; Graham Parry, *The Golden Age Restor'd: The Culture of the Stuart Court, 1603–42* (New York: St. Martin's Press, 1981), 1–9; and my discussion of the Londinium Arch in *The Politics of Mirth: Jonson, Herrick, Milton, Marvell, and the Defense of Old Holiday Pastimes* (Chicago: Univ. of Chicago Press, 1986), 64–67. For imperial analogues, see Roy Strong, *Art and Power: Renaissance Festivals 1450–1650* (1973; reprinted Berkeley: Univ. of California Press, 1984), chap. 2, "Images of Empire: Charles V and the Imperial Progress," 75–97; and Stanley Applebaum, ed., *The Triumph of Maximilian I* (New York: Dover Publications, 1964).

6. Lever, ed., *Measure for Measure*, xxxi.

7. Richard Levin, *New Readings vs. Old Plays: Recent Trends in the Reinterpretation of English Renaissance Drama* (1979; reprinted Chicago: Univ. of Chicago Press, 1982), 171–93. For materials linking James and the duke, see Lever's edition of *Measure for Measure*, xlviii–li; and the interpretations in Josephine Waters Bennett, *Measure for Measure as Royal Entertainment* (New York: Columbia Univ. Press, 1966); David L. Stevenson, *The Achievement of Shakespeare's Measure for Measure* (Ithaca: Cornell Univ. Press, 1966); and more recently, Jonathan Goldberg, *James I and the Politics of Literature*, 231–39; and Leonard Tennenhouse, *Power on Display: The Politics of Shakespeare's Genres* (London: Methuen, 1986), 154–59; along with Tennenhouse's important earlier article "Representing Power: *Measure for Measure* in Its Time," in *The Power of Forms in the English Renaissance*, ed. Stephen Greenblatt (Norman, Okla.: Pilgrim Books, 1982), 139–56.

More generally, I am also indebted to Jacqueline Rose, "Sexuality in the Reading of Shakespeare: *Hamlet* and *Measure for Measure*," in John Drakakis, ed., *Alternative Shakespeares* (London: Methuen, 1985), 95–118; and to Paul Hammond, "The Argument of *Measure for Measure*," *English Literary Renaissance* 16 (1986): 496–519. Steven Mullaney's work on "the place of the stage" in Renaissance London has influenced my own analysis throughout the chapter. See his *The Place of the Stage: License, Play, and Power in Renaissance England* (Chicago: Univ. of Chicago Press, 1988). Studies of law in the play will be cited further along.

8. *Annus Mirabilis*, epistle dedicatory, *The Poetical Works of Dryden*, ed. George R. Noyes (Cambridge, Mass.: Riverside Press, 1950), 23. For standard accounts of the growth and development of London, see Roger Finlay, *Population and Metropolis: The Demography of London* (Cambridge: Cambridge Univ. Press, 1981); and Harold Edford Priestley, *London: The Years of Change* (London: Muller, 1966).

9. Alexander Pulling, *The Laws, Customs, Usages, and Regulations of the City and Port of London*, 2d ed. (London: William Henry Bond, 1854), 221–22.

10. See Patrick Collinson, *The Elizabethan Puritan Movement* (Berkeley: Univ. of California Press, 1967), 86–87, 339–41; for the liberties used as sanctuary, G. B. Harrison, *The Elizabethan Journals*, note 4 above, 1:192, 2:327; and on the liberties and the theater, Virginia Crocheron Gildersleeve, *Government Regulation of the Elizabethan Drama* (1908; reprinted New York: Burt Franklin, 1961). See also Gildersleeve's indispensable discussion of the slippery meanings of the phrases "Liberties of London" and "London Liberties," 142–43.

11. See the discussion in Virginia Gildersleeve, *Government Regulation of the Elizabethan Drama*, 193–94.

12. For the conflict over the Tower, see *Analytical Index to the Series of Records Known as the Remembrancia . . . AD 1579–1664* (London: Francis and Co., 1878), 426–35; and *Calendar of State Papers Domestic*, James I, 8:452 (dated Aug. 21, 1608). Other areas of conflict are recorded in the *Analytical Index*, 4–6, 17, 56, 70–71, and 94. Some of the key cases at law are collected in Edward Coke, *The Twelfth Part of the Reports of Sir Edward Coke* (London: for Henry Twyford, 1656), 26–27. For a more general view of the conflict, see Carolyn A. Edie, "Tactics and Strategies: Parliament's Attack upon the Royal Dispensing Power 1597–1689," *American Journal of Legal History* 29 (1985): 197–234; and Derek Hirst, "Court, Country, and Politics before 1629," in *Faction and Parliament: Essays on Early Stuart History*, ed. Kevin Sharpe (Oxford: Clarendon, 1978), 105–37.

13. Richard Helgerson, "The Land Speaks: Cartography, Chorography, and the Representation of Power," *Representations* 16 (1986): 50–85. I am grateful to Mr. Helgerson for graciously giving me access to his work in manuscript.

14. *Analytical Index to the Remembrancia*, 438.

15. See the analyses cited in note 5 above.

16. See the survey of canon law approaches in Jonathan K. Price, "*Measure for Measure* and the Critics: Towards a New Approach," *Shakespeare Quarterly* 20 (1969): 179–204; and for individual studies of the play's use of law, see in addition to the sources in note 7 above Peter Alexander, "*Measure for Measure*: A Case for the Scottish Solomon," *Modern Language Quarterly* 28 (1967): 478–88; James Black, "The Unfolding of 'Measure for Measure,'" *Shakespeare Survey* 26 (1973): 119–28; John W. Dickinson, "Renaissance Equity and *Measure for Measure*," *Shakespeare Quarterly* 13 (1962): 287–97; Wilbur Dunkel, "Law and Equity in *Measure for Measure*," *Shakespeare Quarterly* 13 (1962): 275–85; Darryl J. Gless, *Measure for Measure, the Law, and the Convent* (Princeton: Princeton Univ. Press, 1979); George W. Keeton's study of equity in *Shakespeare's Legal and Political Background* (London: Pitman & Sons, 1967); and Margaret Scott's reminder as to differences between canon law on the Continent and in England, "'Our City's Institutions': Some Further Reflections on the Marriage Contracts in *Measure for Measure*," *ELH* 49 (1982): 790–804.

For a lively sense of the ecclesiastical courts' flexibility in terms of legal practice, see R. H. Helmholz, *Marriage Litigation in Medieval England* (Cambridge: Cambridge Univ. Press, 1974); and F. G. Emmison, *Elizabethan Life: Morals and the Church Courts* (Chelmsford: Essex County Council, 1973). The new canons are recorded in Anthony Sparrow, *A Collection of Articles, Injunctions, Canons, Orders, Ordinances and Constitutions Ecclesiastical . . . of the Church of England* (London: for Robert Cutler and Joseph Clarke, 1671), which reprints the 1604 edition of the canons in English translation. The canons in question are on p. 28 of the 1604 reprint. See also the background material in John Strype, *The Life and Acts of John Whitgift, D.D.*, 1:232; 2:377–510, and the Appendix (separately dated 1717) to the 1718 one-volume edition of Strype's *Life of Whitgift*, 222–23.

17. See Lawrence Stone, *The Family, Sex and Marriage in England 1500–1800* (New York: Harper & Row, 1977), 32–35; Christopher Hill, *Society and Puritanism in Pre-Revolutionary England*, 2d ed. (New York: Schocken Books, 1967), 298–343; and Peter Laslett and Richard Wall, eds., *Household and Family in Past Time* (Cambridge: Cambridge Univ. Press, 1972). For examples, see

Paul Hair, ed., *Before the Bawdy Court . . . 1300–1800* (London: Elek, 1972); and F. G. Emmison, *Elizabethan Life: Morals and the Church Courts.*

18. Ferdinando Pulton, *A Collection of all the Statutes Now in Use* (London: for John Bell and Christopher Barker, 1670), 973.

19. Christopher Hill, *Society and Puritanism in Pre-Revolutionary England,* 298–343; John Strype, *Life and Acts of John Whitgift,* 1:266, 2:383–84, 397–99, 428–30; and F. G. Emmison, *Elizabethan Life: Morals and the Church Courts,* 10, 20, 30, 40–41.

20. Patrick Collinson, *The Elizabethan Puritan Movement,* 347–49. The particular characterizations of the church courts are cited from Luther as quoted in Strauss, *Law, Resistance, and the State,* 217; and Phillip Stubbes, *The Anatomie of Abuses* (1583), as cited in Hair, ed., *Before the Bawdy Court,* 57. See also Emmison, 310–13.

There is disagreement among historians about the extent to which city and town reform movements coincided with Puritanism. For the controversy, see the essays in *Order and Disorder in Early Modern England,* ed. Anthony Fletcher and John Stevenson (Cambridge: Cambridge Univ. Press, 1985), especially M. Spufford, "Puritanism and Social Control?" 41–57; and S. D. Amussen, "Gender, Family, and the Social Order, 1560–1725," 196–217. For an amusing account of one "outburst of reforming frenzy," see David Underdown, *Revel, Riot, and Rebellion: Popular Politics and Culture in England 1603–1660* (Oxford: Clarendon Press, 1985), 59.

21. Strype, *Life and Acts of John Whitgift,* 2:376; see also the colorful list of examples, Appendix, 222–24. The abuse was not, apparently, corrected until much later, despite parliamentary and ecclesiastical initiatives. For later and more blatant examples, see Gellert Spencer Alleman, *Matrimonial Law and the Materials of Restoration Comedy* (Philadelphia: Univ. of Pennsylvania Press, 1942), 36–50.

22. See Anthony Sparrow, *A Collection of Articles, Injunctions, Canons, Orders, Ordinances,* reprint of 1604 edition of the canons, 28; Lawrence Stone, *The Family, Sex, and Marriage in England 1500–1800,* 33–35; and the detailed discussion in Gellert Alleman, *Matrimonial Law and the Materials of Restoration Comedy,* 34–35.

23. Hill, *Society and Puritanism in Pre-Revolutionary England,* 298–343; Ronald A. Marchant, *The Puritans and the Church Courts in the Diocese of York 1560–1642* (London: Longmans, 1960), 143.

24. Gellert Alleman, *Matrimonial Law and the Materials of Restoration Comedy,* 58–59; for statutes against fornication, see *An Abstract of the Laws Already in Force against Profaneness, Immorality, & Blasphemy Together with the Laws and Ordinances against the same by the Parliament . . . 1640 to 1656* (London: R. Baldwin, 1698).

25. Alexander Pulling, *The Laws, Customs, Usages, etc. of the City and Port of London,* 253–54, 540; John Stow, *Survay of London* (London, 1603), 190–91. In the Middle Ages, the ecclesiastical punishment had been closer to London's, but with time the church courts relaxed the strictness of punishments for sexual offenses. See R. H. Helmholz, *Marriage Litigation in Medieval England,* 182–83. Other towns asserted similar privileges; see Hill, *Society and Puritanism in Pre-Revolutionary England,* 333; and James A. Brundage, *Law, Sex, and Christian Society in Medieval Europe* (Chicago: Univ. of Chicago Press, 1987), 442–44, 469, 482–87, 491–93.

26. See Lever's edition of *Measure for Measure,* 4n. On the Continent, "the

terms for common justice" would imply canon law; in England, the law which collected local laws together into a single body of precedent was the common law.

27. See the *Dictionary of National Biography* under Popham and Coke; for other literary examples of the counterpoising of local law and "Imperia" to the disparagement of local justices, see David Bevington, *Tudor Drama and Politics: A Critical Approach to Topical Meaning* (Cambridge, Mass.: Harvard Univ. Press, 1968), 267–86; Lever, ed., *Measure for Measure*, xlvii; my discussion of Jonson's *Bartholomew Fair* in *The Politics of Mirth*, 38–63; Leonard Tennenhouse, "Representing Power: *Measure for Measure* in Its Time"; and Susan Wells, *The Dialectics of Representation* (Baltimore: Johns Hopkins Univ. Press, 1985), 103–32.

28. Mark Eccles, ed., *A New Variorum Edition of Shakespeare: Measure for Measure*, 299.

29. C. H. McIlwain, ed., *The Political Works of James I* (Cambridge, Mass.: Harvard Univ. Press, 1918), 291; for the idea in Roman law, see, among other similar discussions, Gerald Strauss, *Law, Resistance, and the State*, note 4 above, 71. Strauss's discussion uses another common term for the same idea— the emperor as *lex animata*.

30. R. H. Helmholz, *Marriage Litigation in Medieval England*, 17–22, 127–34; for a corrective to Helmholz's essentially positive view of the system, see the discussion of post-Reformation complaints in Ronald A. Marchant, *The Puritans and the Church Courts*; and Christopher Hill, *Society and Puritanism in Pre-Revolutionary England*, 298–343.

31. Cited in John W. Dickinson, "Renaissance Equity and *Measure for Measure*," note 16 above, 287–97, from William Lambarde's *Archeion* (before 1591).

32. Mark Eccles, ed., *A New Variorum Edition of Shakespeare: Measure for Measure*, 234.

33. For Elizabethan and Jacobean examples of the ritual, see John Nichols, *The Progresses and Public Processions of Queen Elizabeth* (London: John Nichols, 1823), 2:138–43; and G. B. Harrison, *A Jacobean Journal: Being a Record of Those Things Most Talked of During the Years 1603–6* (London: George Routledge and Sons, 1941), 224–25 (the king's 1605 entry into Oxford). In *Measure for Measure*, there is a minor inconsistency between the duke's order to the officials to meet him a league below the city and the actual place of meeting, nearer the gates; as Escalus has earlier complained, "Euery Letter he hath writ, hath disuouch'd other" (TLN 2273).

34. My discussion is indebted to Philip C. McGuire, *Speechless Dialect: Shakespeare's Open Silences* (Berkeley: Univ. of California Press, 1985), 79–96; and more generally to David Bevington, *Action Is Eloquence: Shakespeare's Language of Gesture* (Cambridge, Mass.: Harvard Univ. Press, 1984).

35. See, for example, Josephine Waters Bennett, *Measure for Measure as Royal Entertainment*, 174n.6. Isabella is the only nonroyal character in Shakespeare besides Caesar to use the royal "we": "More then our Brother, is our Chastitie." See Warren D. Smith, "More Light on *Measure for Measure*," *Modern Language Quarterly* 23 (1962): 309–22. That usage could link her with Elizabeth, or with some other regal personage; another possibility will be discussed in the next section.

36. Roy Strong, *Portraits of Queen Elizabeth I* (Oxford: Clarendon Press, 1963), 156. The statue was quickly removed, probably because of court objections to its iconography (the interpretation of which is mine). Strong

calls the statue "one of the strangest of the posthumous representations of the Queen."

For civic liberties and *Lucrece*, see the "Argument," cited from *The Complete Works of Shakespeare*, ed. David Bevington, 3d ed. (Glenview, Ill.: Scott, Foresman, 1980), 1545–46; and Clifford Chalmers Huffman, *Coriolanus in Context* (Lewisburg, Pa.: Bucknell Univ. Press, 1971), 34–50.

37. See Gerald Strauss's detailed study *Law, Resistance, and the State*, note 4 above; and for the Hapsburg lands in particular, R. J. W. Evans, *The Making of the Habsburg Monarchy 1550–1700* (1979; reprinted Oxford: Clarendon Press, 1984), 82, 103–5, 112; Roger Lockyer, *Habsburg and Bourbon Europe 1470–1720* (London: Longman, 1974), 187–218; and Hermann Rebel, *Peasant Classes: The Bureaucratization of Property and Family Relations under Early Habsburg Absolutism 1511–1636* (Princeton: Princeton Univ. Press, 1983), 167.

38. For sources and analogues, see Mark Eccles, ed., *The New Variorum Edition of Shakespeare: Measure for Measure*, 301–93; and Geoffrey Bullough, ed., *Narrative and Dramatic Sources of Shakespeare*, 2 (New York: Columbia Univ. Press, 1958), 399–530.

39. See Mark Eccles, "*Measure for Measure*, Montmorency, and Sardou's *La Tosca*," *Comparative Drama* 14 (1980): 74–78. My thanks to Margaret Lacy for kindly supplying the reference.

40. Don Pedro Calderón de la Barca, *Obras Completas I: Dramas*, ed. Luis Astrana Marín (Madrid: Aguilar, 1951), 523–53. For the reference in context, see H. G. Koenigsberger, *The Habsburgs and Europe 1516–1660* (Ithaca: Cornell Univ. Press, 1971), 81. See also Edward Fitzgerald, trans., *Six Dramas of Calderón Freely Translated*, ed. H. Oelsner (London: Chatto & Windus, 1909), 337–406. For analysis of similarities between the English and Spanish stage, see Walter Cohen, *Drama of a Nation: Public Theater in Renaissance England and Spain* (Ithaca: Cornell Univ. Press, 1985).

41. Gerald Strauss, *Law, Resistance, and the State*, note 4 above, 56.

42. Eccles, ed., *Variorum Edition*, 21n; Lever, ed., *Measure for Measure*, xxxi.

43. See George W. Keeton's reading in *Shakespeare's Legal and Political Background*, 374–76; and, among many general histories which detail the Hapsburg events, Roger Lockyer, *Habsburg and Bourbon Europe*, 317–29.

44. For a sense of just how close ties were between English and Hungarian Protestants, I am indebted to the session on Hungary, Annual Conference of the Renaissance Society of America, Tempe, Arizona, March 1967, particularly to the paper presented by Gyorgy Szonyi, "English Books in 16th and 17th Century Hungary."

45. See Josephine Waters Bennett's discussion of the duke of Holst, *Measure for Measure as Royal Entertainment,* note 7 above, 8–11. She misses the topical reference to division among the Hapsburg archdukes, but gives a good sense of the contemporary preoccupation with Hungary.

46. Eccles, ed., *Variorum Edition*, 22n; Lever, ed., *Measure for Measure*, 9–10n.

47. Mark Eccles notes that parallels have been found between Shakespeare's duke and Vincentio Gonzaga, duke of Mantua, a cousin of Rudolf II (*Variorum Edition*, 3n.). The connection is certainly possible. However, that duke was not particularly well known in England; the topical resonances with Shakespeare's duke, if any, would not have been strong. Moreover, by 1623, the Vincentio who was duke of Mantua had been dead for eleven years.

48. R. J. W. Evans, *Rudolf II and His World: A Study in Intellectual History* (Oxford: Clarendon Press, 1973), 80–82.

49. Most of these details are taken from English gossip and letters. See *The Letters of John Chamberlain*, ed. N. E. McClure, note 3 above, 1:50, 103, 115; *Calendar of State Papers Domestic*, Elizabeth I, 5:49 (May 8, 1598), 76 (July 31, 1598), 160 (Feb. 5, 1599). See also Ch. Potvin, *Albert et Isabelle: Fragments sur leur règne* (Paris: A. Bohné, 1861), 62, 148–70; and the less hostile account in James Shaw, *Sketches of the History of the Austrian Netherlands* (London: for G. G. J. and J. Robinson, 1786), 302.

The topical associations with Isabella of Spain and her flamboyant religious asceticism cast an interesting light on the patterns discussed in Carolyn E. Brown, "Erotic Religious Flagellation and Shakespeare's *Measure for Measure*," *English Literary Renaissance* 16 (1986): 139–65.

50. H. G. Koenigsberger, *The Habsburgs and Europe 1516–1660*, 200–201; *The Letters of John Chamberlain*, 1:81.

51. *Calendar of State Papers Domestic*, Elizabeth I, 5:263 (July 29, 1599); H. G. Koenigsberger, *The Habsburgs and Europe*, 200–201; Albert J. Loomie, S.J., *Toleration and Diplomacy: The Religious Issue in Anglo-Spanish Relations, 1603–1605*, The American Philosophical Society, n.s. vol. 53, pt. 6 (1963), 15 (pamphlet).

52. *Calendar of State Papers Domestic*, Elizabeth I, 4:157 (1595?), 5:68 (June 1598); 212–13 (letter from Robert Parsons, June 15, 1599); 220 (June 27, 1599); 398 (Feb. 26, 1600); 460 (Aug. 13/23, 1600); James I, 8:1 (March? 1603). See also C. H. McIlwain, ed., *The Political Works of James I*, Introduction, pp. l–li.

53. Charles Howard Carter, *The Secret Diplomacy of the Habsburgs, 1598–1625* (New York: Columbia Univ. Press, 1964), 12, 53–55. Elizabeth herself had expressed cordiality toward the idea of peace, but temporized, probably sensing that to conclude a peace before she was safely succeeded by a Protestant ruler in England would be dangerous. For contemporary rumors, see also *Calendar of State Papers Domestic*, Elizabeth I, 4:169; 5:172 (March 24, 1599); 267–68 (July 30, 1599); 402 (Feb. 29, 1600); 6:71 (July 1601); 180 (April 27, 1602); 271 (Dec. 25, 1602); James I, 8:145 (August 1604); and *The Letters of John Chamberlain*, 1:202.

54. On the Archduke's policy and reputation, see H. G. Koenigsberger, *The Habsburgs and Europe*, 203–4; Roger Lockyer, *Habsburg and Bourbon Europe*, 251–52, 407; and M. de Montpleinchamp, *Histoire de l'Archiduc Albert* (Brussels: Société de l'histoire de Belgique, 1870), 558–59. Belgian historians' accounts of the Archdukes are nearly as variable as those in seventeenth-century England. For Isabella's promise to defeat Ostend, see the letter from Dudley Carleton to John Chamberlain, *Calendar of State Papers Domestic*, Elizabeth I, 5:407 (Mar. 2, 1600).

55. On London efforts to aid Ostend, see *Calendar of State Papers Domestic*, Elizabeth I, 6:61 (July 6, 1601); 114 (Oct. 31, 1601); 187 (May 8, 1602). For the Archdukes' hollow victory, see Ch. Potvin, *Albert et Isabelle: Fragments sur leur règne*, 101–31. This is a hostile account, but quite close to a wide current of contemporary English opinion. One contemporary quipped that the archduke killed his soldiers instead of paying them, *Calendar of State Papers Domestic*, James I, 8:27 (Aug. 3, 1603).

56. For James's cordiality toward the Archdukes, see Albert J. Loomie, *Toleration and Diplomacy*, 10; and for James's speech, see C. H. McIlwain, ed., *The Political Works of James I*, 274.

James made a deliberate policy of deception toward the Catholic powers;

see Loomie, *Toleration and Diplomacy*, 10–13, 23. In order to gain their support for his title to the English throne, for example, he let it be understood that if he received the English crown, he would have his son Henry brought up as a Catholic (p. 12). These tactics came back to haunt him once he had acceded to the English throne—hence, perhaps, some of his emphasis on royal sincerity. But there was also nervousness at the other end of the spectrum: some of the Anglican bishops feared he would be too lenient toward the ultra-Calvinists.

57. For comparisons between the English church courts and the Inquisition, see John Strype, *Life and Acts of John Whitgift*, 2:135, 497–98. The matter came up several times at the Hampton Court Conference in 1604, and also in Parliament that year, where there were violent attacks on the ecclesiastical courts, particularly the High Commission. The same Parliament also objected to James's use of the title of emperor. See William Barlow, *The Svmme and Substance of the Conference . . . at Hampton Court. Ianuary 14, 1603* [new style, 1604] (London: for Mathew Law, 1604), 89; Wallace Notestein, *The House of Commons 1604–1610* (New Haven: Yale Univ. Press, 1971), 40–42; and R. C. Munden, "James I and 'the growth of mutual distrust': King, Commons, and Reform, 1603–1604," in Kevin Sharpe, ed., *Faction and Parliament: Essays in Early Stuart History* (Oxford: Clarendon, 1978), 43–72. Munden sees ecclesiastical policy as the single most important factor in the "growth of mutual distrust" between king and reformers. For other important studies of the Hampton Court Conference and its aftermath, see Patrick Collinson, *The Elizabethan Puritan Movement*, note 10 above, 455–67; and M. H. Curtis, "Hampton Court Conference and Its Aftermath," *History* 46 (1961): 1–16.

58. *Calendar of State Papers Domestic*, James I, 8:101 (Apr. 27? 1604).

59. See the detailed discussion of the environment and negotiations leading up to the peace in Loomie, *Toleration and Diplomacy*, 10–31. Some of the quotations I have used are from slightly earlier: see *Calendar of State Papers Domestic*, Elizabeth I, 5:2 (1598) and 5:262 (July [27], 1599).

60. Loomie, 12, 21–27, 30–38. The report that the Spanish ambassador had been mobbed in London was dated Jan. 31, 1604 (*Calendar of State Papers Domestic*, James I, 8:72). Philip III of Spain (who had succeeded Philip II) suspected that the letter was counterfeit, but that may have been overoptimism on his part as to popular reception of the peace in England.

61. See G. B. Harrison, *A Jacobean Journal . . . 1603–1606*, 156–57; Loomie, *Toleration and Diplomacy*, 36. Precise dating and details of the day's events vary in different accounts. For the text of the treaty, see James F. Larkin and Paul L. Hughes, eds., *Stuart Royal Proclamations*, Vol. 1, *Royal Proclamations of King James I 1603–25* (Oxford: Clarendon Press, 1973), 91–92.

62. James F. Larkin and Paul L. Hughes, eds., *Royal Proclamations of King James I*, 91–92; the 1605 proclamation is on pp. 114–17. For later reactions, see Loomie, *Toleration and Diplomacy*, 48; Loomie gives more credence than Larkin and Hughes (or I) do to the Spanish ambassador's report of the treaty's popularity in London. For additional evidence, see also A[nthony] W[eldon], *The Court and Character of K. James* (London, 1650), 26–27, 32–33, 36–37.

63. See R. Chris Hassel, Jr., *Renaissance Drama and the English Church Year* (Lincoln: Univ. of Nebraska Press, 1979), 23–25, from which the Collect excerpt is cited.

64. See Lever's discussion of the passage in terms of the Treaty of London, xxxi–xxxii.

65. For the pro-Catholic play, see David Bevington, *Tudor Drama and Politics*, 293–95. On the treatment of the 1632 folio, see Robert Stevenson, *Shakespeare's Religious Frontier* (The Hague: Martinus Nijhoff, 1958), 44–45. Only a year after the Treaty of London came news of the Gunpowder Plot—scarcely an event to improve the lot of English Catholics.

66. Virginia Gildersleeve, *Government Regulation of the Elizabethan Drama*, note 10 above, 36–43.

67. See the discussions in Eccles, ed., *Variorum Edition*, 3–6; and W. W. Greg, *The Shakespeare First Folio*, 354–56. Even Pompey, curiously enough, bears a name associated with Rome and military conquest.

68. Among the many recent studies of *Coriolanus*, I am particularly indebted to E. C. Pettet, "*Coriolanus* and the Midlands Insurrection of 1607," *Shakespeare Survey* 3 (1950): 34–42; the extensive discussion of topicality in Geoffrey Bullough, *Narrative and Dramatic Sources of Shakespeare*, 5 (New York: Columbia Univ. Press, 1964), 456–60; Clifford Chalmers Huffman, *Coriolanus in Context*, note 36 above; W. Gordon Zeeveld, "'Coriolanus' and Jacobean Politics," *Modern Language Review* 57 (1962): 321–34; and Janet Adelman's psychoanalytic study of the climate of hunger in the play, "'Anger's My Meat': Feeding, Dependence, and Aggression in *Coriolanus*," 1978; reprinted in *Representing Shakespeare: New Psychoanalytic Essays*, ed. Murray M. Schwartz and Coppélia Kahn (Baltimore: Johns Hopkins Univ. Press, 1980), 129–49. My brief analysis intersects Adelman's at several points. I am suggesting a political dimension for her analysis of phallic aggression and hunger.

I am also indebted to Stuart Kurland, whose work in manuscript presented at Midwest MLA, 1986, helped get me thinking about the play, and to Jonathan Dollimore, *Radical Tragedy: Religion, Ideology and Power in the Drama of Shakespeare and His Contemporaries* (Chicago: Univ. of Chicago Press, 1984), 218–30; Jonathan Goldberg, *James I and the Politics of Literature* (Baltimore: Johns Hopkins Univ. Press, 1983), 186–93, 202; Leonard Tennenhouse, "*Coriolanus*: History and the Crisis of Semantic Order," 1977; reprinted in *Selected Essays on Renaissance Drama*, ed. Clifford Davidson (New York: AMS, 1985); Kenneth Burke, "*Coriolanus*—and the Delights of Faction," in *Essays in Shakespearean Criticism*, ed. James L. Calderwood and Harold E. Toliver (Englewood Cliffs, N.J.: Prentice-Hall, 1970), 530–47; James L. Calderwood, "*Coriolanus*: Wordless Meanings and Meaningless Words," also in *Essays in Shakespearean Criticism*, 548–59; and Stanley Cavell's amplification and reinterpretation of Adelman in terms of the politics of the gift and cycles of nurturance and anality, "'Who does the wolf love?': *Coriolanus* and the Interpretations of Politics," 1984; reprinted in *Shakespeare and the Question of Theory*, ed. Patricia Parker and Geoffrey Hartman (New York: Methuen, 1985), 245–72.

69. See the series of interesting encounters recorded in *Analytical Index to the Remembrancia*, note 12 above, 426–34. In a petition to Queen Elizabeth, the mayor, aldermen, and commonalty of the City of London had protested that the city enjoyed sole right to the "survey, search, assay, examination, weighing, and trying of all kinds of goods, merchandize, victuals, etc." brought to the city either by land or water (p. 436). In 1603 some of the London guilds also complained about wrongs done by His Majesty's purveyors (p. 94).

70. Mark S. Kishlansky, *Parliamentary Selection: Social and Political Choice in Early Modern England* (Cambridge: Cambridge Univ. Press, 1986), 3–9. Although Kishlansky's attack on the "Whig" interpretation of the early modern

electoral process has aroused controversy among historians, he convincingly demonstrates that a locus of tension in *Coriolanus* is the breakdown of a traditional system by which a candidate's selection is validated by popular acclamation, but in which that acclamation is actively invoked through the candidate's "courting" of the people.

71. Geoffrey Bullough, ed., *Narrative and Dramatic Sources of Shakespeare*, 5:518.

72. I am indebted for the reference to the 1610 Parliament to Annabel Patterson, personal communication, June 17, 1986. The Fable of the Belly and the Members, of course, came up regularly in political discourse. See, for example, the aftermath of the Essex affair, in which the fable was used to argue that citizens have to support their prince lest all be slaughtered, *Calendar of State Papers Domestic*, Elizabeth I, 5:405 (Feb.? 1600); and for another example within a Roman Catholic context, Camden's *Remaines* as excerpted in Geoffrey Bullough, ed., *Narrative and Dramatic Sources of Shakespeare*, 5:551–52.

On the monetary connection between banqueting and city "liberty," see E. K. Chambers, *The Elizabethan Stage* (Oxford: Clarendon Press, 1923), 2:480. For parliamentary debates over supply and purveyance, see, for example, R. C. Munden's discussion, "James I and 'the growth of mutual distrust,'" 52–72; Wallace Notestein, *The House of Commons 1604–1610*, 96–106, 186–210; and W. Gordon Zeeveld, "'Coriolanus' and Jacobean Politics," 324–34. The phrase "Tribunes of the People" and references to the "head" and the "members" were used frequently during the debates to refer to members of the House of Commons who took the populist side against purveyance.

73. The text of the 1608 charter is printed in *The Historical Charters and Constitutional Documents of the City of London*, rev. ed., ed. Walter de Gray Birch (London: Whiting & Co., 1887), 139–50. For an account of the charter's limitations, see Valerie Pearl, *London and the Outbreak of the Puritan Revolution: City Government and National Politics, 1625–43* (London: Oxford Univ. Press, 1961), 27–33. Needless to say, despite the new royal guarantees, the royal encroachments continued.

74. Cited from *Coleridge's Shakespearean Criticism*, ed. Thomas Middleton Raysor (London: Constable, 1930), 1:89.

75. Adelman, "Anger's My Meat" in *Representing Shakespeare*, ed. Murray M. Schwartz and Coppélia Kahn, note 68 above, 144–45.

76. Kenneth Burke, "*Coriolanus*—and the Delights of Faction," note 68 above, 532.

EPILOGUE

1. See David Piper's discussion of this and other metamorphoses of the image of Shakespeare in *The Image of the Poet: British Poets and Their Portraits* (Oxford: Clarendon Press, 1982), 102.

2. Paul Ricoeur, *The Conflict of Interpretations: Essays in Hermeneutics*, ed. Don Ihde (Evanston: Northwestern Univ. Press, 1974), 23.

3. I have borrowed the phrase "ongoing cultural activity" from Alvin Kernan, *Printing Technology, Letters & Samuel Johnson* (Princeton: Princeton Univ. Press, 1987), 313.

Index

Adelman, Janet, 209
Aeneas, 121
Agincourt, 77
Alcalde de Zalamea, El (Calderón), 185
Amazon, 76, 82, 93–94, 99, 104–5. *See also* Elizabeth I of England
Andrewes, Lancelot: *XCVI Sermons,* 3, 16–17 (figure 9), 18–19
Androgyny, 58–61; in Shakespearean comedy, 102. *See also* Cross-dressing; Elizabeth I of England; Gender roles
Anglican church. *See* Church of England
Anjou, Duke of (Alençon), 59, 68, 72–73 (figure 13), 74, 85
Anjou, Duke of (later Henry III of France), 68. *See also* Henry III of France
Annus Mirabilis (Dryden), 165, 210
Anti-Scottish prejudice, 122–25, 130–31, 146, 154, 245n.30
Anti-Stratfordians, 20, 34–35
"Archdukes, the," 190–200
Arches of Triumph (Harrison), 170 (figure 16)
Armada of 1588, 54–87 passim, 128; plays about, 80
Armada portrait, 62, 65, 81; attributed to George Gower, 65 (figure 12)
Armada speech (Elizabeth I of England), 54–55
Arraignment of Paris, The (Peele), 27
Aske, James, *Elizabetha Triumphans,* 62–66, 82
Astraea, 53, 83, 135. *See also* Elizabeth I of England
Audience: at court, 27, 98, 148–58, 197–200; for First Folio, 21–38, 43–44, 237–38n.79; humanist construction of, 21, 30; for "localization," 214–17; for pageants, 115–16; in Renaissance theater, 25–26, 33, 37, 41, 69, 160–61, 227–28n.2; for speeches of Elizabeth, 56–58. *See also under individual plays*
Augustus Caesar, 109, 126, 135, 246n.44

Authorship: in avant-garde theater, 39; in *Hamlet,* 47; and intentionality, 42; as new Renaissance institution, 3–50 passim, 108, 112–13, 206, 210–16; in twentieth century, 31

Bancroft, Archbishop, 127
Bartholomew Fair (Jonson), 22
Basilikon Doron (James I), 111, 163
Bawdy courts, 173, 175, 178, 194
Bercé, Yves-Marie, 90
Bertie, Peregrine. *See* Willoughby, Lord
Bible, 2, 3, 62, 85, 157, 163, 174, 222n.6. *See also* James I of England
Blake, William, 2
Boccaccio, 126
"Body natural" of the monarch, 54, 102, 157
"Body politic" of the monarch, 54–74 passim, 103, 141–42, 157, 246n.39
Book of Bounty (James I), 112
Book of Sports (James I), 112, 156
Booth, Stephen, 129
Boxing Day, 154
British empire. *See* James I of England
Brute (legendary founder of Britain), 121
Buckingham, Duke of, 28
Burbage, Richard, 116–17
Bye plot, 191

Cade, Jack, 93
Caesar, Julius (Elizabethan Master of Requests), 66
Calderón: *El Alcalde de Zalamea,* 185
Calvinism. *See* Protestantism; Puritanism
Camden, William, 72, 230n.22
Canon, the literary, 31, 33, 52
Canons of 1604, 172–74, 179. *See also* Marriage, validity of
Catherine de' Medici, 72
Catholicism: Catholic League, 63, 72, 78; and church courts, 173; and cult of Elizabeth, 67, 84–86; fear of in England, 66, 72, 162–64, 190–92, 202; in

Compositor:	G&S Typesetters, Inc.
Text:	10/13 Bembo
Display:	Bembo
Printer:	Maple-Vail Book Mfg. Group
Binder:	Maple-Vail Book Mfg. Group